Private Lessons With Jesus
from A Course in Miracles

All rights reserved. No part of this book may be reproduced or transmitted in any form or by any means, electronic or otherwise, including photocopying, without express written consent of the author.

Copyright © 2021
Myrna Skoller
soulsearchpublications@gmail.com

Published by
Soul Search Publications
www.soulsearchpublications.com

Editing: Blue Horizon Books
www.bluehorizonbooks.com

Design: Morninglite Book Design
www.morninglitebookdesign.com

Publisher's Cataloging-in-Publication data:
Skoller, Myrna

Private Lessons With Jesus: From A Course In Miracles
ISBN: 978-1-7369594-0-4

Praise for
Private Lessons With Jesus

In Private Lessons with Jesus, Myrna has gifted our world with an invaluable resource. The teachings Jesus gave Myrna to accompany her study of A Course in Miracles, though personal, are of universal relevance and applicability. Whether you utilize her book as a companion to your study of ACIM or just want to receive Jesus's wisdom and love, this book is a shining gem.

Robert Schwartz, author of Your Soul's Plan, Your Soul's Gift, *and* Your Soul's Love: Living the Love You Planned Before You Were Born, *international speaker and practitioner of between-life and soul regression*

Private Lessons With Jesus is inspirationally powerful. Myrna represents her deeply personal connection to Jesus in a true, authentic fashion, so that anyone searching within themselves can move forward toward a more loving and peaceful state of mind.

Elyse Scheiner, Educator

Private Lessons With Jesus keeps feeding my heart, like food for the soul. I believe my heart knows the truth when it hears it, even if my mind is slow to follow. I can feel my heart grow fuller with each new lesson.

Karen Helburn, Owner
Just Hatched, Children's Luxury Goods

Private Lessons With Jesus offers the reader a uniquely true and genuine style of writing. It is a look into a world where love is inescapable, and judgment is non-existent—the heart of Myrna's book.

Corey Scheiner, Accounts Manager/ Information technology

Truly inspirational and written from the heart, Myrna's book is very creative, spiritual, and emotionally motivating. I find it to be an enthusiastic and inspiring read.

Michael Geringer, Investment Broker

This book is very, very well-written. It is at the same time challenging for a lay person as myself to identify with the philosophy espoused. I read several essays from Jesus and I look forward to reading this one in its entirety.

Allen Goldstein, Retired Educator

May we always be focused on the "light" and all that is good. Myrna's book profoundly expresses this and more. Through the years we have spent many hours sharing our thoughts, our love, our life. This will be yet another opportunity to take us further along our path to oneness.

Gloria Altman, Retired Investment Broker

What a pleasure to read Myrna's wonderful book. Each lesson is a meditation, a joy, and a soul-awakening gift.

Jael Klein Coaracy, Artist,
Psychologist, and Author

To grasp this material on a deeper level, beyond the intellect, is awe-inspiring. Myrna's words remind me who I really am—a part of God, unconditional love, a miracle worker. I thank her for helping me to remember who I really am.

Susan Michel, Dedicated Proponent, Teacher,
and Speaker of ACIM Studies

I found *Private Lessons With Jesus* inspirational, meaningful, and packed with wisdom. As I was reading it, I felt completely uplifted and peaceful. This is a book I am recommending to everyone I care about and one that I will read over and over again. Congratulations, Myrna, on this amazing book. You are a true inspiration.

Linda Baratz, Founder of Kindness Angels,
Helping to Care for the Homeless and Hungry

Over the years, my spiritual sister Myrna and I have had numerous discussions about her journey with A Course In Miracles, and mine with Kabbalah. We have discovered similarities that exist through both avenues. Her spiritual path has brought her to a higher sense of creativity. The book will surely have an extended life. Kudos to her.

Shirley Camhi Goldblatt, Renowned Artist (NAWA)
and Interior Designer

Eye-opening and mind expanding. Lots of beautiful information in one place. The author has an approach that is engaging and refreshing.

Denise Gobin, Realtor

Private Lessons With Jesus

---

from
A Course in Miracles

MYRNA SKOLLER

*This book is dedicated
to my beloved Brother, Jesus.*
Love, Myrna

In memory of

*Charlie,
my wonderful and amazing husband
who believed in me more than I believed in myself.*

*Betty Schwartz,
my beloved sister and life-long friend,*

*and Beth Mesika,
who was so much more to me than a step-daughter.*

FOREWORD

Private Lessons with Jesus by Myrna Skoller is a must-read for all who wish to enjoy a positive, peaceful life full of joy and free of anxiety. She is promoting staying in the present, in the realm of God's grace. Martin Seligman in his book *Learned Optimism* found that by focusing on the positives even Olympic swimmers could improve results. The National Science Foundation suggests that 80 percent of our 50,000 daily thoughts can be negative, which can lead to dwelling on the past, feeling unhappy and stuck.

What Myrna so brilliantly explains to us is that we are all given the opportunity to have more peaceful days and nights by following her teachings. By studying her concepts, we can become reborn.

John Tompkins, MFT, author of *Not Crazy Yet? Then Start Talking To Yourself Differently*, teaches us that to grow and prosper in relationships we need thoughts that are positive and free of blame and drama. His "Green Language" returns us to the present, empowering us to truly see, hear, and connect with others—an experience we can choose to make harmonious and joyful. Myrna not only gives us the foresight about creating our own future peace but also gives us the spiritual background that makes this reality-based.

Myrna has devoted enormous study to her beliefs and her book is not only an important contribution to the well-being of all but also teaches us how to avoid the pitfalls we often face. *Private Lessons With Jesus* can certainly change your life.

Cheri Florance, Ph.D.
Brain Scientist and Founder of Brain Engineering Labs

INTRODUCTION

A Course in Miracles is a gentle yet powerful teaching that inspires love, forgiveness, and spiritual awakening. It helps us remember the beauty we embody and the absolute magnificent souls that we are. Although it teaches us to become God-Realized on a much deeper level, unless it is practiced regularly, it is so easy to fall back into feelings of separation, time and again.

I came upon A Course in Miracles in the early 1990s when my quest for spiritual awakening first began. It was then that I began to experience snippets and pieces of memory calling out to me. I was awakened to the knowledge that we are much, much more than we perceive ourselves to be. Yet little did I know, spiritual awakening is only the beginning. It is the journey towards learning and absorbing its deeper meanings that brings us to God-Realization. Although words appearing here, such as Jesus, God, Christ-Mind, and Holy Spirit, seem to be religious terms, they are also spiritual in nature. For those not familiar with A Course in Miracles, the following words are seen over and over in The Course and also in this book as follows: "Sonship" (all equal members of humanity), "brothers" and "sons" (male and/or female), "Self" (all a part of the One Mind, God), "vision" (true sight).

"3D consciousness," as mentioned in this book, recognizes that there is a massive planetary shift currently taking place, which actually began in December 2012. The Earth is in an ascension process, elevating the planet from the lower 3D consciousness into fourth- and fifth-dimensional consciousness. It is a time of massive awakening, the opportunity to enter into that which connects our spiritual nature to the Divine.

Introduction

I grew up in the 1950s and 60s in a world steeped in third-dimensional consciousness. It was an era where war, violence, anger, hatred, racism, judgment, bullying, misogyny, and everything else which spoke in terms of separation was the norm.

A Course in Miracles, also referred to as "The Course," was scribed by Helen Schucman. Helen was a Professor of Medical Psychology at Columbia Presbyterian Hospital in New York City in the 1960s when a strange thing happened. It was an occurrence which she never could have predicted. Because she was frustrated by the way her colleagues were disrespecting one another, as arguments and conflict became common practice, it was William Thetford, a close friend and colleague of Helen's, who one day said to her, "There has to be another way." This was an invitation to something which Helen could never have anticipated. She began hearing a voice which identified itself as Jesus. At first, she was thrown by this unexpected phenomenon, but with the assistance of Bill Thetford, she realized she was going to comply with what she now felt compelled to do, which was to take down what she was hearing. This inner dictation by Jesus, which Helen and Bill were transcribing, later became known as A Course in Miracles, written from 1965 to 1972, and published in 1976. It has now been translated into more than twenty languages, and over 3,000,000 copies have been printed. The Course consists of 1,200 pages, including a text, a teacher's manual, and a workbook, which consists of 365 lessons, one for each day of the year.

I have been a student of A Course in Miracles for over thirty years and have completed the lessons several times. One day, when I was about to embark upon another 365 days of lesson repetition, I suddenly brainstormed into trying it a different way. I asked Jesus if he would give me "private lessons." I wanted him to explain what the lessons should mean to me personally. What I learned from this request is that we definitely get what we ask for. Our intentions are carried far beyond our imagined limitations, and what I received in answer could never have been predicted at the time.

Each day, in preparing to do another lesson, I would sit down at the computer, type in the heading of that day's lesson, close my eyes, and retreat into the deepest part of myself. Except for the title of each lesson, I pretty much put the ACIM book aside, and embarked upon my own intimate excursion with Jesus. My fingers would roll along on the keyboard, and I would transcribe the thoughts that were coming to me. I cannot say it is a distinct channeled voice which was speaking to me clearly and audibly. It was but a combination of thoughts, feelings, and words, all manifesting into that which felt undeniably true. I knew that what was coming to me was being fueled by a Higher Power, and I loved it.

What was magical were the feelings of intense love that this renewed connection to Jesus was bringing about. Afterward, I would re-read the same lesson over and over. It was the last thing I would read before going to bed, and the first thing I reached for the following morning. It showed me another part of myself that I did not know existed. What inspired me to continue more than anything was that I was getting so many new insights pertaining to love, peace, forgiveness, and healing. It was as though I was unlocking endless vaults of new teachings which I voraciously consumed. Although the lessons were spoken to me on a personal level, I believe its messages have universal appeal, as we are all a living part of the same God.

These 365 days I spent with Jesus in compiling the lessons was an amazing journey into the Self, one which I could never have accomplished alone. I asked for guidance, and I received it.

Myrna Skoller
soulsearchpublications@gmail.com

1

**Nothing I see in this room
(on this street, from this window, in this place)
means anything.**

On Earth, everything you perceive seems real, but in truth the world is an illusion. Because you play a part in the world you must depend on that which you perceive as real or you could not live in the world. The mind translates what your eyes are seeing. However, it is within your purpose to stand in your own truth, not another's. In this way you come to learn what is real and what is not, what makes you happy and what does not. True vision is apart from what you seem to witness here. While you are in a physical body, of course you must rely on what the body's eyes see for that is what perception is. Yet not to take what you are perceiving so seriously is a learning process. What needs to be taken seriously, however, is love, for love is the core of everything you are. You were created One with God, still perfect, forever changeless. This is why nothing has any true meaning except what is revealed to you through Spirit.

Love, Jesus

2

**I have given everything I see in this room
(on this street, from this window, in this place)
all the meaning that it has for me.**

The world's foundation is built on illusion. Everything you see in the world is a manifestation of thought. If this could be recognized as true, the world would be relieved of much distress and unhappiness, for what you think, you create. Imagine if you could separate truth from illusion how much happier you would be, for you would not believe all that you perceive. Everything you give meaning to which is not lasting, is also not real, for what is real is indestructible. Consider love, peace, and kindness to be indestructible qualities of the human spirit. Everything you see has the importance, or lack thereof, by the meaning you give to it.

Love, Jesus

3

I do not understand anything I see in this room (on this street, from this window, in this place).

How can anything be understood if it has no reality? You believe that everything you see is true, yet only some of what you see bears any truth at all. In reality, they are but illusions, for nothing outside of God-Consciousness can be counted on to be true. And if so much of what you perceive has no truth, how can you understand anything at all? It is your worldly experiences which give rise to your thoughts, and thoughts are but manifestations of your experiences. Happiness, love, kindness, and all else which bring feelings of peace and well-being have far greater meaning than anything the world paints with its glittered colors and life-like pictures, making promises that cannot be kept. And so, you must wonder why you are often unhappy and disillusioned. Follow your bliss past all your illusions and come to the light of truth. Rest in the knowledge that only that which comes from God can be truly understood.

Love, Jesus

4

**These thoughts do not mean anything.
They are like the things I see in this room
(on this street, from this window, in this place).**

The thoughts you hear the loudest come from an egoic thought system and not from the part of you that resonates peace. Ego thoughts speak in platitudes and never with absolute certainty. This leaves too much room for doubt, for the mind wants to be sure of itself. Doubt inhibits the part of the mind that yearns to be sovereign, to choose the thoughts which bring creative ideas into focus instead of damaging ones—spirit versus ego. Thoughts that take you away from peace, you can be sure are not aligned with the part which identifies with God. The ego worships its own false beliefs, but God would have you know only truth. What you perceive through the ego's eyes cannot mean anything, for they are not true. Practice peaceful thoughts coming from a place of stillness, and that is what you will experience. Whatever thoughts come to you which keep you away from peace also keep you distanced from love, for love and peace are entwined.

Love, Jesus

5

I am never upset for the reason I think.

What you think you are thinking is not always accurate. Patterns of erratic thoughts come from the ego and not from the part of the mind which is peaceful. When you are upset, you believe that someone else is the cause of it. No one has the power to overtake your peace. However, you are giving your power away to the one you believe is responsible. It is only you who can divert a bickering war with yourself, and only you are to blame for giving away your peace. What causes your distress is that you are aligning yourself with the part of the mind that does not desire to know peace, and anger appears to be more pleasurable than peace, for to forgive would seem to mean you have lost. A distorted picture now unfolds. You are either aligning with peace, or fear. It is one or the other. When you allow a peaceful state of mind to rule, it is because you have joined with love which is your natural state. However, when fear comes storming in and your peace is compromised it is because your power has been lost to you. Retain your peace and relinquish your power to no one.

Love, Jesus

6

I am upset because I see something that is not there.

You thought you belonged to a world which you believed was your true reality. But what the world sees are merely frantic beliefs perceiving what is not really there. The world you see is a magician's trick called the ego. It is a world of misguided thoughts running rampant. Right-minded thoughts come naturally when you focus on love, which is always followed by peace. Truth can only be known when the world is seen from a different perspective. Nothing outside yourself can be relied on to provide peace, so when you are upset it is because you are dreaming thoughts that have no reality. Give God your full attention as He gives you His. Nothing you see outside yourself seems safe when you rely on the world's unsteady beliefs to provide you with peace and security. Instead, look deep within yourself to find it. Your purpose in the world is to offer it love. That is the only true reality the world can hold for you, for nothing else is there.

Love, Jesus

7
I see only the past.

The ego thrives on its ability to show you false pictures of a past that is not real. Its ability to make you believe in guilt is how it thrives. If you did not have thoughts of a guilty past, it would be impossible for the ego to intrude upon your freedom. But because the ego was made by your very belief in it, it will never cease its hold over you, as long as you give it the power to do so. It will always attempt to bring forth painful memories of a past which in truth has no reality, for the past is dead and buried. To give up ego thoughts, which are all based on past thoughts, takes vigilance. When you focus on God's Love, see how quickly the ego cowers before Him for it has no reality in His Presence. Nothing but love exists in God, and in you. Always remember, it is the ego's main purpose to keep you feeling unloved. When you release past thoughts, the ego is no longer the ruler of your thoughts. Everything you see in the world is based on what you believe, and not necessarily what is true. If you believe you are lost, you will be lost. The past is gone. In truth it does not exist except to the mind which deemed it valuable.

Love, Jesus

8
My mind is preoccupied with past thoughts.

Past thoughts are old habits that arise when the mind appears to be idle. But the mind is never idle for the ego's chattering indulges itself in constant thought. When the mind is busy with chatter, it is because you are dreaming of a past. The mind continually wavers from truth to deception and back again. It is only in the present moment that there are no cares or worries. To be in the present is to be at peace, for that is where all healing takes place. It is in this place where your higher consciousness dwells. The present eliminates the past. To maintain such a state of consciousness is a blessing indeed. If you allow the ego's relentless attempts to intrude upon your peace, how can the mind restore itself to peace? Give your full allegiance to the present. Because the ego and God are apart, you cannot live in two worlds. Of course, there is only one option, but it entails persistence. When you have decided to no longer be preoccupied with past thoughts, it is because you have chosen instead to be happy.

Love, Jesus

9

I see nothing as it is now.

How can anything be understood if its truth is not recognized? The present exists in timelessness, for only "time," not timelessness, is linear. Each moment out of time brings forth the present. When each moment is linked to the present and so on, therein lies peace and peace brings about healing. When the mind focuses on past thoughts, the present is denied and so you deny yourself peace. In the present there is no pain, as pain is associated with fear, and there can be no fear in the here and now. The ego depends on your belief in its illusions for it could not exist without them. When you are entrenched in the past, you are seeing nothing as it is now. By letting go of the past and recognizing that only the present is true, your mind shifts to a higher level of awareness. The more the ego is allowed to pursue you with its false beliefs, the harder it will be to put it to rest, for it does not give up easily, as your higher consciousness is its demise. Everything you will ever come to know as joyful and happy can be found only in the here and now.

Love, Jesus

10
My thoughts
do not mean anything.

Thoughts cannot mean anything when they are not in tune with reality. What is real is to know your purpose by understanding that thoughts of past regrets or misgivings do nothing for they are meaningless. They are neither good nor bad. They just remain hitherto. They do not resonate with truth for they are not in sync with right-mindedness. All thoughts make up a world you see as real, but in truth it has no reality, although this is not easily understood. "New" past thoughts just add more nothingness to the collection, for they mean nothing and remain without purpose. To be presently focused is to return to miracle-mindedness which leads the way to the best possible outcome. In this realm of greater wisdom, everything unfolds differently. The present restores peace and lifts you to higher levels of self-awareness. Leave your past behind, for it serves to hinder your progress. The past is past, and it can never be returned to the present. Past events just shackle the mind, impeding it from greater pursuits which can only be found in the present.

Love, Jesus

11
My meaningless thoughts are
showing me a meaningless world.

Thoughts are meaningless when they are tied to past beliefs that are untrue. In yesterday's lesson, I emphasized that the past is meaningless. This is so because it keeps you from knowing true peace, which is found in the here and now. The past, too, brings about feelings of guilt which are untrue, for God sees you as sinless, as there is no sin in

God. When you began to experience peace by letting go of a meaningless past, you became willing to practice letting go with greater surrender. You learned that without a tainted past inflicted upon yourself, the art of forgiveness was better understood. Guilt no longer had meaning because you were able to see yourself without sin, as does God. Through years of studying The Course, and your desire to receive my tutoring, you have come to understand that in keeping your state of mind in the present, it strengthens your endurance to cope. Your days and nights are more peaceful, for you no longer have ties to a past that caused you so much unnecessary suffering. You did find the truth by seeking answers. With this recognition, you were re-born.

Love, Jesus

12

I am upset because
I see a meaningless world.

A meaningless world remains meaningless while suffering and hate take precedence over love. In such a world, love cannot reveal itself. You have the power to give the world meaning when you recognize that forgiveness is the only remedy strong enough to cure the world's ails. The body, which houses the ego, does nothing to empower the human spirit. In such a world how can happiness be known? The mind, separate from the body, has the choice to see a different purpose in the world. This can only be realized through forgiveness. The mind has the capacity to change from fear to love when forgiveness is practiced. Because your mind is One with Spirit, you have the power to change the world by offering it love which opens up the portals to peace. Forgiveness understands the strength of love, and love brings peace to the world.

Love, Jesus

13

A meaningless world engenders fear.

God did not create a meaningless world. You did. The world is founded on false beliefs which in themselves create fear. Belief in sin, guilt, and hate, does indeed engender fear. Until the decision to change is practiced, a fear-based world creates more of the same. Spirit, which is inherent in everyone, reveals a different world. This is undiscovered while one sees only that which he/she wishes to make real, instead of what IS real. Raise your consciousness and see how the world changes from a darkened unreality to one of peace. The only real meaning the world has for you is boundless love, which is of God. Awareness of love comes from Spirit, while fear is confined to the limitations of the body when it is lost in wrong-minded beliefs. Absent fear, you need not be limited. Take your mind out of the sand trap of darkness and into the pureness of light where it breeds love, peace, and happiness. Go far and beyond your perceived limitations and know that the world need not be a fearful place, but one of peace. Change your beliefs and change the world.

Love, Jesus

14

God did not create a meaningless world.

In yesterday's opening statement I stated, "God did not create a meaningless world." Thinking that past injustices are meaningful can only lead to pain, and therefore cannot be rationalized correctly. A world which ravages itself with sin, guilt, and fear, are but illusions. Any idea which prompts such imaginary scenarios, where one's anger is justified for what they seem to witness in the world, are meaningless beliefs. Harsh reprisals set forth by the ego are also false, for they instill fear. Such beliefs and patterns of thought lead nowhere. The world you see is full of folly and frolic, and also fearfully insane, for nothing which creates illusion can also be real. It is time to come to a place of truth. The mind has the capacity to change from fear to peace. Thoughts made up of worldly beliefs, which exclude forgiveness and kindness, deny God. Give up the false and examine the real. That is the way back to your true reality, which is not found in a world of fear.

Love, Jesus

15

My thoughts are images that I have made.

Thoughts are created by images in the mind and the constant chatter never ceases. The brain is constantly at work. Everything you see are images of thought, whether you are awake or asleep. Thoughts are reflections of that which the mind reveals to you. Yet the world's foundation is built on fear. It is hard to imagine that this is true but indeed it is, for everything you see outside yourself are illusions. All thoughts are reflections of the imagination and create the world you have invented. When you are feeling peaceful, it is because you are choosing thoughts that are serving you well. When you can believe that everything you see is illusory, it makes you wonder why you spend so much time toying with magic beliefs. There is a far deeper recognition as to what is true and meaningful. Look past made-up images and into your heart, for peace comes from within. Go beyond the images you see in the world to find reality. Teach yourself to think happy thoughts—joy, kindness, compassion. All of this falls under the umbrella of love, which is all that is true.

Love, Jesus

16
I have no neutral thoughts.

Every thought has bearing on something, for each thought creates your reality. Obviously, happy thoughts produce better results. Such is the law of cause and effect. Every single outcome you experience is the result of the thought which produced it. Each thought urges various feelings to be stirred up. Your mind is always busy dictating your thoughts. They are not neutral, for neutrality is the absence of expression, and you are constantly expressing your thoughts one way or another. This never ceases. The power of thought creates a myriad of various outcomes. There is a cause and effect outcome attached to every thought. Nothing you think is solitary or confined. Thoughts move about constantly creating more of the same. Cause and effect are the two main energies that make up your world. How you think is crucial, based on the outcome you wish for. It is this which determines whether it was from love or from fear. Every thought has a goal. If it is not from love, you can be sure it is from fear.

Love, Jesus

17
I see no neutral things.

Today's idea rests heavily on neutrality. Everything you have ever valued are ideas which seemed to have more importance than they should. The furniture you buy, the clothes you wear, the car you drive, are all founded on the importance you give to them. Materialistic things are relied on very heavily in this world. The world's greed runs rampant because it is believed that possessions have greater value than life. The insanity behind such beliefs seems totally rational according to what the world is founded on. Every single thing we own is deemed so important that, because we fear its possible loss, there is a lack of trust, fearing others may take it away from us. How can anything that eventually frays away to nothing be so misunderstood in terms of the value it is given? How foolish it is to place so much importance on such things, that we are willing to give up our peace to protect it. It is sometimes realized that when you did give something up which you thought meant so much, it suddenly had no real importance at all. Truth, love, happiness, kindness, and compassion are priceless gifts by comparison. In moments of stillness, be in gratitude that you have come to discern the valuable from the valueless. The more you feel that emotion, the more you will come to understand what is truly valuable.

Love, Jesus

18

I am not alone in experiencing the effects of my seeing.

What you choose to see is how thoughts become manifest, as they circulate through the collective consciousness. Thoughts are not private, although it may seem that they are. We are all a part of the One Mind, the Creator of All. Every thought's outcome is revealed by the level of its power, and it carries itself into the world's frequencies. Because minds are joined, thoughts are constantly exchanged. Thoughts cannot be contained by a single individual; they are shared. That is why it is essential that your thoughts be controlled. As your thoughts become elevated through love, kindness, forgiveness, and sharing, so is your consciousness elevated. What you think affects the entire Sonship—all of Humanity—for we are all part of the Greater Consciousness, God. When you are feeling a kinship to another, it is because you are receiving loving energy. Emotions are transmitted just like radio air waves, which also come through the power of energy. That is why positivity on a collective level works for the good of all. In fact, it works well enough to heal an entire planet. Because all thoughts are connected to the One Mind, as the world receives high energy impact on a collective level, the effects are no less than astounding.

Love, Jesus

19
I am not alone in experiencing the effects of my thoughts.

Negativity brings fear into the subconscious. Illness, depression, sadness, and low energy all stem from fear. You are obviously energized by right-minded activity and this works on a collective level, for thoughts are shared. They cannot remain confined to one individual because all minds are joined. Thoughts may appear to be private but do not be deceived. Thoughts that are aligned with positive beliefs will bring forth positive outpour, such as wellness, joy, happiness, and peace. What you think becomes manifest into physical reality, as thoughts create the visible world. When thoughts are positive, they are quite powerful, and operate on a higher plane of energy. If you allow your thoughts to fester in negativity, you are sending out those signals that are called into your reality and you will see it in others, for negativity is as equally powerful as positivity. Elevated consciousness recognizes positive energy and reacts according to those signals. You are all a part of the Greater Consciousness, whereby the energy of your thoughts is shared. Whichever seeds you plant will sprout new growth as if sewn into a giant field of energy, all a part of the same magnetic force of combined consciousness.

Love, Jesus

20
I am determined to see.

True vision does not come from fantasies or illusions stemming from the ego's beliefs. Images depicting fearful scenarios such as crime, brutality, war, racism, hatred, unkindness, and a constant barrage of media news, produces fear if you allow it to intrude upon your freedoms. Such distortions are doled out without conscience. That does not mean there is a need to jump into a hole and pull the hole in after you. When you rely on a deeper, more meaningful thought system, which is your inner truth, you will not be a slave to such meaningless ideals. That it is best for you to rely on your own intuitive beliefs, is true. But it is also important to share your gifts, for they are the by-products of those truths. The deep dramas you see in the world reduces the ability to differentiate between what is true and what is false. True vision comes from a deeper recognition which reaches beyond the misguided interpretations that many would have you believe. If something causes you to be fearful or threatened, there is no need to fatigue yourself further. By maintaining a continued connection with Source is what keeps you feeling safe. Let no outside obstacles stand in the way of what you know to be true.

Love, Jesus

21
I am determined to see things differently.

You had been well taught in how NOT to think. You grew up with ideas and teachings completely opposite from the free soul you are created to be. Because you were constantly judged, you became insecure and confused, having had no memory of your Spiritual Roots. And so, you did not begin to exercise your own better judgment until adulthood. Because you were sucked into controlled thinking, there was no way you could recognize the truth within yourself and so you were headed in a direction that did not suit your intended purpose, which was indeed painful. Although you now have strong recognition of who you truly are, still lingering is the fear of what others might think. The spiritual world is your home, but the true comforts of home are felt when you are sure of how to take command of your thoughts and to express them. Although you have come far, you are still reticent about speaking your mind even though it is incumbent upon you to do so. Spiritual thinking differs from the world's constrained thinking. Your intuitive thoughts are much more reliable than what you had been taught, as you had been badly taught. Trust your intuition and speak your truths. Although you may not get agreement, you will make a dent in the minds of others who are perhaps unwilling to change, but deep within they know what is true. Keep your beliefs undeterred and learn to speak your mind without fear of being judged. It does not matter that those who still possess their old world judgments disagree. Be true only to yourself.

Love, Jesus

22

What I see
is a form of vengeance.

How can a loving God allow the world to linger in hate, fear, and pain, one wonders? The answer is, He does not. Thoughts create the world you see. All thoughts manifest into reality by how they are projected. Thoughts are erratically formed when chatter of the mind persists. They are perceived to be perfectly rational, but how can erratic thoughts make sense of anything? This is exactly what occurs because they are rationalized as true. Because they are not sound, they have no real meaning. God created you perfect. Do not think for a single moment that God could allow such insanity to take the place of His Divine Love. All thoughts are manufactured in the subconscious. The mind is a magnificent instrument, despite the ego's main objective, which is to play havoc with your sanity. Love is known when you feel it rising within and moving into your heart. If you cannot feel love's energy it is a form of vengeance.

Love, Jesus

23

I can escape from the world I see
by giving up attack thoughts.

The material world is made manifest by your thoughts. Everything you see is a reflection of the thoughts you choose to accept into your world. You have become well-versed on how your thoughts make real the world you see. Your eyes have been opened to a new you. Before you undertook the practice of giving up attack, you walked a dismal road. It was only then that you sought to focus your thoughts differently, for pain is a stern teacher. By learning to love yourself, you first had to change your thoughts about yourself, your brothers and sisters, and the world. By pivoting your thoughts into a far better reality, you experienced healing. With God's help you were able to do the necessary work required to heal. Hateful thoughts bring on attack, and sadly, you attack no one but yourself. Such feelings invariably fan the fire keeping fearful thoughts alive and well. Attack thoughts lock you into feelings of hopelessness, for there is no hope where hate prevails. Your thoughts create the world you see, and also how you see yourself. To escape from such a sorry state requires practice and willingness. Escape then is not only possible, but inevitable.

Love, Jesus

24

I do not perceive my own best interests.

Mere perception is based on thoughts and not what is factual. It is no more than a system of belief, neither true nor false. The way you think is impacted solely by what you see and what you hear. Fragmented bits and pieces of information coming from outside yourself, which is the material world, alters perception and changes with the wind. Yet facts do not change moment by moment, such as perception does. Facts are facts and remain just as they are, for they are true. Manipulation by those who believe themselves to be in higher standing than yourself will try to seize control of your thoughts if permitted to do so. If you put yourself in the hands of those who desire to seek control of you, false perception will most likely be the outcome and fear follows. The world is going through a pivotal change of consciousness now, as more people are less likely to accept false ideals planted by advertisements, news media, and others as a means of control. Collectively, your brothers and sisters are beginning to recognize it is far better to place their beliefs into that which serves the best interests of all, than to buy into the ideals of those who are self-serving. Within the Mind of God, you are given the tools to perceive correctly and this you must do, for all else leads away from truth and into despair. Many still do not rely on their own truths, but instead allow others to manipulate their truths for them. True perception allows the heart to interpret for itself, independent of outside influences. Be loving, be peaceful, and be true to no one but yourself.

Love, Jesus

25
I do not know what anything is for.

The ego gives you ideas which you think serve your best interests. In fact, its intentions are just the opposite. Every morning begins with agendas set forth by the ego and hurls you immediately into the world of time, not paying much mind to that which exists only in the present. The first thing you do each morning is look at the clock. Immediately, you are busy with things that really serve no real purpose when you think in terms of what is truly meaningful by comparison. You are very often focused on mindless projects which do not support your higher consciousness. Ego thoughts have you jumping from place to place with a myriad of things to do, really intended to keep you distanced from your real teacher, which is Spirit. Is it not best to wake up in the morning with no cares or worries? Is it not more meaningful to spend time enjoying the serene beauty of nature, taking some quiet time for meditation, taking a few minutes to think of those you love, and to just be present within yourself? This requires no agenda, and it will bring you more peace than anything the ego can tempt you with. The ego keeps you focused on its own agendas and is intensely preoccupied with everything except that which is truly worthy of you. Where you need to be is in the here and now, and nowhere else. If you remain true to yourself, you will know what to do, and where you need to be. You need but be still and allow your inner teacher to guide you. All peace is found within the truth of Spirit.

Love, Jesus

26

My attack thoughts are attacking my invulnerability.

The ego amplifies attack thoughts and prescribes it in enormous doses, for that is what it does best. Love is impossible to project when the mind is continuously invaded, for you have given it a dual purpose. One part feels compassion, while the other is intent on attack. It is not until you finally become aware of the ego's propensity towards such distorted thoughts that it is recognized. It is only by paying close attention to your thoughts that you see how often it occurs. It does not have to be overt to be recognized. It can be so subtle you barely notice it. But until you become aware of how often it occurs, you cannot maintain a peaceful state of mind. Although it occupies such a vast amount of your free thinking space, you are not aware of its magnitude. For if you were, you would see the insanity behind it. You might believe that attack thoughts are only thoughts, and therefore harmless. But they are deadly. This has become obvious to you by now. Peace and attack cannot live side by side. One or the other must go. It is only until pain, guilt, and depression become too hard to bear that another choice is not only sought, but imperative. If a thought arises that hinders your peace, letting it go is the only way.

Love, Jesus

27
Above all else I want to see.

What you see in the world is not true reality. To be able to see outside the ego's interpretations of the world requires dedication and practice. What you see day by day are not your eyes giving you true perception, but thoughts manifesting what you believe your eyes are beholding. All thoughts create the world you see. A fearful mind will see fearful pictures which make up your world. Each person's reality is separate and apart from another's and captures their vision through their own filters. The way to true vision is through forgiveness, and only this works. Now, with a forgiving heart, the world has purpose. When you perceive that you have been unjustly hurt, you will view it as an attack unless you perceive through the lens of Spirit, and not the eyes of the ego. True sight is revealed when you can see that the world you live in is no more than an illusion. How you dream your part in this world is that which will determine the outcome. If you see an attack as justified, this is not vision, for you attack yourself. Peaceful thoughts bring about peaceful scenarios. Attack is never the way to true vision, which comes from the desire to live in a peaceful world. If you can comprehend that the way to rise above the world and see a world built on love, that is what you will see. You are all a creation of the One Self, joined as one with your brothers and sisters.

Love, Jesus

28
Above all else I want to see things differently.

You came into a fearful world and so fear is what you experienced early on. You had to assimilate into a society which had little or no spiritual understanding. You suffered trauma at the behest of family, teachers, and even bullies who were your peers, and so your world became dismal and seemingly without purpose. So, you pushed your way through those growing up years with a great deal of sorting out to do. Your society was a harsh teacher, for it inhibited the expression of thought, God-Awareness, and freedom of spirit. Yet it was through those very experiences which brought you to see the world from a whole new perspective, as the adult you are today. However, even as a child you were fortunate, having some of degree of God realization in your memory. This gift of faith enabled you to come into a greater spiritual awareness then, and now. You were always treasured by God, irrespective of your poor behavior and how little you thought of yourself. God gave us all free will so that we may stand true to ourselves. Today of course, you see things differently, no longer the damaged being you once perceived yourself to be. Nothing in your life warms you more than the light of God's Love in your heart. And by this awareness you now live. Shadows of a fearful past no longer hold you hostage and you have entered into a shining new reality. You have made incredible strides as you hold the world up to a brand new standard.

Love, Jesus

29

God is in everything I see.

Behind all form is vision. With vision everything you see is recognized as God. When you see yourself not just as a body but as a connection to all things in the Universe, you will stay in the light of self-love. Everything in the world as seen through the body's eyes is ephemeral and not lasting. Real vision, having nothing to do with physical sight, is how God is seen. It is within this spiritual connection to your Creator that you are connected to all things. He is the light within us all. Because God is everywhere, He must be in all things, expressing Himself to the fullest. The painting you love was inspired by an artist, your favorite chair was made by a craftsman, the bed you sleep in offers you comfort, what you eat in a restaurant is prepared by a chef, and so on. Everything has meaning when you see beyond what appears to be only density. Every single thing in the world has consciousness. That is why God is in everything you see. Because He is everywhere, He must live in every person, every place, and in all things.

Love, Jesus

30
God is in everything I see because God is in my mind.

God is in your mind because He shares His with you. In studying The Course through the years, you have come to learn that its basic and most important lesson is forgiveness. Until you became tutored by your brother Jesus on the strength of forgiveness, you did not know that it was the prime ingredient leading the way to peace. You never knew the impact an unforgiving mind had on your own outlook, which was a perception of a dismal and sorrowful world. The world is made up of the thoughts you project into it. By giving up the thoughts you do not share with God, you become free in spirit and your heart is lightened of its heavy burdens. It is easier to forgive another when you are not in judgment of him. When thoughts of hate are projected, you do not see yourself in God. You can only become enriched by letting God shine away your fears. He is indeed in everything you see because He is in all things.

Love, Jesus

31
I am not a victim of the world I see.

Victims are those who choose to accept themselves as frail and unable to cope. No one is a victim. What you see happening in the world via the news media are brainwashing techniques in a ruling society. It is hard to overcome perceptions of helplessness when you believe they are true. Because your early training taught you to see yourself as powerless, you could not get past your own limitations. When you stand true to yourself you can conquer anything, for nothing is impossible. Although many saw me (Jesus) as a victim, that is not the lesson I came to teach. The lesson I tried to instill was that if I had overcome what appeared to be such unspeakable treachery, then no one need fall into the ego's trap of victimization, for I never saw myself as a victim. There is no need to live in fear when there is nothing that can keep you in the shadows of your illusions but your own false beliefs. Free will allows one to choose whichever reality they wish. You have entered into a new level of consciousness since first studying The Course with me years ago. You no longer live in the shadows of a dark belief system which once had the power to fill you with fear and self-doubt. There are no victims. There are only those who perceive themselves as such. Be happy you have come to learn this lesson.

Love, Jesus

32

I have invented the world I see.

All thoughts are viewed according to how your ego perceives them. If a person irritates you in thought, it is because you are perceiving something about him/her which does not exist. Today was a perfect example of such a person. She was brought up in conversation which had to do with the viciousness you believe she is guilty of. Although you already know that judgment is a perception, you added to the illusion by bringing up past memories which served to vilify her even further. You listened mostly, but you also intimated that you knew of the pain and suffering she caused to those she had control over. Yet what you saw was in the past. Such thoughts are bits and scraps of information persuading the mind to think them true. Although it is sometimes difficult to see the God qualities in some people, it serves no purpose to speak of them unfavorably. Perhaps such an individual needs your love all the more because they are denying it to themselves. How frightening it is to live without the most precious life-sustaining need there is, which is love. Think of this person and send her light. Even a small glimmer can be carried further than you can possibly imagine.

Love, Jesus

33
There is another way at looking at the world.

There is a different picture of the world that can filter into your reality by a kind and forgiving heart. To forgive past grievances and focus on the present serves as a springboard into the future, for the future is the effect of the present made manifest into your awareness. That is how you create the world you see, for you choose the outcome. Within the whirling and twirling of a changing world you begin to move forward into a higher dimensional frequency. The world seen anew no longer recognizes the shadows of the old. As a new awareness is born from the elevated consciousness of one person, it finds its way into the collective consciousness of many. When this happens, its force of power is so great it can change the world you see. When you begin to perceive differently, you gain momentum and things start happening at a faster pace. You might find yourself in the midst of a lot of chaos and unexplained phenomenon while these changes are occurring. This should not be viewed as fearful. As you adjust to the changes within yourself, it is important to keep your mind focused on the positive and know that your higher consciousness is bringing about a changed world, replenished with love and absolved from sin.

Love, Jesus

34
I could see peace instead of this.

The world's news media is not a friend of truth. When news anchors, politicians, business people, and the like attempt to promote fear in the world it preys upon the vulnerability of so many. Although they speak of the terrible crisis which lurks in the midst, they say nothing of a world dedicated to peace and love. They do not tell you this, for they do not know it themselves. And so, they relentlessly try to instill fear in those who are steadfast in sharing those same beliefs. The world is indeed in a state of chaos if you choose to see it this way. There are those in your society who are dedicated to creating fear for it is thought to be a means of control. But to deny the freedom of others is to deny it to yourself. For how can freedom be found anywhere in an unfree world? The world's beautiful energy is inexhaustible. If you rely on your own truth and do not succumb to the beliefs of those who deny peace to the world, it is shown to you. The consciousness of the masses is changing. Many in the world are now joining together with a new purpose. No one can find peace in a world which breeds havoc, mistrust, and fear. You have risen above the battleground, for you are aware that the greater consciousness is moving towards peace because you have found it in yourself. Those who succumb to the false conditioning of those promoting disaster are left at the starting gate deprived of a world radiating love, peace, and all good.

Love, Jesus

35
My mind is part of God's. I am very holy.

Each person learns of his or her holiness when the truth of who they are is seen. You have learned to settle into the comforts of God's peace when you saw the healing it brought you. You are His beloved child and you have been shown the light within yourself. You are not always completely convinced of this, but I assure you that the light can be seen well beyond your limited acceptance of it. You have come through a long and arduous journey of fear and self-doubt, unrecognizable to yourself. But these emotions no longer intrude upon your will to see the truth. You came here for reasons unknown to you until you questioned. And you were given the answers because you longed to hear God's Truth, for that is all He knows. Your holy Self is in the Mind you share with God. Your past served as lessons which enabled you to come into your higher purpose. God created you in likeness to Himself so therefore how can you be anything but that? If you truly embodied this, there would not be a single question you would not know the answer to. This is the time to expand your vibrational skills to one of love, for its light is luminous. Forgive yourself for forgetting the light you hold. With forgiveness does all memory return. By coming away from lower patterns of thought your skills are heightened. Give up all doubt about yourself and come completely into your holiness where God welcomes you.

Love, Jesus

36

My holiness envelops everything I see.

Your holiness is as much a part of you as the One Who created you. The world does not teach you this. There is a sacred dwelling place inside of you, undeniably inherent in you. It is there because God put it there. There is nothing which culminates from within that you cannot understand when your awareness is heightened to this reality. To recognize God's holiness in yourself does not come from thought, but from a "knowing" that you are God's holy child sent as a beacon of light to help save the world. Everything you behold in the world manifests from thought. What you have been taught, what you hear, and what you believe, gives rise to the world you see. But it is only when thoughts turn to emotion, and the creative process begins, that all knowing takes place. When you use your creative abilities to enhance and to expand, there is nothing that can keep you from your God-Given purpose. You know this because you feel it in your heart. You are part of a creative force so great it envelops all things. Just as God created you, you have the power to create all good in the world. Use it to change the world.

Love, Jesus

37

My holiness blesses the world.

Today is a day of faith, for God does indeed guide us towards the healing of an ailing world. You have taken on a newness in perception. Your role now is to concentrate on healing the world through the projection of positive thoughts. The world's chaos leaves much to be desired. Many are coming together as brothers and sisters, willing to stand up to those misguided ideals. The masses are now recognizing all destruction in the world is caused by the misuse of power using hatred and fear as weapons. You are witness to the rise of new thought patterns coming about. Those who censure themselves and live in the shadows of old world beliefs do not yet understand that they too have the power to bring about change, for each is empowered to bless the world. You see how your own thoughts are moving away from a fear-driven society towards a newer and greater level of consciousness. The world has been steeped in darkness for too long. You are correct in perceiving that there is a shift in planetary consciousness taking place. You are feeling a certain calmness inviting love, peace, and kindness to enter. Higher consciousness does not relate to rioting, thievery, killing, fighting, lying, and stealing. For how can peace be found in a world such as this? Mistakes are being corrected by the greater consciousness, moving up towards higher ideals. Your days of fear are over, for a new reality is beginning to cover up the old. You recognize your holy brothers and sisters, as they do you, for many now join with a common purpose—to change the world from one of fear to one that is blessed.

Love, Jesus

38

There is nothing my holiness cannot do.

If God empowered you with abilities that the world could not, does it not seem that all your accomplishments come from a separate Source? You were dazed and uncertain and so you sought God, for you were in need of Him. It is because you were created holy that you heard Him. With God nothing is impossible. Yet without this knowing, there is only a dismal belief in yourself and belief in God can only be dim. This is not who you are. God is the only Source by which healing is possible. Because you are made holy and holiness is of God, you must rely on your inner wisdom for answers that cannot be found elsewhere. What God Wills is what you want, for where else can peace be obtained and what else could you want once you have found it? In recognizing your holiness there is peace. This is not learned or acquired on a whim. It is bestowed by God when it is truly sought. Because God deems you holy, you cannot be lost. But many are deceived, believing that God is indifferent and cares not if they are lost. The ego tries to tempt you with its worthless invitations by giving you periods of peace in fragments, but nothing lasting. Only in Him does your holiness reveal itself to be eternal.

Love, Jesus

39
My holiness is my salvation.

What is consciousness but the frequency by which your thoughts manifest into reality? Lower levels of thought such as fear, hate, attack, unforgiveness, and the like produce lower levels of frequency within the world. A higher level of consciousness lifts the world to freer and happier experiences which are called "miracles." The more you allow your lower consciousness to rule, the more it keeps your higher vibrational skills from developing. You are a holy child of God, a lightworker in the making. Come to recognition of your purpose. See a changed world just by changing your mind about the world, which are misconceived ideas gone awry, and live a fuller life. When your mind is conditioned to a more loving presence, you bring about new changes in yourself and in the world. Your emotional state is enhanced because you begin to experience greater happiness and you also observe it in others. When this is recognized, the world becomes more attuned to miracle encounters which occur faster and much more often. When you see the holiness in yourself, you see it in others, as they recognize it in you as well. Within this rise to greater recognition of your holiness lies your salvation.

Love, Jesus

40
I am blessed as a Son of God.

You are a blessed being indeed for you are not just a body, but a holy incarnation of All That Is. You are obviously not a son. God does not see gender, only the magnificence of His creations, whether they be young or old, male or female. Put simply, you are One with God and this makes you nothing less than Pure Consciousness, which connects you to all living things. Be courageous and strong in this belief. To be blessed is great, but to FEEL blessed is greater, for it is the gift of life recognized. A blessing is bestowed by God, but it is you who must be impassioned enough to manifest it into your reality. It is through this greatness in creativity, which joins you to love's vibration, which you are now experiencing to a greater degree. Be true to yourself and live in the glory of all that you are. Be loving in nature and strong in your convictions. There is nothing that can take this from you, for what can be more sustainable than God's blessings? They lift you up to the highest understanding of who you are and thus your purpose in the world becomes clear. When you understand your purpose, it paves the way for it to be fulfilled. Blessings are also meant to be shared. They are miracles in the making. A blessing shared by one is a blessing to all.

Love, Jesus

41
God goes with me wherever I go.

The history of your life has taught you that without God you could not be healed from painful misgivings. You came into the world with many tall orders to fill, for your trials and tribulations were quite daunting. This is true. Because you experienced abandonment early in life; the death of your father, the absence of your mother, it came to be one of your most important undertakings in the undoing of pain. You have fulfilled your purpose because you have seen beyond all doubt that you were never alone or abandoned. So, rejoice, for you have become keenly aware, and finally awakened to this reality. God holds you in the highest esteem, for in truth, abandonment by God is impossible. Your steps were carefully monitored throughout your life and you were guided by the healing power of His Love past all fear and grievances. Forgiveness, in all respects, was indeed a mighty triumph, for your willingness to do so was long in the making. To be in the moment is to discover all things you inherently know but had forgotten. Memory returns to you, knowing you are One with your Creator. Where you are, is He.

Love, Jesus

42

God is my strength. Vision is His Gift.

The strength of God is that which has been brought forth into your reality. You had many issues not knowing where your strength lied. You were trapped within a chaotic thought system, while real Vision was hidden behind dense walls of fear, and hardened beliefs in sin. He gently helped you find your strength when you realized there was nothing in your power to sustain you. Of yourself, you are indeed small and powerless. For where would you find the means to acquire any sustainable answers on your own? God lends His strength to those who find it too hard to deal with the struggles they encounter in the world. The hopeless battles they fight to save themselves are to no avail. Vision brings peace and healing to the forefront. He is the safety net and protector of all who seek to find it within themselves. When all hell breaks loose and peace seems lost without any hope of regaining it, the strength of God is within reach. You have received the Gift of Vision which you now hold precious. It is the Creative Force within, guiding and restoring you to wholeness.

Love, Jesus

43

God is my Source. I cannot see apart from Him.

Not to see God as part of yourself, is not to see God at all. To think that God is apart from you inhibits your abilities to recognize all that you are. The conditioning you had received from your early teachings, mainly unsound beliefs and untruths about yourself, painted a poor image of the larger picture. This diagnosis of yourself grew into disillusionment for you could not know God as the Energetic Creative Force in all that you are. The magnificence of His Plan includes you as a living manifestation of the Greater Consciousness. To fulfill your obligations by understanding your purpose can only be shown to you when the mind releases itself from lower dimensional misperceptions. When you are still linked to thoughts of hatred, mistrust, and worldly dogma, you cannot know the reality of your purpose. You then give up your abilities to bring into your world greatness of power such as healing, wellness, truth, happiness, and joy. Seeing the connection to your Source helps you to recognize that you are one with all creation. Creative energy keeps you in view of God at all times. Not to see apart from Him is the understanding that you are never outside of the One Universal Mind.

Love, Jesus

44

God is the light in which I see.

With God's light, vision is the means by which you can see your brothers and sisters sinless. When a brother irks you for whatever reason, it shortens your senses and takes away your ability see him as he truly is. Remember, he is not just a body, but light. When you cannot see him as your brother in Spirit, it is because you are not fully awakened to the light that exists within both of you. This is when you need to bring yourself to a place of truth. Today was an example of how vision can be obstructed, for you were not totally at peace with a particular individual. In fact, she happens to be a longtime friend. This is because you are not yet willing to see her oneness, as she was created. She is the perfect lesson for you, waiting to be learned. By not seeing her as yourself indicates you are still making judgments, for there is a part of you that remains unhealed. When you can see the light in another without the ego's condemnation, you will also see it in yourself. You know you are healed when you project a deeply felt loving affection which of itself offers light, or love, as they are one and the same. Until then, you will still see her as separate and apart from Source. Light cannot be seen where darkness dwells. This is a lesson which is incumbent upon you to learn, for this must be your goal. To see the light in another is to see beyond the limited aspects of yourself and into the vastness of Self.

Love, Jesus

45

God is the Mind with which I think.

Because God's Mind is joined with yours, to think with God is actually freedom of the mind, and not the opposite. For where God is, so are you. To think apart from Him is to think not at all. For God only recognizes His Own Voice in you. Because God is in you, thoughts separate from His cannot be maintained on the level of true happiness. To let yourself slip away from God is the attempt to hide from truth, for the ego instills beliefs of a punishing God, one not easily reached. Yet how can peace be found with such fearful interludes of thought invading your mind? It cannot. Yet what you are most often hearing, is a non-thinking ego mind. Although you want the truth, you will not know it until you understand it is the cornerstone within your mind. There is a part of you that knows this to be so, but it can only be revealed if God is welcome there. When fearful and guilty thoughts plague the mind, it locks God out. Yet peace and healing are restored when the mind decides to accept God's thoughts over the ego's chattering. So, you see, God's peace is never lost to you. It is only misplaced, yet safely stored until you return to it. Give all your thoughts to God, those that are loving as well as those that are injured. Let them shine back to you completely covered over with Love.

Love, Jesus

46
God is the Love in which I forgive.

With God's Love you have learned that forgiveness brings peace, and peace is a treasured goal. Forgiveness is the most important rule to follow, yet the hardest one to adhere to. To forgive another's evils does seem to imply a weakness in character by the one who forfeits anger in the name of forgiveness. Yet forgiveness does not come from weakness, but from strength. Actually, it was finally your strength which brought you to the core of your pain and a desire to heal. When you finally decided to exchange pain for love, you increased your ability to forgive the past. If one shred of unforgiveness still lurks within the corners of your mind, then love has not triumphed. But when there are no traces of fallout left behind to gnaw at you, it is because the decision was made to let the past go and choose love's fulfillment instead. By now you know there are no victims, only the false belief in victimization. You carried the scars which festered over time, but you did uncover this most important lesson which you came to learn, and I came to teach. The scars which you carried are no longer visible to you. With God's Love, truth has come to take its place.

Love, Jesus

47
God is the strength in which I trust.

When you trust in God you can then trust yourself, for His Strength is demonstrated through you. The ability to forgive without holding another accountable for your own weak misgivings exhibits great strength of character. The ego's thinking is that to forgive somehow implies weakness. But the ability to forgive sends a better message. It is actually a sign of strength because it creates loving energies acknowledging your own well-being. People are drawn to such a lovely vibrational aura. Once you start living this, you will possess the strength required to bring peace and love into the hearts and minds of others, because it is recognized in you. In such a state of grace you can see Angels. To be among the Angels is to project peace, kindness, love, wellness, and joy, into a world much in need of it.

Love, Jesus

48

There is nothing to fear.

When ego thoughts permeate the mind, it brings fear to the forefront. What is fear but a series of emotions crashing into one another with no discerning purpose? Fear stems from anger, hate, guilt, disappointment, and a host of endless judgments. Yet when thoughts align with right-thinking ideas, fear is contained. You are coming to the point where you are experiencing the extraordinary truth to this. There is no doubt in your mind that God is always there. With this recognition, what is there to fear? This world, which is predicated on fear-based principles, can be changed by bringing positive thoughts to the forefront instead of fearful ones. You bring yourself out of the density of lower thought vibrations by projecting peace and tranquility. Joy, happiness, wellness, and all the rest become invariably part of your world thereafter. The Love of your Creator fills your senses and this you are experiencing daily. With God, there can be no undercurrents pulling you down beneath the surface once you have broken free of fear. When the sun takes over the clouds, the clouds are no longer visible. This is God showing you there is nothing to fear, for His Love is all there is.

Love, Jesus

49
God's Voice speaks to me all through the day.

With God's Voice comes the recognition of truth, for you inherently know of it. When the mind is fragmented, nothing is audible except the chatter of a troubled mind. The ego's voice is the one which speaks loudest, yet still meager, as it comes from the limitations of an unhealed mind. Truth comes from the One Mind which is in all things. What can be learned from a fearful voice? One which tells you frightening untruths—that you are guilty, you are sinful, you are not worthy of forgiveness, you are evil? These are the fears that attach themselves to you when your confidence is shaken, for you have been guided wrongly. Yet God's Voice assures you that you are a magnificent vibration of your Creator, and so you need never, ever doubt. When you are kind, loving, and peaceful, you become a vehicle which carries the echoes of His Truth to all, for everyone is drawn to it. When you surrender to His Voice you cannot be sick, nor fearful, nor guilty. God's Words manifest through you. All you need do is speak them in thought. The peace of God is within you to share. When your mind is attuned to His Voice there is nothing that can take away your peace. All you need do is tap into the magnificence of Self as you are created, and hear His Word spoken to you.

Love, Jesus

50
I am sustained by the Love of God.

It is only with God that life becomes purposeful. For in truth, you have the map which guides you to your purpose. With thoughts of anger, hate and guilt, you can only forage deeper into the wilderness. While you traveled this road, you did not look up, so you could not know how lost you were. Without God's map you are directionless, and without direction, you do not know your purpose. What purpose is there when dense fog covers over you and you are alone? When you fell into this sorry state where there was no peace, no love, and little joy, you became depressed and fearful. You knew you needed peace for you could not live this way, tired and afraid. In life, broken promises to yourself do not sustain you, nor does false hope, for empty promises hold no hope. What matters is you. Did you see it when all the aforementioned engulfed your spirit, and depression became your identity? When all else failed you looked for God. You found that He willingly and without judgment lit the way for you. He was not hard to find. For you found Him where He dwells, within the deepest part of you. You have since come to realize that your capacity to love was merely covered over. With God there is only Love, and that is all you need to sustain you, for nothing else will.

Love, Jesus

51

(Review) Nothing I see means anything.

1. (1) - Nothing I see means anything.

What you see in the world is perception of thought. As you think, so it shall be. Everything you see only holds the meaning you give to it. But true vision shows you a far better way in which to live. Project love, and that is what you shall experience. See the world as hateful, and so it shall be. Your thoughts become manifest according to your own reality. Fear is in you and not God, for God is only Love. When fearful thoughts take over, it is because you feel broken off from Spirit and do not know there is another way. The "trick" is to sustain yourself by recognizing that a solution to all problems can be found when you turn your fears over to the One Who is never apart from you.

2. (2) - I have given what I see all the meaning it has for me.

Nothing means anything when thoughts invent the world you see. The material world is not sustainable because it is not true. It is but the way you think that brings rise to what you see as real. When you place too much reliance on possessions, as they are often never enough to satisfy, you are not experiencing true peace. Peace rises from deep within. There is a richness of spirit within the core of every person which is made manifest by thoughts of love. All thought creates the real as well as the unreal. God has given us free will to choose the experiences we wish to bring into our existence.

3. (3) - I do not understand anything I see.

You do not understand what you do not know. What could you know of something that has no meaning? What can you rely on which offers no hope? In the world, hopes and beliefs are based on snippets of information deciphered as plausible, but they often mean nothing. Learn to turn away from that which you do not understand. In this world even though you must follow baseless rules, you do not need to live by them. You need not believe what you hear or read by those whose gains are predicated on your fears such as the news media's violent interpretations at worst, and misleading at best. Live only by that which offers you understanding and not which denies your right to it. It is best to spend your time practicing your given purpose, which is to offer loving kindness to a world so bereft of it.

4. (4) - These thoughts do not mean anything.

The only thoughts that mean anything are those which bring you peace. Thoughts in contemplation of truth can be far more satisfying than thoughts exchanged with those who use many words to express themselves but say nothing. To sit quietly and ponder is where great accomplishments originate. The world is in turmoil and many people are allowing themselves to be controlled by the disdainful voices of those in high places causing pain to many, for they are blind to the obvious. Speak your own truth, for truth is the discovery of self on a deeper, and more profound level. The mastery of truth through self-expression and understanding is indeed a great step forward.

5. (5) - I am never upset for the reason I think.

Thoughts are not always truthful, and so we become perplexed, sad, and fearful as a result. Yet we do not see ourselves as the cause of our own misfortunes and so we transfer the blame where it does not belong. When someone else is perceived to be the cause of our unhappiness we find it hard to forgive, and so an entire mountain of hate festers which then becomes a breeding ground for depression. It is only when we can see the light and realize that to hold another responsible for our unhappiness does nothing to heal our pain. It only sinks us further into the mire of mistrust and confusion. We need not judge others for our saddened dreams. Open your heart to the understanding that healing begins with the ability to forgive those whom we falsely believed were the causes of our pain. You alone are responsible for your feelings. Who would want the agony of pain when peaceful solutions can be decided upon instead?

Love, Jesus

52

(Review) I am upset because I see what is not there.

1. (6) - I am upset because I see what is not there.

At times you will become upset by a dream, although you know that dreams are fantasies. Yet when you awaken from a saddened dream you feel sad. Frightful dreams are frightening. Happy dreams make you happy. The dreams you see as you sleep come from the same illusory thoughts as your waking dreams, only the waking ones seem real, while they too are fantasies of the mind. When a thought arises out of a past long gone, you manufacture a false perception of it. Everything you perceive is an illusion. The only place to be is in the present where there are no dreams and only in this place can peace be counted on, for here is where truth is found. Your goal is to release yourself from thoughts which disrupt your present state of mind. You do not need to revisit a past that has no validity except in dreams, sleeping or waking. When such a thought arises, it is but an illusion. Let it dissolve into the nothingness that it is. To do this takes vigilance in your practicing. Turn your thoughts over to a lovely song, take a walk in nature, call someone with a kind word, go within and cite a spiritual affirmation. There are many ways to unhinge a thought which robs you of your peace.

2. (7) - I see only the past.

The past is unkind for it retraces steps that are meaningless at worst, and partly true at best. Time wasted on past regrets leaves you bereft of peace with no room to understand the concepts of self-expression which is your given purpose. Discovery of self is found in creativity of thought, not illusion of thought. The holy instant which I (Jesus) have referred to many times in The Course, is that enriching moment which touches the senses, and you know beyond all doubt that you are living your truth. It is extremely liberating because it transcends all perceived mistakes which causes guilt and opens up the channels whereby you come unto yourself, reborn. It is in the stillness of Spirit where you awaken. Be in the present and see yourself thrive in recognition of your true self magnified.

3. (8) - My mind is preoccupied with past thoughts.

What the mind sees are past thoughts. They show up minute by minute and they are unyielding. The ego mind will rule at every opportunity. If you allow it to control your thinking, it will also take control of you. Thoughts allowed to roam free hear the echoes of incessant chatter, leaving very little room for growth. When you meditate it does serve to still the mind momentarily. But it also takes vigilance to stop persistent mind-disturbing activity. You have devoted much time to practicing this awareness and you have come to understand that it does take persistence to withdraw from old habits which cause your thoughts to run amok. Divisive habits are formed in early childhood. Most of the time much pain and suffering occur before the cause is recognized, but it is never too late to change it. You have since learned to quiet your mind, which took devotion and practice before the shadows of sin, guilt, and fear, were finally seen for what they are. Today you are well beyond such suffering for your thoughts are contained much more easily now. How wonderful it is that you have learned not to succumb to the ego's blustering assaults. This is because you know there is no judgment in God. You are a loving soul who has rendered herself free from preoccupation with past thoughts and have yielded to a higher frequency of consciousness.

4. (9) - I see nothing as it is now.

When you are seeing only the past, you are not seeing at all, for the past robs you of present pleasures. "Now" is the only time there is. Think about how much time your brain ponders your choices, continually questioning itself. This of course is the ego's ploy to keep you concentrated on past regrets and forever doubting. Yet ideas which come to you in present moments are your best revelations. Keep your thoughts aligned with the power of now and resist the dark shadows of past choices which do not bring you peace. Stillness of the mind is where peace is found, and this is where all creativity and wisdom come alive in you. See the present and see your true self aggrandized.

5. (10) - My thoughts do not mean anything.

The thoughts that do not serve you, inspire you, or induce you into a better state of being, are not your real thoughts. What good are thoughts which cause you to undermine yourself and can do nothing to change what was? Today you felt twinges of guilt when thoughts of past misgivings ensued as you reminisced with a friend. When the past is brought up and brings back memories of events that are not particularly uplifting, it is best to recognize that you actually were gifted by those experiences. Understand that they give you insights as to who you thought you were then, as compared to the one you now know as you. Healing has come to take its place and past events no longer serve you. Today you realized that you are blessed to be in a far better place. You have risen above the level of unloving patterns of thought, and that you never need to return to it. Today is a new day. Let us forget the old and praise the new, for the past is nothing more than an illusion.

Love, Jesus

53

(Review) My meaningless thoughts are showing me a meaningless world.

1. (11) - My meaningless thoughts are showing me a meaningless world.

Thoughts are meaningful only to the one who thinks them true. Thoughts are neither right nor wrong. They are no more than reactions to brain impulses. A healed mind will produce thoughts that bring peace, not fear, into a conflicting situation. But troubled thoughts will cause anger to flare if you indulge them. Keep your thoughts aligned with peace and forgiveness, even under trying circumstances. Do not delude yourself into thinking that a harsh reaction towards someone already in a state of turmoil will end on a positive note, for it never does. You have come a long way in your learning. To react poorly in any situation is indeed meaningless. The person who lashed out at you did not perceive himself as loving or he would not have followed the urge to pursue anger even though you thought it to be unprovoked. What can give the world meaning when thoughts of aggression are spiked, leaving no room for a positive or peaceful outcome? By reacting angrily to someone who is already feeling unloved will show you both a meaningless world. Because all minds are joined, one healed mind can only serve to bring healing to another's mind with loving kindness.

2. (12) - I am upset because I see a meaningless world.

What can give meaning to a world steeped in chaos? Fear pours from the narratives of TV news commentators who rant and rave, as they are paid to do. They do nothing but promote devastation and urgency to those who are unaware that they are being fed a steady diet of untruths. Who can feel safe in such a world, and who can live in peace when greed and self-serving intentions call you away from your right to peace and well-being? Such addiction to the news serves no purpose but to cause states of agitation. Only peace can bring happiness. And although everyone seeks it, they do not know that it is within their own capacity to know of it. You need not buy into that which the broken few are selling to the world. Seek peace in nature, be creative, and spend time with those who help to lift your spirits. Everyone can assist in creating a more meaningful world by not allowing the false beliefs of others to become their own. Do not get caught up in daily routines by those who feed into the censorship of truth. Stay centered, and let no outside influences take you away from that which is truly meaningful.

3. (13) - A meaningless world engenders fear.

To know and to feel peace is a place of great expansion. What we are witnessing in the world today is much apprehension as the world is in the midst of great chaos. The world as such is becoming unrecognizable as it seems to be moving out of control. Because there is so much disorder, it would seem impossible that anything positive will come out of the shadows, and nothing ever will for those who render themselves helpless and afraid. But there is a new and better world awaiting those who choose to be a part of it. When nothing is ever questioned, nothing ever changes. Many are no longer willing to give into the fears that the world forces upon them. Before peace can come to fruition, necessary changes must come first. Within these changes, new realizations sprout, leaving illusions of the past to wither away and die. Those in fear must come to realize that they do have choices and the choice to be free is a decision. You need not live by the standards of those who choose to wrap themselves in cloaks of fear and hide their heads, believing they will be safe if they do not question. Never deny your feelings. Whatever you choose to believe that brings you peace cannot engender fear.

4. (14) - God did not create a meaningless world.

The world you see is a manifestation of thought. Every thought you ever had, or ever will have, creates the world you see. You are either trapped by your thoughts or liberated by them. Every outcome you perceive comes from the thought that created it. You do not need to be the perpetrator of fearful beliefs when peace is your greatest desire. Fear always gives way to peace and peace gives you the power to bring happier experiences into your life. You have the choice to bring either harmony or ill will into the world. In its present state, this is not the world God created. Because God creates with you, how can this be all that you are? What you truly are is far greater than the limitations you place upon yourself. You were designed to bring loveliness and light into the world. Nothing is meaningless when you choose to live your purpose.

5. (15) - My thoughts are images that I have made.

If your mind is not at peace, it is in darkness. For what can fearful thoughts be but painful images? All problems stem from images that seem to culminate from outside yourself. But in truth there is nothing beyond yourself. The mind cannot serve a dual purpose; one is self-serving, while the other is Spirit. The images of the thoughts you create are the ones you must live by. If your thoughts are in tune with your God-Given realities, they can be expressed creatively. But if you allow your thoughts to cause havoc in your world, fearful scenarios become your reality. The Holy Spirit is the interpreter of your true thoughts and what He understands He can heal. He does not believe ego interpretations, and by yourself alone, you are left to grope in darkness. Thoughts that are creatively expressed bring you towards a true and everlasting purpose. God created you to think independently. But it is only through self-awareness that He can reach you. It is a choice as to whether you use your thoughts creatively or misdirect your thoughts by aligning them instead with false images.

Love, Jesus

54

(Review). I have no neutral thoughts.

1. (16) - I have no neutral thoughts.

Thoughts are never neutral because each thought has the power to create or to miscreate. Thoughts as such are all powerful. Each thought determines what the outcome shall be—the way you feel, what you wish to happen, and how you react in a given situation. If a thought displeases you, it will create a displeasing result. If a thought is harried, it will create an urgency of sorts. If a thought is peaceful, it will create calmness. All thoughts have the power to bring something either positive or negative into your reality, right, wrong, or indifferent. It makes no difference, for the Universe judges not. But it is incumbent upon you to keep your thoughts "well maintained." Each thought brings a new reality into the playing field. Therefore, outcome is a choice. When you are peaceful you attract loving conditions into your reality. Your happiness depends upon your commitment to this truth.

2. (17) - I see no neutral things.

What is vision but true thoughts revealed? Vision does not aspire to what the body's eyes see, but what the mind beholds in thought. True vision comes from thoughts that are purposeful which signify balance, wellness, and peace. What your eyes see is what you perceive to be true but not to be relied upon if the ego chooses for you. What the mind projects is made manifest through the body's eyes. Each thought brings you closer to truth if you think with the part of the mind that understands salvation. When you have come to the point where you are experiencing total peace, you know that your vision is serving you well, for you are trusting in it. Give your thoughts freedom to express creatively. Those are the thoughts God returns to you, thoroughly polished and free from strain. The truth of who you are is actually belief in yourself. You are very capable of interpreting what your mind reveals when you stand in your own truth.

3. (18) - I am not alone in experiencing the effects of my seeing.

The reason you are not alone in your experiences is because your thoughts are not private; they are shared. All thoughts create a different energetic frequency. What you experience depends on the vibrational energy of your thoughts. Lower levels of thought hinder the mind from exploring greater truths. When you are feeling happy, you are raising your own vibrations and joining with others who share the same elevated consciousness. By allowing yourself to be influenced by thoughts due to anger, fear, worry, and sickness, it brings your energy level down and you operate at a lower vibrational frequency. Now perceived as separate and apart from your brothers and sisters, you lose the ability to see them as one with you, sharing the same goals. Hone your skills in keeping pace with others who desire to change the world by changing the world's frequency from fear to love.

4. (19) - I am not alone in experiencing the effects of my thoughts.

Thoughts are energetic vibrations transmitted through brain activity. Because thoughts cannot be detected in the physical sense, they would appear to be isolated, separate, and hidden. What you see or touch would seem to have greater reality than your thoughts. Yet, whatever you see and touch is made manifest by the very thoughts that make up the world you see. Think how the world would thrive if thoughts reflected kindness, love, and peace on a collective level. That is why each individual's thought process collectively impacts the whole, and why thought maintenance is so imperative. To reach lasting peace is a place of great expansion. Your goal and your purpose is to bring an atmosphere of peace and love into the world which goes well beyond that which you think are your limitations. Love knows no boundaries, for the effects of your thoughts are boundless.

5. (20) - I am determined to see.

Determination to see is the willingness to bring lies to truth, and weakness to strength. Seeking awareness, changes old, distorted thinking habits to newer and more advanced ones. You are not yet fully aware of the magnificent energetic frequency your body holds. It was always there, but for the recognition of it. It was by your determination to know true from false—for lies can become too much to bear, and weakness too depleting—that you decided to look for better options. Old, distorted images of yourself were cleared away, and new realities took their place. Where you were once blinded to the perfection of Self, you have awakened to a far better reality. To feel peace is a place of great expansion indeed. You found your peace by your determination to see the truth.

Love, Jesus

55

(Review). I am determined to see things differently.

1. (21) - I am determined to see things differently.

Presently, you are determined to remain free, both spiritually and emotionally, and you have made great strides in your efforts. The story that unfolds today shows you a different side of the tapestry you previously thought was representative of all you believed in. You are now more at peace and your guides are with you always—this you have come to realize beyond all doubt. Do not inhibit yourself from revealing what is true for you. Stand in your own creative artistry. Do not deny yourself happiness when no sacrifices need be made at the cost of it. Allow your imagination to spin gold from straw, for this is indeed possible. You are the author of your own story. Write the story in accordance with how your mind would picture it to be. The picture you create is the one you will live by.

2. (22) - What I see is a form of vengeance.

Ego thoughts come from every direction. They are a boxing match of emotions at the behest of the ego. Vengeful thoughts bring out the worst in all of us. Throwing punches in defense of one's self in response to a perceived attack is not the answer. Send them light, send them peace, and muster up enough of your Self to send them love.

To bring peace into a situation where you feel attacked and not give in to vengeance is a lesson well learned. Do not ingest anger for you will choke on it. To energize attack thoughts only brings grief. This is where all errors come to truth. When you hold yourself up to higher standards and leave no room for the ego to dictate its worthless solutions, you will then experience greater peace. This will keep your attack thoughts harnessed and enlighten you in the process.

3. (23) - I can escape from this world by giving up attack thoughts.

What a magical concept it is to give up attack thoughts and escape from a world of hate. But it is the truth. Beneath the surface of attack thoughts, there is peace. If you do not use attack as a necessary defense, it enables the mind to understand how the world can be seen from a different perspective. When you join with your Higher Self, you find peace. There is no sacrifice by choosing to give up attack thoughts in preference to feeling peace. Peace is assured when you can find it in your heart to give way to another's call for help, for this is what they are asking. They are in need, so what can your anger accomplish? The world you have escaped by giving up attack thoughts rises above the clouds and settles into a heavenly form of release making it new again.

4. (24) - I do not perceive my own best interests.

What we sometimes think is in our own best interests is just the opposite of what is true. When the ego paints pictures of wonderful gains at the end of a rainbow, it is reeling you in with false promises. It isn't about finding a pot of gold at the end of a rainbow, it's about finding your inner truth which reveals where the "real" gold is. If decisions are made on an egoic level, you will suffer disappointment and heartbreak. Even if you think you have won, you have in truth lost because there is no peace to be found in poor choices. The ego does not think, it reacts. If you listen to your inner truth you will feel the gentle breeze of peace wash over you. This is what true perception is about and there is no greater accomplishment than this.

5. (25) - I do not know what anything is for.

Open your heart and understand what love is. Never do anything impulsive when you are in a state of unknowing. Anger, bewilderment, hurt, and other negative feelings, all fall under the heading of "fear." Ask instead to heal the past in order to establish the future and know that you are moving towards your purpose and not away from it. Do not make decisions while you are playing on the ego's turf. All thoughts that are not centered and in line with peace are fear-based. You want to disable pain, not strengthen it. And how can you know which decisions best serve you when you are in a state of flux? Be with Spirit in these moments of uncertainty, for peace is always found just a bit beyond.

Love, Jesus

56

(Review). My attack thoughts are attacking my invulnerability.

1. (26) - My attack thoughts are attacking my invulnerability.

Because God made you One with Him, you are invulnerable, for what can threaten the greatness of such love? When you undermine yourself in thought and in deed, and you cannot move away from your need to be right at the cost of your happiness, then your allegiance is to the ego and not to Self, which God created pure and changeless. We suffer the agony of pain and sickness when we cannot recognize our own invulnerability. If we did, attack would not be such a necessary option. For this would mean the release of attack in exchange for peace. The ego does not advocate peace as a healing method and would rather stick to its own agendas. That is why forgiveness is such a mighty antidote working against the ego's cravings. A forgiving heart does not need to attack, for it has no desire to strengthen the ego. Do not give away something as priceless as your invulnerability for a worthless substitute and sacrifice it for the innocence by which you were created.

2. (27) - Above all else I want to see.

What better gift can there be than the gift of vision which differs from how the body sees. Without vision, you are groping in darkness, no different from when your eyes are closed, and you are off dreaming elsewhere. To see the light is to awaken to a new world; one where there is no darkness, no pain, no remorse, no regret. Your mind is free to create when you open yourself up to true vision. Depression is the manifestation of the belief in sin, but sin is an illusion of the mind, for God did not put it there. It is a manifestation of the ego which cannot be trusted to show what is really there. You will know that the choices you make are the right ones as you move closer towards inner peace. Asking for guidance gives you the vision to make the choices which are right for you. Then, there is nothing to fear, for you are now walking on solid ground and the way home can be seen.

3. (28) - Above all I want to see things differently.

The world perceived in its current state is indeed chaotic, and widespread fear seems to be running rampant. The world is in a sorry state of affairs, yet those in peace are the ones who can rise above the mire by choosing to see things differently. A peaceful mind creates an atmosphere of security and well-being which serves to raise consciousness to higher levels, as fear dissipates and peace abounds. You need not see a world in turmoil. You can create a different experience by appreciating the exuberance of life itself—a walk in nature, a day at the beach, a hike in the woods. Whatever fills your senses. There is so much happiness and joy to be seen if you focus on loveliness instead of heartbreak. Nature is a wonderful resource in changing one's perspective into seeing gentler and more peaceful times ahead. Stand uplifted and do not let your peace be compromised. This can't always be avoided. But what can be avoided are those small setbacks which seem to be stripping you of joy and peace. Instead of giving in to its irritations, change the aura of your thoughts to one of happiness and well-being.

4. (29) - God is in everything I see.

God is in everything you see because God is in all things. When you are disturbed by a brother it is because you do not see the God in him, and with some, it is no doubt hard to see. But such individuals do not understand that they are created from love as we all are and cannot yet see it within themselves. It is indeed in your best interests to see it for them. To get past those barriers and to see the God in all is to see it in yourself. It is important to peer through the tough exterior of some of your brothers and sisters without judgment. You do not need to covet their space, nor they yours. You simply need to feel the kindred spirit that you all share, so that they too may come to know it as well. Remember, there are no private thoughts. To judge others for your false perception of them is unworthy of God's child. Turn your thoughts away from judgment and understand that the best medicine is to forgive.

5. (30) - God is in everything I see because God is in my mind.

If God is in everything you see, He must also be in your mind. And because this is so, He works with you to solve dilemmas you might think are unsolvable, and they usually are when they are not coming from a deeper sense of Self. Of yourself, you cannot solve a potentially dire situation because emotions run high and thoughts leap out of control. But when you bring God into the equation, then everything else is brought to fruition. God is only Love, and so He brings Love into the separation where healing is needed. The ego will always attempt to seize control in place of Him. With God, your thoughts and words come from truth. Even if you question, the heart knows what is true. Whether you are aware of it or not, God is always in your mind, and as such, He is in all things.

Love, Jesus

57

(Review). I am not the victim of the world I see.

1. (31) - I am not the victim of the world I see.

Because you are a creation of free will, it gives you all freedom to pursue whatever your heart desires. The exuberance and energy you are always reaching for is a natural desire. The world you see does not provide happiness, for of itself the world is a dry and thirsty land. But it is incumbent upon you to provide it with the nourishment it needs which is brought forth through kindness and love. You came to the world not as a victim, but as a participant. You are a creative energy forever seeking new ventures and ideas. Bring joy into the world so that you may experience the best of it. God does not deem you a victim, for you were created to express yourself freely. It is only you who can think yourself something other than what God created you to be. You thrive best when you are fulfilling your life's purpose. Give the world what you came to do so that it may experience the best of your intentions.

2. (32) - I have invented the world I see.

The reason you are not a victim of the world is because you are the creator of everything in your life and the inventor of each outcome. To create something can also mean to miscreate. Fearful thoughts will bring down a fearful reality. Everything manifests according to how you perceive a given situation, good or bad, right or wrong.

You need not be a victim of your thoughts. Thoughts which make you sad can be dissolved, but only when you see there is nothing to be gained by savoring them. When you embody the idea that you are a child of God, created One with Him, why would anything other than this be your chosen reality? A peaceful mind presents the best outcome in all situations. By maintaining this belief, you are free to grow and become a creative force in the world as you are meant to be.

3. (33) - There is another way of looking at the world.

Peace is always on the horizon if you choose to welcome it. When you cannot let go of guilt, anger, frustration, and hate, for you believe someone has caused you pain, it is never about them, it is always about you. When you feel such emotions, you have it within yourself to change the picture and see it from a different perspective. It is not the deed or the crime of the other that needs rearranging, it is always you. All you need to do is forgive the "sin," so not to make it yours, for the burden is a heavy one, tiring at best, unbearable at worst. You do not need to carry such a burdensome weight, for it is so much better to transform your emotions into the weightlessness of peace. The other person then has the chore of determining how he or she will choose to see, for the onus is no longer yours to carry. This is what we mean when we say, "You are the master of your own fate." When you choose to see the world condemned, that is how it shall be. When you can experience the glory of peace, it is because you have chosen it.

4. (34) - I could see peace instead of this.

Controlling your thoughts is how peace enters in. When you are juggling difficult issues and you are not in a loving, peaceful state of mind, you know it is time to re-adjust your priorities, for no positive outcome can come of this. The ego will storm in and tempt you with "justified" reprisals, but to no avail, because it will not change anything. It is at this point you must make conscious adjustments by taking control of your beliefs. Once you regain a feeling of peace and centeredness, it enables Spirit to take charge, and only then will truth unfold, and the answers given will be understood. But if you race ahead of yourself, it robs you of the opportunity to choose peace over pain. Only in stillness is there peace. You cannot raise your consciousness when you are in the depths of raging emotions. If you give it a rest, peace has room to enter, and healing is allowed to occur.

5. (35) - My mind is part of God's. I am every holy.

Because your mind is part of God's, it enables you to think as He does, for your true thoughts are blended with His. But the ego, which keeps us bound to littleness, is how we define ourselves. We cannot accept the truth that we are created as exalted beings in God. Therefore, we believe we think apart from God. By not accepting our holiness, we keep ourselves locked away in the ego's thought system, unable to comprehend how truly free we are. True grandeur lies in the recognition that we are all holy creations of God. And as God's holy sons and daughters, our true home is not in the world of physicality as we are convinced we are, but in God's Mind. Where else can greater peace be found than in knowing that our True Identity and holiness is established in God? Be not afraid to go beyond the limited aspect to see yourself as He does and delve into the holiness of the One Mind which is the only place that is truly safe.

Love, Jesus

58

(Review). My holiness envelops everything I see.

1. (36) - My holiness envelops everything I see.

It is within your reality to understand you are forever loved and cherished by the One Who created you holy. With this recognizable truth comes great freedom for your holiness gives you a world absent of sin, as holiness IS the absence of sin. In holiness there are no impurities which keep you apart from understanding God's Love, for it is deeply ingrained. Lay down your differences and come to God with your hands bare, for in holiness also lies your innocence. Nothing more is needed. Bring forth all your goodness and leave behind the sinful person you thought yourself to be and come into the person you are in truth. The world is at rest as your holiness is recognized, for nothing is threatened when peace is at hand.

2. (37) - My holiness blesses the world.

In holiness what can there possibly be to threaten your peace and hold it hostage? In holiness comes the recognition that with God all is well, for you are loved and protected by a Force far beyond your own limitations. How can anything come to take the place of such greatness? What the ego sees is a dismal portrayal of who you really are. Your holiness rises above these dim perceptions, for how can you not be anything but holy when God Himself assures you it is what you are? Give back to the One Who blesses you by rising above the temptation to retreat into the dark corners of your mind. Your peace is guaranteed by your unwavering resilience. To look away from such blessings delays you in finding your truth and so the world waits on a promise long ago made. Look beyond such needless dallying and seek the light which forever flickers within you.

3. (38) - There is nothing my holiness cannot do.

You can never make what is false true, though the ego consistently does so in its attempts. Only this realization can be counted on to bring you peace. The peace you seek exists within the Mind you share with God, for here is where the truth of your holiness is assured. When you come to a fork in the road, you must stop and discern your bearings. The trail is much more dependable now that the journey is almost over. You have come to understand that all answers are within the part of you that knows the truth, yet it is easy to be tempted to trade away peace for illusions. Retaliation, even when it seems fair and warranted is not the answer no matter how hard you try to justify it, for it cannot be justified. The answer is never to try and satisfy the ego's hunger for redemption for it can never be satiated. You must now stay on course and let only the truth of who you are rule your actions and your thoughts.

4. (39) - My holiness is my salvation.

How comforting it is to learn that holiness and salvation are one and the same. It is the understanding that to be holy is to make holy, for only when you feel the strength of its greatness does the world respond to the love and peace it offers. By holding the vibration of your holiness in your heart you become free—free from fear, free from guilt, and free from all conflict in your mind. All of this, your holiness brings, for you have accepted it as true and thus the miracles of healing are now in motion as the decision has been made. If you can have peace over the untamed grievances of the ego why would you choose the latter? Is it not insane to choose pain when healing is the only sane choice? Feel the strength of the One Who made you holy and offers you salvation as well.

5. (40) - I am blessed as a Son of God.

As a blessed Son of God, you are always guided and protected. Ask any brother or sister, no matter the degree of their awareness, if they feel blessed. Their answer is almost always "yes." In God there is only love, so how can even the slightest notion of His love not be felt? Within this scope of divine energy, blessings become manifest, for they are finally recognized. When you are angry, resentful, unhappy, or fearful, blessings go unnoticed. It matters not what you do. It is only within the capacity in which the heart is given to express itself that blessings are seen, lest they go unnoticed. As a creation born of Him you are indeed blessed.

Love, Jesus

59

(Review). God goes with me wherever I go.

1. (41) - God goes with me wherever I go.

God is never apart from you, for He is always aware of you. What terrible mishaps can possibly occur when you know that God holds the key to this absolute certainty? As a part of the Living God, and also an integral part of the human experience, you are never alone. Because the body is fallible and prone to error, the human experience cannot always be expected to be perfect as well. But you can bring it to near-perfection by trusting in God's Unconditional Love, which is always shielding and protecting you. You can change any misperceptions about this by focusing more on the God-Experience, which is all about peace and love. As you move into this realm of consciousness you cannot help but to become more aware that God is with you wherever you are. Keep this amazing thought close to you at all times. This in itself will create the greatest good possible within the human experience.

2. (42) - God is my strength. Vision is His gift.

At times of sadness when you want to comprehend why something happened which caused you pain, this is the time to question what it was for, and not to question why it happened? This is where God's Strength and His Vision become the Source from which you can draw your own strength. It is where you get a truer picture of how a given situation is best seen. The Holy Spirit which guides you through such altercations is the One Voice that you can hear, for His words and thoughts speak for God. Feelings are often a mix of emotions hard to interpret if you get caught up in their frailties. Be certain, however, that there is a gift within the heart of every experience, even if you find it injurious to your feelings. It is actually a blessing, for He holds your hand as you wait for a bigger picture to emerge. Look to Him for strength, for that is where it is found.

3. (43) - God is my Source. I cannot see apart from Him.

Give God your complete willingness to see as He sees. Although you are striving to reach your full potential here, you are nevertheless still sorting out unresolved issues. Yet, sorting out cannot be done alone, for alone there can be no successful outcome. As such, the ego rushes in and feeds on the power it is given to exalt itself. It recognizes it as an opportunity to take you away from the peace of your Father, for you believe your peace comes from a better source. Step back and feel your closeness to The One you are never apart from. This, however, can only be seen in the stillness of your mind. It is important to be centered and resist any retaliatory outbursts in your head, for they serve no purpose. Look away from the grievances of the day and smile with your Creator, your Source, and the One who knows your real thoughts, as they are also His thoughts. You need only to keep in stride with the peace of God within. Apart from Him, you cannot see.

4. (44) - God is the light in which I see.

Healed thoughts reflect God's light, as do your words. Know that there is a gift in all things, no matter the upheavals which sometimes come to take away your peace. It is an important concept to remember. You are not lost, just realigning yourself when disturbances of a particular sort come and overtake you. Your heart knows God's thoughts, for here is where they are deeply felt. To distance yourself from the ego is to find the place within where you can "just be." A beach outing, stillness in a garden, or just a simple walk, are ways to silence the ego, even if only temporarily. For now, you have regained your centeredness and once again you have found the quiet place where nothing can intrude upon your peace. This requires patience, diligence, and desire. The more you practice, the more proficient you become. The light of God's Grace shines bright so that it can be seen.

5. (45) - God is the mind with which I think.

You cannot think apart from God, although you think you do when your thoughts become compromised. Thoughts are either with God or with the ego. Those thoughts that cause you conflict are obviously not the thoughts of true awareness, and so they are ego-based. With God, thoughts are flawless, yet without flawed thoughts, you would not understand the greater glory of your true thoughts by comparison, and not see the magnificent light you behold. It is this recognition which brings you to a higher place in your conscious development. This is where all healing, pleasure, and heartfelt goodness come together, for here is where you need to be, and nowhere else. When you are in a place of stillness, the meditative state, God fills you as your mind and His become joined. The more you practice, the faster your mind will grasp the glory of the thoughts you think with God.

Love, Jesus

60

(Review) God is the Love in which I forgive.

1. (46) - God is the Love in which I forgive.

Forgiveness is of the heart and it is the heart's energy which connects you to God. Below the arc of forgiveness there exists a lower realm of energy which is the ego. It knows not of love because it suppresses, it does not embrace. To truly forgive another is to render the heart free. Where there is forgiveness of the heart there is also love. Forgiveness offers the freedom to love, while the soul ignites the heart's energetic goodness. God's Love is pureness of Spirit. This is what you are, and only this. It is the ego which is the foreigner here and as such it speaks a foreign language, inaudible and strange. It professes to love, but it knows not love for it spews unloving words and unkind thoughts. And where there is hate, how can love be present? Love's true home is of the heart, where forgiveness is bountiful. Hold yourself up to the heart's natural environment, which is where you must be and nowhere else.

2. (47) - God is the strength in which I trust.

What greater strength to rely on but from the One who offers it unconditionally? Your strength can be drawn from Him, for where He is there is only love. You desperately need His strength, for you are steeped in a world bereft of love and it is the strength of His Love which provides it for you. Although love is everywhere, it is not recognized often enough and seen by so few. By accepting His Love, you can then become one of many who do know of it because they have found it and shared it among the rest. This opens a path for those who yearn to know of it, yet still remain unfulfilled. But they too can learn of its truth when you give to them as you have received. Leave your past behind and come into a new and beautiful reality where love abounds and happiness dwells. It opens up a future whereby love is felt by every heart because it was bestowed freely and thus kept.

3. (48) - There is nothing to fear.

Worldly dysfunction inhibits peace. From where you come, fear is non-existent and only love exists. Although you came to Earth with the blessings of Heaven you became conditioned in the ways of fear and did not recognize your inherent nature, which is love. You were not born of fear, you merely blocked the energy to love's presence and so fear became instilled. The lower frequencies of this world are sorry teachers, for it indoctrinates fear into the hearts of many who feel lost and bewildered. But protection and safety are discovered when love is practiced, and healing is experienced. With this great connection to love's presence, a heavenly glow drops into your heart, for there is nothing to fear and nothing worthwhile exists outside of it. Stay focused on this truth and know that nothing can come to threaten your peace when you do not let fear linger in your heart.

4. (49) - God's Voice speaks to me all through the day.

God's Voice is with you all through the day. If your mind is at peace, it opens up the channels in recognition of His Voice as He speaks. When your mind is actively involved in worldly distractions, God's Voice which is broadcast all through the day cannot be heard, for you are not tuned into the frequency by which it comes. The part of the mind which picks up ideas and thoughts are turned off. You then miss out on opportunities which are meant to guide and serve you. His Thoughts come to you in that "aha" moment when the message is understood, and you have learned something perhaps you always knew but had forgotten. This then becomes the moment when you move up another rung on the ladder to higher understanding. His Voice is always available to you. All you need do is be willing to hear it.

5. (50) - I am sustained by the Love of God.

The Love that comes from God sustains us, for it does not wane or shift or die; it is eternal. In your desire to awaken to this reality you became strengthened, for it helped you to understand more fully your purpose in the world which always comes from a place of Love. You heard the Call and awakened to it. Had you not, you would never know the all-powerful, all-loving, creative being that you are. You thought yourself to be small and weak, for the world conditions us to believe this great distortion of truth. You came to fulfill a purpose which was thwarted early on and so you suffered in darkness, for the weak suffer much. In this three-dimensional world of density and fear, it is difficult to comprehend the enormity of our true capacities and the roles we are here to fulfill. Be joyful now, for the world is coming into a new "waking reality." As you open yourself up to its resounding effects, illusions of the past will be seen no more, for you will see a happier world where fear is contained, and Love surrounds you.

Love, Jesus

61
I am the light of the world.

Light is life, just as darkness is the opposite. Because you were created in light, you have the power to illuminate through the darkness which lurks in the shadows of a fear-based world. The light in one is powerful enough to ignite the flame in many, as it replenishes and creates more of the same. Love brings forth more light, for that is its purpose. It is a great and abundant source of energy to be used openly and freely in a world which is rapidly accelerating to a higher level of consciousness as it raises love's vibrations. It reflects back to you in appreciation from all who experience it. If you demonstrate kindness, whether by choice of words or deeds, or both, so too shall you feel the breath of love within the abundance of its light. That is why it is of the utmost importance to keep your thoughts positive for that is what light responds to. You will know yourself as the light of the world when it reveals itself by the satisfaction it brings you, and you can love yourself in the process. Your purpose in the world is to reveal your light. You need do nothing more than this, for you are living your purpose.

Love, Jesus

62
Forgiveness is my function as the light of the world.

As the light of the world, you are given the understanding of your true function, which is to forgive. It shows you a better world, for you have made it so by your forgiveness. It shows you a healed world instead of a sick and ailing world. Forgiveness is a means by which healing becomes the effect of forgiveness. Imagine if everyone in the world could understand the power of forgiveness—the world would flourish and sustain itself, for there would be no cause to see it sick or ailing. But forgiveness must start somewhere, and so it is incumbent upon those who seek to save the world to shine their light upon it. And so, a forgiven world is no longer a hateful world. To forgive another is not necessarily reason to be physically involved. As long as you can find it in yourself to forgive the perceived perpetrator, that is all it takes to free yourself from the binds that tie you to guilt, and you still retain your power, for you had not forfeited it. From forgiveness comes love and love is light. By this, you are a light worker. Such are those who recognize their purpose. They are the bringers of peace by forgiving the world its frailties.

Love, Jesus

63

The light of the world brings peace to every mind through forgiveness.

Those who are aware of the light they carry walk the Earth lighting a path for those who do not yet see it reflected in themselves. Everyone is a lightworker, but not all are aware of it. Those who are bring the light of peace to every heart through forgiveness. Those who know their purpose are also aware that they hold the light for others to see. In the world there is a great thirst for peace, and forgiveness is the well from which they quench their thirst. This is a time when God's lightworkers are gathering in great numbers for they understand their purpose. The energy on the planet is rising as so many are now joining in awareness of their elevated consciousness. Keep your head above the clouds of fear and allow others to see the peace in you so that they see it within themselves. This is not a time to be fearful but a time to be joyful. Forgiveness is a practice which brings light into the hearts of those who are still fearful, that they may find it in those who are distributing the light of peace by the examples they set.

Love, Jesus

64
Let me not forget my function.

As a sovereign being, it is your right to come away from those who do not make you feel good about yourself or uplift you. When you subject yourself to someone else's demands you cannot see yourself as sovereign. If you allow a sword to be held over your head, you are giving your power away and your strength is denied you. It is a bully who tries to take someone else's power thinking he has a right to it. It is because he sees himself as powerless and by bullying or controlling, he believes he is restoring his own power by taking yours. You cannot know your function if you allow others to take your freedoms from you. Loosen the grip if the binds are too tight and you feel that your peace is being compromised. Let no one use your power to make it theirs, for that is hardly freedom. Send them light, send them love, and focus on forgiveness. To forgive and to also be free is where your sovereignty lies, for then you are living your truth, which is your function.

Love, Jesus

65
My only function is the one God gave me.

The function God gave you is to live your purpose. But first you must understand what it is you are truly seeking. Each individual must determine what salvation means to him. You cannot change another person's beliefs, but you can influence him by believing in yourself. Imagine a ferris wheel and each person riding it is at a different level of expansion. The lower part of the wheel carries a lower vibration than do the higher levels. As such, every person is at a different stage of learning and each one must determine when he or she is ready to fulfill the function assigned to him or her. The function God gave you is easier to understand when you put it in this perspective: Each person is at his own stage of awareness and no one can change another's reality in order to make it theirs. It is for you and you alone to decide what it means to you. The higher you raise your vibration of thought, the closer it will bring you to understanding your function. When you reach it, you can better understand your part in salvation.

Love, Jesus

66
My happiness and my function are one.

There is always a choice to be in a place of happiness or not. You can choose to be forlorn but that is not what you would rather be. Your free will entitles you to go in any direction you wish. But in choosing happiness, you are automatically brought to a place where the air is light and peace is felt. To choose happiness brings you to a place of self-awareness and your function is recognized. Happiness is a state of being; it is who you are in truth. The ego does not allow for long periods of happiness for it is never patient. It seeks your constant attention if you allow it. It has a short attention span, for it cannot stay silent for long. When the ego urges you to come down to its level of distraction—hate, fear, and the like—you are obviously not making the best choice if that is your decision. You have come to understand that you do have choices and that you are free to take control of any situation if you choose to. Practice and diligence are always at play, for every choice you make requires your better judgment. It is up to you to recognize that the ego does have an agenda, as does Spirit. It best serves you to put your energy where your happiness lies. Fill your function by choosing to be happy which is also the home of peace.

Love, Jesus

67
Love created me like itself.

Wherever a situation arises, and expression of thought is your will, your choice of words will make all the difference in how you are perceived. If what you say comes from a presence of love, it transfers over to the one you are speaking to, even if you are not consciously aware of it at the time. Always remember that you are created from the greatest Source of Power in the Universe, which is Love. That is what you are, and only this. Words of attack come from fear and foils any hope for peace as the outcome. You cannot coerce another to think as you do. But if your intentions come from love, then love's energy will flow naturally, leaving nothing to stand in the way of truth. Words are your strongest tools; they reveal your emotions. Only good can be accomplished in the realm of Spirit and in Spirit, words do speak volumes. Created from love, it is your natural state of being. You have the power to transform any situation from fear to love depending on your thoughts and the words you choose to express them. Everything you think and say manifests itself into reality. If you say it lovingly, peace will be the outcome. If it is defensive in an attempt to win, the results will be poor for no one wins. Love comes from love, and where there is love, there is only truth.

Love, Jesus

68
Love holds no grievances.

To see yourself the way God sees you requires great determination of faith. The part of you that is of God knows only Love. To step aside from a grievance and hold yourself up as the immortal child of God that you are, is to let go of that which is unworthy of you. God created you as Himself, but you cannot know yourself this way when you are holding onto a grievance. To nurture your soul is to forgive, and if you cannot forgive, you cannot know Love. Go beyond those thoughts which tell you that you were unjustly treated, and move into the greater part of your Self, your Higher Self. There is a place inside of you that remains undefiled and incapable of hurt. You have become very much acquainted with the part of you which knows Spirit. You need not bow down to condemnation even in circumstances where you believe someone you love has betrayed that love and has wounded you. You do not need to attach yourself to that which seems irreparable when there is really nothing that needs repair. You need do nothing but honor the loving Child of God that you are. As a creator, you can master the art of releasing grievances and feel only love if you dedicate your life to it. You have come to assist in raising the consciousness of the world. That position is still yours. Concentrate on the part of you that is only love and take your place in Heaven.

Love, Jesus

69

My grievances hide the light of the world in me.

As the light of the world, you have come to take part in a brand new celebration. It is a time when you can take a giant step towards reaching your goal. It is a time to connect with all others having the same purpose. They too have come in celebration of a new world rising, and their light is joining with yours. But by holding onto grievances, your light remains hidden. If unforgiving thoughts enter your mind and dawdle there, it is urgent that you see the necessity in letting them go, for there is a far larger picture to consider. It is the recognition that you are working towards a greater purpose, and the light reflected within reveals that it is so. Those who see the light in you will honor it. Those who do not are sabotaging their vision, for they remain in darkness. There will always be someone you will need to forgive for something. Some forms of forgiveness seem more difficult than others. But they are all the same. Your purpose is to strive to stay connected to peace, which makes it easier to forgive and to move forward. Love yourself enough to realize your power, and not give it away by holding a grievance. When you reach the top of the mountain you will rejoice, for there you will be free.

Love, Jesus

70

My salvation comes from me.

There is nothing that you can experience which does not come from you. Your thoughts and ideas can move mountains, for you have been given the power to create. It is you who creates the world you see. Each new thought attracts another, and another, and so on. There are consequences to everything you do. This is the law of cause and effect. Your creative powers determine your actions, and your actions determine the outcome. That which you choose will come to pass. If you choose salvation you need never fear, for the outcome is sure. It is the ego which is relentless in its efforts to destroy that which is your greatest need, which is peace. If your thoughts and deeds come from Spirit, you will receive the outcome you want, for then the ego has lost its grip. To be in a healthy state of awareness creates miracles, one of which is healing. Why then would you choose sickness in its place? You have complete power of choice. So much so, that it is enough to keep your mind and body healthy and free from all sickness. Nothing can intrude upon this, for this IS salvation. Although salvation will one day come to every heart, the sooner you seek it, the closer you will come to it. Bring the light of Heaven where you go and find your salvation in the here and now.

Love, Jesus

71

Only God's plan for salvation will work.

Because you are a creation of God, does this not tell you that it is only God's plan for salvation that can succeed? Any plan in opposition to God's plan cannot work. The need for salvation in the world must be recognized before it can be achieved. You cannot know peace within the confines of the ego's version of it. What you have come to understand is that there is no escape from suffering if you do not see the cause of it. It was not until you discovered its cause in yourself that you were finally able to experience true healing. It was the bond you sought with God which brought this about. When a brother or sister is attacking you, their need for forgiveness is greater than the attack itself. This you can understand because you have been witness to it. There were times you felt unloved because of your own perceived transgressions. With forgiveness, brothers and sisters can see themselves in the light by which you were all created. Anger cannot be fought with anger and then expect that it will bring about harmony. You are a healer. But you can only accept this truth if you accept God's plan, for that is what it takes for salvation to work.

Love, Jesus

72

Holding grievances is an attack on God's plan for salvation.

Holding a grievance is an attack on God, for God knows only Love. When you are strongly connected to the density of the ego's belief system, it is difficult to comprehend how peace can be yours. The ego denies God, and therefore it cannot know true peace. It seems to desire it, but it looks for it in all the wrong places. Attack and peace do not work well together. That is why the ego steadfastly holds onto grievances, for peace is against its innate beliefs. Salvation is the link which connects you to the wonders of creation. Once you have experienced tranquility of the soul, it is much more difficult to accept the ego's agenda for peace, for there is no lasting peace to be found there—certainly not by holding on to grievances. Salvation, which comes from God, must be truly sought before it can be found. To make forgiveness your daily practice instills greater understanding of purpose. It requires placing yourself in another person's shoes, if only for a little while. This takes patience, understanding, and the willingness to become free of the ego's unwise beliefs, which serve no purpose but its own. If you dedicate yourself to all you can be, God's plan for salvation will be easy to understand.

Love, Jesus

73
I will there be light.

You live in a fear-driven society, where many leaders steadfastly attempt to seize control of those who buy into their nefarious agendas. Yet the only control anyone has over another is if it is willingly relinquished. Now is the time where faith is your greatest ally. Because God shares His light with all creation, it is in everyone, yet not everyone knows that they are in possession of it. During these days of struggle and oppression upon the Earth, the light you behold must be shone brightly so that others may see that they too possess the miracles they witness in you. To share light is to be forgiving, loving, kind, considerate, and truthful. The body is not all that you are. It is the light that shines beyond the body which bears witness to all that you are. The world shines anew, for so many are gathering in recognition of the peace and resilience in those who stand true to themselves. Be strong in your efforts and rise above the limitations imposed by those who seek power over others. Instead, feel the love which is inherent in everyone. The world is in need of lightworkers who are benevolent in their words and actions. To be free is to take control of your own power. It belongs to no one but you.

Love, Jesus

74
There is no will but God's.

You cannot help but feel peace, love, joy, and tranquility, just by recognizing that God's will and yours are joined. This is what you always sought but did not know it was what you truly wanted. The safety net of protection you found was unlike anything you knew before. There is no greater state of peace than when you decide to embrace and surrender to it. God knows you only as Love, and for this alone, your best interests are left in His care. Of yourself, you cannot know what your best interests are. If you did, you would not seek God. But to rely completely on yourself is to grope blindly in place of what you now see as truth. You did learn of it when you began to experience the difference, despair versus peace. You cannot know true peace when you are lost in the ego's world. The egoic state of consciousness is to be without God. To escape from the density and drudgery of this fear-driven world requires you to understand that there is nothing outside of God's will. This is the love that brings you into the Heart of God, for you are always invited in. Peace is His will for you, and only there can it be found.

Love, Jesus

75
The light has come.

What is light, but love? Love, deeply felt, is a reflection of the light within. You think you know love. But until you actually experience

God-Love, you can see that there is really no resemblance. To think you know, and to actually know, differs greatly. God-Realization is a knowing that you are all you can be. It brings about experiences coming from greater wisdom, and wisdom is truth. You know this to be so because your experiences have taught you this. You are no longer in fear of the future because the darkness of your past takes on a different perspective and brings you to the present where there is light. Each new experience of this places you on a higher platform of awareness. Your reactions to various situations are now dealt with peacefully. When the light of love enters your heart, a sweet blanket of calm is what you feel. So why would you choose pain when peace is at your doorstep, especially when you realize there really is no other option? God created you perfect and so you are nothing less, nor will you ever be. The light of love is here. You are at an advantage now, for you are now equipped to handle many of the pitfalls that come your way. You know the light has come when you see the endless miracles they bring.

Love, Jesus

76

I am under no laws but God's.

The world is made up of laws. These are the laws by which you must live, for you are bound to them. Many of those laws leave you confused and bewildered. Yet you must abide by those laws for they are written by decree and enforced by government. But God's laws differ from the world's laws in that they provide you with the strength and power to rise above all other laws. These are the laws of true freedom and they deliver to you what the world is incapable of giving you. The ego is one aspect of yourself, but its laws leave you bereft of peace for they are self-serving. Because of this, you are fearful, making no sense of who you are in truth. But the Self which is also you is an expression of God. A mind intent on bringing peace and love to the world knows there is only one law. You cannot serve the ego's laws and God's. There, you must discern your choices—whether to make peace or fear your reality. It is for you to determine which is the best offer. Choose peace, and that is the law by which you will live. Choose fear, and that is what you shall live by as well. Let the truth be known so you can choose to live according to the very laws by which you were created. Therefore, you must choose wisely.

Love, Jesus

77

I am entitled to miracles.

In order to believe you are deserving of miracles, you must first see creation itself as a miracle. And because you are a part of creation, why would you not afford yourself the privilege of believing that you are also entitled to miracles? That is a hard concept for the ego to follow, but it is true. If you cannot believe this, it is your arrogance which denies God over the ego's insolence which emphatically convinces you that you are undeserving of love. You came into the world knowing yourself as God's perfect creation, but somewhere along life's journey you forgot. You did not see the greatness of strength you carried because you could not believe it was given to you. Like a candle flickering in a darkened room, you believed you were too small and insignificant to be seen. But even the smallest flicker of a candle is seen as light. You are a strong, intelligent, and creative being. Believing this, makes all the difference. And to believe you are entitled to miracles is a step taken towards creating them. Keep your mind aware, and never forget that as your birthright, you are entitled to this, and more. How do you recognize a miracle coming your way? You feel the Love of God assuring you that this is what you are entitled to, and nothing less than this is His Will for you.

Love, Jesus

78
Let miracles replace all grievances.

Now is the time you must decide to let your grievances go. Think how important it is for you to choose to do this, for if you do not, you will still be lost in the drama and wasting valuable time. As you know, there are lessons to be learned in everything you do. Those who have hurt you are actually your saviors, for they are the ones from whom you can learn the most. They cause you to search for answers, and the answers you find tell the story behind the grievances you share. Ultimately, this serves to raise your awareness. By going beyond the facade of justifying your anger, you can then understand the part you played in the experience. Every time you let a grievance go, you attract a miracle not only to yourself, but also to the one you are having the grievance with. Healing will occur only when you have worked out the entanglements that you are both tied to. Give up the thoughts which hold you to a grievance and make no one responsible for your unhappiness. It is you and you alone who decides. You cannot change another's mind about their beliefs, but you can change yours. You need not befriend the person; you just need to forgive the person.

Love, Jesus

79
Let me recognize the problem so it can be solved.

There is a solution to every problem, but unless you believe it is so, you will not be aware that every problem is solvable. In life there are always problems, and no one walks the Earth free of them. Sometimes a problem seems unsolvable and far too complex to be fixed. Yet many problems fix themselves. Much of the time when a problem arises, if you do nothing, the problem will simply disappear. The mind is a most amazing instrument. It can accomplish anything, for it is powerful enough to bring healing to itself simply by the thoughts it receives. And what it receives it transmits. Fear is at the forefront of every problem. Do not allow fear to take control of your thoughts. Replace fear with faith and recognize that the strongest antidote to any problem is love. Stay present and do not worry about a future that has not yet occurred. Almost everything you fear that will happen, never does anyway. So why worry over something that has not yet occurred? The best recipe is a steady diet of trust, faith, and forgiveness. With this type of nourishment fed to the soul, no problem is unsolvable.

Love, Jesus

80

Let me recognize my problems have been solved.

If you could truly understand that your problems have already been solved, you would never have a single moment's unrest. Worry, fear, depression, and anxiety would never take such a heavy toll, as it was once the center of your universe. There was a time when you did not understand that all your problems had already been solved. You could have rested, feeling assured, if you had seen yourself as God sees you, completely whole and healed. You would have easily grasped the idea that absent love, there are only fearful outcomes. At this time, because the world is in a serious state of unrest, it is important to understand that the world rebounds where there is love and recoils without it. It is so easy to be caught up in a world that seems to be running rampant in fear and confusion. Yet God, in His infinite wisdom, sees the world as Love. He does not see you swallowed up in a world destined to fail, as the current state of affairs implies this fate. In waking each morning, look ahead and see your day as peaceful, allowing it to uplift your spirits. Trust that whatever problems you perceive, have already been solved. As a creation of love, tap into love's frequency and remain true to it.

Love, Jesus

81

(Review) I am the light of the world.

1. (61) - I am the light of the world.

Do you believe you are the light of the world? For if you did, you would not have a single care or worry in the world. As light, you are only love. To feel the light in your heart is to fulfill your purpose. Even the smallest candle is sometimes enough to light an entire room. You might think of a candle as nothing more than something to be placed on top of a cake. It is not the candle alone which does anything, but it is the heart of the candle, the flame, which is its purpose. When one candle is ignited, its tiny light can ignite another, then another, and there can be no end if it continues to be passed on. The light of one candle strengthens all the rest. That is why it is important to shrug off petty differences when they arise, for they mean nothing as compared to what you can accomplish as the light of the world. This is how consciousness is raised. If one corner of the world brings light to itself, it would eventually impact its entirety. Love is the most extraordinary light there is, for it cannot be extinguished where it is felt.

2. (62) - Forgiveness is my function as the light of the world.

Forgiveness, without giving it a second thought, is indeed a tall order. But without it there can be no real peace, for peace is only a present luxury, not a past one, as the past is non-existent. As the light of the world, you are an expression of love. Yet you cannot feel love when you are too grounded in your convictions. This is to say you would rather be right than happy. Forgiveness is not only the way to peace, but it frees you from being tied to a painful history where there was no peace at all. When you cannot let go of a grievance, you have not yet recognized that you are caught in a thought system which insists it is more satisfying to harbor anger than to feel love. It is a gift to yourself when you can move to a place where you see forgiveness as a welcome friend. You know you have forgiven a grievance when you are at peace, for now there is rest, and sleep comes easily. As the light of the world, you are here to fulfill your function, and this where your purpose is best served.

Love, Jesus

82

(Review) The light of the world brings peace to every mind through forgiveness.

1. (63) - The light of the world brings peace to every mind through forgiveness.

To forgive is to love. When you can forgive wholeheartedly, it is because you have come to truly understand the concept of forgiveness and what it does. Think of a happy world. Imagine how wonderful it would be to recognize that it came about because forgiveness was understood as the central idea which brought it love. The world then, would be a haven for peace. Imagine living in a world where forgiveness is no longer needed, for love outshone the need for it. Imagine such a world and you shall have it. If you held no grievances and forgave every person whom you held responsible for your distraught thoughts, you would see a new world, radiant with peace. Forgiveness is the central means by which such a world would come about. As the light of the world, it is incumbent upon you to bring light into the world by demonstrating it in yourself, first through forgiveness, and then through the love which binds it.

2. (64) - Let me not forget my function.

Your function is forgiveness. If you forget this one central ingredient to peace, you will have lost your way again. This, you understand, is because you have found the peace within yourself which was once buried deep within the debris of self-condemnation—guilt, depression, and fear. You did not know what it was, but you knew its weight was crushing. Because peace is what you looked to find, you did find it by learning the art of forgiveness, first in yourself, then in the world. It is a long and arduous road sometimes before forgiveness is understood as the method by which to heal. It is also the only answer to all your unresolved issues. You are an example of this, but examples need to be set for others to follow. This is how you fulfill your function.

Love, Jesus

83

(Review) My only function is the one God gave me.

1. (65) - My only function is the one God gave me.

Happiness is your true function. It is essential that you recognize where it comes from and not look for it where it does not exist. To look for it in the world leads to unhappiness for there the search is futile. The ego's idea of happiness comes from worldly possessions. According to the ego's beliefs, the more you have, the more it takes to make you happy. Look at the world and see how greed has not made it a better world, but instead has created greater hunger for more, while it is never satiated. It is somewhat like a dog chasing its tail. It chases after something that is impossible to reach, and what cannot be reached cannot make you happy. Happiness does not come from the materialistic indulgences of the ego. God is the Source from where your happiness lies. Before you can be truly happy, you must seek what is lasting. What is not lasting is not of God.

2. (66) - My happiness and my function are one.

Happiness is your function for it is attained when it is drawn from Source. Do not look elsewhere except from where it comes. God is the Source by which happiness manifests. It is denied to no one who truly seeks it. There is no greater feeling than owning your own power. And to find happiness is using your power to the fullest. To have it and not know you possess it is to deny God-Consciousness. For you cannot really know you are happy without understanding that God is the Source by which it is provided. There is nothing that can threaten its presence when this is truly understood. Besides love, happiness is the greatest power you own, for happiness and love are joined. And because it cannot be contained, it moves about for others to sense, feel, and sometimes even see the vibration it holds. With this recognition, it is easy to understand that your happiness and your function are one and the same.

Love, Jesus

84

(Review) Love created me like itself.

1. (67) - Love created me like itself.

Without love, there would be no creation, for God would not exist. The entire spectrum of the Universe is made up of love. This indeed is an awesome thought, for it is the answer to every mystery the world looks to unfold but has yet to unlock. For if it did, the power of its energy would be so great, you would understand every aspect of creation without so much as leaving your chair, for you would not need to go out and search for it. You would find it just where it was placed, in you. Like Himself, God created you from Love. If you were completely invisible, you would be seen as pure energy for that is all you are. If this is true, and I can assure you it is, would it not show you that you are indeed created from love, and that love is what you are? The body was not created by God and therefore it is an abject creation, void of love. It was made to separate itself from God and therefore, separate from love. When you are in touch with the energy of love, it can heal the body because the body does not think, it only obeys.

2. (68) - Love holds no grievances.

Because you were created from love, love is your inherent nature. While it is a great accomplishment to know it in yourself, a greater accomplishment is to recognize its presence beyond yourself. It is not about hiding your dislike of someone that makes it all okay, it is the actual dislike of the person which causes you to lose sight of love's presence that makes it not okay. You can uncover this facade by not necessarily excusing wrong behavior, but to forgive it and to recognize the inherent love we all share. Everyone is made of the same substance, yet not everyone is aware of the very substance by which they were created. In order to stay in love's frequency, it is precisely the reason you must hold no grievances, for then there would be no barriers to keep it hidden.

Love, Jesus

85

(Review) My grievances hide the light of the world in me.

1. (69) - My grievances hide the light of the world in me.

Light was given to you to shine upon the world. When you do, it brings more love into the world and overturns the false belief that you were powerless to bring this about. Light is love and love is what you are. Grievances block the path to love's presence. And because love is perfect, there can be nothing imperfect to mar it. This is a time of great opportunity, for expanded energy shifts you to higher planes of consciousness. Just go with the flow and let it lift you up, just as the world lifts itself out of its chaotic and tumultuous frequency. If there are any impurities floating around in your head, give them up now. Let nothing stand in the way of all that you stand to gain at this time of spiritual awakening. In so doing, you bring light into the world, whereas before, there was not enough of it. Know only peace, for lasting peace is granted to those who assist as lightworkers. As the population of the world is finding its way into a brand new world, it is inevitable that those who stand in their light will bring it about with greater speed.

2. (70) - My salvation comes from me.

Salvation comes when beliefs that we are helpless victims are no longer perceived. This must come from you, for nothing outside yourself can be depended upon as true. When you are at peace you do not see yourself as a victim. In fact, you see yourself in a position of strength, no longer weakened by the fear that your survival is threatened. Peace brings healing to those who somehow find it within themselves to withdraw from the belief that they are weak. To see the innocence in another is to witness the strength in yourself. Healing is always a condition of a peaceful mind. It is an energy which speaks volumes, for once you have experienced the truth of its effects, you never want to return to the ravages of a chaotic mind again. There is a place inside of you that is sacred and untouched. When you are at peace and realize that there is nothing outside yourself that can come to claim it, you then see the silver lining behind the clouds where light has taken the place of darkness.

Love, Jesus

86

(Review) Only God's plan for salvation will work.

1. (71) - Only God's plan for salvation will work.

God's plan for salvation signifies that by offering yourself to help another is an important lesson. By holding a light for someone else to find their way is a loving attribute. The only way for those who are lost to find their salvation is through kindness, not retribution. It is your willingness to understand what it takes to bring healing to the world and thus, make it your mission. You must teach that which you have already learned, for teaching and learning are really the same. Be gentle, compassionate, and loving, and teach this by being a true example of it. Most of all, understand that with a forgiving heart you will also learn what it means to love yourself, for you become a beacon of light when you practice true forgiveness. In the end you will see that it cost you nothing to forgive even the most unkindly act, for there is never a cost when you profit. By giving up your grievances you help others discover their salvation just as you did.

2. (72) - Holding grievances is an attack on God's plan for salvation.

When you attack your brother or sister, you are attacking God. God's plan to save the world is all that can work. To seek salvation is to recognize that it must come from forgiveness. To forgive is to bring peace to all. When anger is permitted to threaten your peace, it is the ego which has won victory over God, but only in the sense that it believes it has triumphed. When the ego has its way, peace is lost and when peace is given over to any grievance, it topples the entire house of cards, and so you must start rebuilding that which has already been destroyed. A grievance does not inspire love, for love and attack cannot work in unison. Attack brings about grievances, and peace begets love. When you attack, you are not feeling love. Such is an attack on God for God knows only Love. Forgiveness brings healing to the minds of those who accept salvation as their function. This would be to fulfill their purpose in the world. To bring love into the hearts of others establishes your place in the Heart of God.

Love, Jesus

87

(Review) I will there be light.

1. (73) - I will there be light.

Light shines love's presence into the hearts of all who witness it in others. Because light is matter and because light and love exist as one, all that exists is matter. We know that matter is the "stuff" that makes up the Universe. When you think light, you can also feel the power of its energy. And when you acknowledge the light within yourself, you bring love's energy into the open. Such energetic frequencies enrich the soul. When you are feeling that energetic flow and your self-awareness is at high-pitch, you bring love's frequency into the hearts of many. The light of love's awareness reflects the magnificence of all that you were created to be. Those who are in your presence feel the light you carry and so they respond in likeness. Light is in everyone. When they see it in you, they must acknowledge the power of its energy within themselves, just as you are aware of the light in yourself when you see it in another. Think love, and there you will see light. Think light, and there you will see love.

2. (74) - There is no will but God's.

The will of God is what you seek, because you want what God wills. When you see rioting, chaos, hatred, bigotry, and fear, thinking it to be front and center of all that is happening, understand that it is not. Love reaches beyond all else which appears to be sordid and unloving. When you seek to make the world a happier place, you have God's blessing as you play out your part in His plan for you. God's will is that the world be free of all those unloving ideals, but it starts with those who use their own free will to bring it about. When enough people join together in so doing, world ascension occurs. We are all made up of different complexities of emotion, but it is in each of us to use our emotions soulfully in order to bring peace and love into this complex world. There is a far better world waiting to show itself. Be all that you are by bringing it light. This you must do, because it is God's will, and yours.

Love, Jesus

88

(Review) The light has come.

1. (75) - The light has come.

"The light has come" is an extraordinary affirmation. It exemplifies the fact that you are living your purpose. When you do not allow the ego to be in control, and you are awakening to your magnificent divinity, it would indicate that the light within has been acknowledged, and once acknowledged, it is cherished. Light is the energetic frequency which springs you to the next level of ascension, for it is love. When you are living within the power of your own light, it is a way out of the darkness forever. When you become acquainted with the light within, the darkness is no longer to be feared, for it is gone. Now you may move on to all you are meant to be in this lifetime. It means you have earned your degree at that level and are ready to move up to higher degrees of learning. Overwhelming feelings of love have the power to take you to that next phase. As light, you are seen as light, for who can help but be drawn to it, for it reflects the energy of love. Remember, light represents love, love is energy, and energy is God. Therefore, so are you.

2. (76) - I am under no laws but God's.

Free will gives you complete sovereignty of choice. Choices are continuous and each new choice brings you either closer to peace or moves you away from it. You are constantly deciding which choices seem best suited to you at the time. They are the choices which will alter your direction forever, occurring moment by moment. The laws of God, however, are all in the here and now, for there is nowhere else. It is only in the present that God is revealed to you. The laws of God are simple to follow but difficult to adhere to when you are not at peace, for then you are not with God, but confined to an egoic thought system. Attack thoughts seem to come uninvited, but they are still choices, nevertheless. Yet God's laws come without attack, without disturbance, and without fear. Thoughts are either true or they are not. Attack thoughts may seem harmless, but they are quite the opposite, for you cannot know you are attacking yourself. Attack in any form is apart from God. There can be no error when you choose to practice God's laws.

Love, Jesus

89

(Review) I am entitled to miracles.

1. (77) - I am entitled to miracles.

Understanding entitlement is to recognize the source by which miracles are created. You are entitled because you are an integral part of this great White Light of Love which is the source of all miracles. When you commune with God you are feeling a miracle, for you are experiencing such overwhelming joy that it is almost too much to contain you. It is of such great magnitude that you are sometimes perplexed by it. Miracles enrich the soul as you receive them. Each new day brings you closer to new miracles, for they are unending. Stay peaceful even in times of turmoil, and do not allow doubt to tug away at your faith as you see the grandeur of a miracle outshine all fear. Be staunch in your efforts to make peace and love your everyday mantra and experience the miracles they bring by remaining steadfast in your constancy. Accept each miracle in gratitude. They are bestowed to you just because you are entitled to them.

2. (78) - Let miracles replace all grievances.

Each time you give up a grievance, a miracle moves in to take its place. This is because letting go of a grievance requires the willingness to forego that which builds, festers, and destroys. Miracles come when you are ready to move past all self-destructive attitudes and hold no grievance sacred. Those who hold onto their grievances believe in them, not realizing they are in direct conflict with truth. First, it must be understood that grievances have no purpose. How can one find the way to peace when the ego is more recognizable than Spirit? You know yourself as Spirit when you are at peace and allow no boundaries to limit your awareness. Let miracles replace all grievances and move another step closer to your divine purpose, which is to be free of ego-imposed limitations and know your own divinity. When you are truly able to give up every grievance, holding none dear, miracles blow towards you like the wind.

Love, Jesus

90

(Review) Let me recognize the problem so it can be solved.

1. (79) - Let me recognize the problem so it can be solved.

When you hold onto a grievance, the problem you are faced with has not yet been solved because it still lays heavily upon you. You cannot see a problem having been solved if you do not see its cause. It is all about letting go of that which has caused you to lose your peace. All problems are solvable because every problem has a solution. It is letting go of the need to hold another person responsible for your lack of peace. When you can genuinely forgive the so-called perpetrator, peace fills you like a delightful cup of hot chocolate on a cold winter's day, giving you that "all-is-well" feeling. But that is precisely the reason it is so difficult to part with a grievance. To forgive the one you are holding a grievance against also releases him from guilt. To many, it is preferred that they suffer the tortures of the damned by holding onto their anger, than to forgive another their "unforgivable" deeds. Forgiveness is the act of simply letting go. You need not even come face to face with your partner-in-crime if you care not to. It is never about the other, it is always about you. Anger carries itself through the airwaves of consciousness as does peace. Once you release another from their guilt through forgiveness, it releases you as well. If you can do this, it means you have signed on for another miracle.

2. (80) - Let me recognize my problems have been solved.

Let me remind you that the power of the Universe and all that is are interconnected. So, actually all problems must also be interconnected, although they appear different in content. Because the Universe operates in perfect synchronization with consciousness, so must you as well. As you raise your consciousness higher, you are also connecting to higher realms of understanding and thought. If all souls are joined, do you not understand that all problems have already been solved because there is only perfection in all? Because you live in a world of time and because you see yourself separate from your brothers and sisters, it would also seem that your problems differ. That is why it is important that you see your brother/sister as yourself, although not in the sense that you must carry the weight of their worries on your shoulders. But if you can see your brothers and sisters as yourself, you can better understand that they ARE you. This you do not yet fully understand, but it is something you must recognize as true. Whatever problem is causing you distress, given over to God, you can be sure that it is solved.

Love, Jesus

91
Miracles are seen in light.

If you could only see the light your body holds, you would never want to leave its beautiful aura, not even for a single moment. Light is the source from which you were created. What can offer you greater peace than to be aware of this undeniable truth? If you could see beyond the flesh, you would also see that the body's limitations keep you from recognizing the remarkable strength you possess, although you are not yet fully aware of it. Because miracles come from Source, you would not be aware of them unless you opened yourself up to the light from which your strength is drawn and recognized. Light can be seen by looking inward and into the heart. Let your light reflect out into the world where others may witness its power. In so doing, you help them remember that we are all one with God, for light is the energy which connects us all as one. If it were possible to dispel the light, you would see only darkness, for in darkness God would not exist, just as darkness could not exist where there is light. Shine your light into the world and find yourself in the midst of boundless miracles.

Love, Jesus

92
Miracles are seen in light, and light and strength are one.

Miracles are seen in light and it is God's light by which you see only truth. The light of His Love reflects the strength that you hold. Do not be fooled by troublesome scenarios which are playing out in the world indicating that you must tread very carefully or die. Walk the world in innocence and rely on your God-Given strength in everything you do, think, and say. Do not believe those who tell you there are nefarious forces lurking all around you. Innocence lies in strength, as does light, for they are one and the same. Only what is real emerges victorious. And what is there to fear when you are coming from a place of truth? There are no nefarious forces out there, except that which is fed into accepting minds. You are protected by your strength which is seen as light, and this you can indeed count on to keep you immovable and steadfast. Live in light, for your strength is carried in light. Never allow yourself to be challenged by anything which causes you to doubt this. There are countless possibilities from which you are free to make choices. Whichever choices you do make are the right ones, for there are no wrong choices, only frivolous ones made in haste. Continue on your course to greater happiness, for what is there to keep you from it?

Love, Jesus

93

Light and joy and peace abide in me.

When you came to Earth you lost sight of your true heritage, for you were now in a place of darkness and density, far from home. You did not know that God never left you alone and helpless and so you paced aimlessly, fearing the worst, and thinking yourself lost and without purpose. In loneliness you sought peace, for you did not know yourself as God knows you; you thought little of yourself. You knew of Him but could not remember the truth of who you are. And so, you traveled a long and winding road, alone and misguided. With snippets of memory coming back to you, you sought God, and in so doing you could then recognize the strength of the light you hold. You thought you had wandered aimlessly, but as it turned out you were not lost at all. You found your salvation in Him, and in asking for forgiveness you found Love. Because manifestations of thought are real, in choosing kindlier and more loving ways to project your thoughts, joy and peace entered. You are a child of God with memory of your birthplace now etched in your heart. When you found your peace, you also found a piece of Heaven.

Love, Jesus

94

I am as God created me.

God created you as Spirit, not as a body. As you take your rightful place in the world, unless your body is attended by Spirit, you cannot know yourself as pure creation. You are recognizable to yourself and others only as a body. But to God, you are soul, and therein lies a treasure trove of beauty and goodness. Because you are so much more than the limitations of your body, the light within can be depended upon to raise you to unlimited heights, for this is where your holiness is recognized. Within this treasure trove of all that you are, and because you are one who loves to explore and discover, why not delve further into the world of Spirit where there is a wealth of peace, love, joy, and happiness, waiting to be discovered? When you look for the best in yourself, you need not venture very far, for it is in all that you are. Just as one hand cannot wash itself for each depends on the other, it is the same with mind, body, and Spirit. When your mind, body and Spirit unite as one, you remain as God created you. You are one with God, incarnated into the world. Bring a part of Heaven into the world experience, and find a pyramid of peace, love, and joy surrounding you.

Love, Jesus

95

I am one Self, united with my Creator.

The self you made is not the Self you share with God. Your Higher Self exists within the body, just as the ego does. But the ego-self does not recognize that it shares its body with your God-Self. Because you possess the strength to heal yourself, it is true faith which gives you the ability to do so. Although God did not create sickness—for nothing imperfect comes from God—He did give you the power to heal through awareness of Self. You alone decide whether to live in wellness, or sickness, for you own the decision to determine which it shall be. As your body is rearranging itself moment by moment, so is your mind. To believe little of yourself is to give away your power, not fully recognizing your True Self which is all-power. What you believe as true, manifests into your reality. You cannot serve two thought systems. One is Self and the other is ego. Which you support is of your own free will. To align with Self is to become aware that you are united with your Creator. Why choose littleness over magnitude when there is a choice? You may think it is not a simple choice, but when you consider what is truly at stake, it should be simple indeed.

Love, Jesus

96

Salvation comes from my one Self.

You knew yourself as only one presence, for you were not within the understanding that there was a much larger and more profound Self which also exists as you. If you knew your Self as you were created, you never would have been so intent on painstakingly building an image of yourself, different from the one God created, and believing it to be all that you are. There is an underside to your One True Self, and that is the ego. The ego will rest comfortably, thinking it cannot be challenged, until it is threatened. It then becomes erratic and troublesome. It cannot relinquish control, for then it would die, and so it fights to stay present. Your truth lies in the recognition that your One Self, which is the home you share with God, knows no opposite. It knows only Itself, pure and holy. The ego-self is an illusion for it has no allegiance to God. When you arrived on the planet you knew only your Self as you were created, but then the ego rose up and sought you. And so, you forgot who you were, why you were here, and what your true purpose must be. You did learn of it, but it took many, many years of pain, suffering, loss, denial, depression, and even hate, to bring you to truth. You were always in the presence of the Almighty, but you did not know Him, for you had forgotten your roots. With memory of your One Self returning to you, you then became proficient in your learning, for you yearned to feel God's Love once again. What is salvation but the understanding that you are One Self, joined with your Creator? Your mission on Earth is to fulfill your purpose and to forgive yourself for forgetting the truth of who you are.

Love, Jesus

97

I am Spirit.

Spirit is energy, and as such, it makes up the entirety of all creation. You have it within yourself to recognize Spirit, for God gave you the mind to understand, and the resources to explore, the truth of who you are. And if you are all that you are created to be, how could you be anything other than Spirit in form? It is incumbent upon you to know your true existence in all of its vastness. Love embraces you like the rays of the sun drenching you in light. And what is light but love? And because you are Spirit, given the awareness to understand that God is only Love, you can be no less than this. Once you embody this truth, there is no need to return to any other belief which lies vacant in the knowledge that Spirit lives within the heart of all creation. Spirit is you, yet this could never be explained accurately in words, for you could never imagine the true splendor of what this truly means. The gift of faith is to know that you are Spirit incarnate, and you will remain as such forever. Because you are an integral part of all creation, you have the ability to lift yourself up to higher frequencies of thought and to decipher what is true from what is false as you learn to differentiate. The affirmation "I am Spirit," keeps you focused on your true heritage, which simply put, is you.

Love, Jesus

98
I will accept my part in God's plan for salvation.

Because the Universe is synchronized perfectly with all of creation, does this not tell you that everything is created with exact precision? True perception is the understanding that there is a Master Plan which works for the good of all. Each person has it within himself/herself to accept their part in God's plan for salvation, yet not all have awakened to the understanding that if they seek it, they shall have it. There are those who do not yet understand what salvation is for, and so they live fearfully when in truth there is nothing to fear. There is no need to live this way, yet fear is handed out in large doses by those who create it for their own nefarious causes. Without salvation, we will ourselves apart from love, yet love lives within the heart of everyone, although not all are accepting of it. There is so much help within reach which serves to restore our faith and relinquish our fears. God's plan for salvation is all that will work. This must be recognized, now more than ever, as the world appears to be engulfed in chaos. Lightworkers are now showing up in massive numbers by offering their help and their love. And so, the world is lifting out of its current state of lower consciousness, which is the home of fear, to higher elevations of consciousness. God indeed does have a plan for salvation, and every soul has a part in it, but first it must be recognized. As each person accepts their part, so it shall be a means to recognize and fulfill their given purpose.

Love, Jesus

99
Salvation is my only function here.

You live in a world where forgiveness seems to be the most difficult rule to follow, yet it is your saving grace. Peace comes from the willingness to forgive, let go, and not look back. A forgiving mind is one that is at rest. That is why forgiveness is stressed so heavily here. It is a cornerstone for everything, for its treasures are unsurpassed. You can save one thousand years or more in karmic payback with those you have spent lifetimes trying to work out those resolutions. Is this not worth sacrificing your disdain for a deal so great you can save centuries in time? True forgiveness offers you a golden opportunity to move out of the gloom of misperception, for then there is nothing to stop your evolution to higher plateaus. Free will opens up doors of possibilities and choices. Yet there is only one door of choice to walk through, and that is the one forgiveness offers. It releases you from what you believe your brother or sister has cost you. They do not know that they stand in the way of your peace, for you are the one who carries the burden of its weight. Now they are left to deal with their own burdens, for you have learned the meaning of salvation, while they have perhaps not yet learned it. That should be enough reason to give up your need to hold your brother or sister responsible for something they know not of. Be steadfast in your desire to rise above the world's temptations and settle into the comfort of peace. That is your only function.

Love, Jesus

100

My part is essential to God's plan for salvation.

Nothing can be complete if a part of its whole is missing. A food dish loses its taste if an important ingredient is absent. A chain is incomplete unless every link supporting its wholeness is included. A play cannot be successful unless each actor is present. And a puzzle, missing even one piece, is far from complete. Although these are miniscule examples of a much greater picture, they are concepts by which to help you understand your part. You may think that you are insignificant, but you do play a major role in God's plan for salvation, not really comprehending how essential it is. To understand this concept, even slightly, is to keep your emotions well-maintained and not allow your mind to wander to the point that it takes you away from your true thoughts, which are God-Thoughts. If you linger too long, your consciousness becomes lowered, and you cannot complete your role at that crossroad. It is incumbent upon you to reel your thoughts in when they roam far and away from the present. God waits, giving you all the time you need to become ready to fulfill His plan for you. But why wait? The moment is here and now. You are indeed a part of all creation, which assures you ownership of will. When you allow your will to be misguided, you cannot fulfill the most essential part in God's plan for salvation.

Love, Jesus

101

God's Will for me is perfect happiness.

Your happiest moments come to pass when you are at peace and world situations are set aside. It happens when the voice of the ego is hushed, even if just for a little while, for less is better than none. Imagine finding that state of contentment whenever you seek it. Imagine living in that warm place of fulfillment where true happiness abides. You need not venture into the ego's territory when it beckons you with its insanity. To choose unrest over peace is indeed insanity, but you can be sure that the ego's playground is not a place of normalcy. Yet, you go there for safety because you believe it offers you more than the grace of God, for why would God welcome you where you believe you do not belong? When you detach yourself from your natural state, which is to be happy, it is because you have chosen thoughts of an unhealing nature, all of which are manufactured by the ego. You need not be held hostage by the ego's erratic moods when God offers you perfect happiness. When you follow the ego's dictates, you are choosing fear over God's Will, preferring the valueless over the valuable. Never think yourself undeserving of happiness. Because God wants only perfect happiness for you, you can be sure it is because He wills you nothing less. To believe this truly is a gift to yourself, unsurpassed by any other.

Love, Jesus

102

I share God's Will for happiness for me.

God's Will for you is happiness. He bestows it to you because He Loves you. Yet love is difficult to analyze, for it seems to appear in different forms. Some days we love, and some days we do not. If we think it has been earned, we bestow it graciously. If we do not believe it is earned, we terminate it. That is the thinking of the world, but not God's Will. Of course we want to be happy, and it gives us joy to see others share in it, but we do not realize that love and happiness are one and the same. Love is the most basic rule to live by. Yet so many are struggling to find it even though it is at the very core of who they are. We are all created as Love and by Love. Therefore, happiness is every person's right, for God wills it to all. Unfortunately, some do not recognize it because they think themselves unworthy of God's unconditional Love. Share your love openly and learn what it is to be truly happy. If you share it, it shall reveal itself to you. To share happiness does not imply that you must give it away at your own expense. If you think you are sacrificing your happiness for someone else, neither of you can benefit by it, for it is lost to both of you. God's Will for you is perfect happiness. This is a most important concept to embody, for it must be believed. Say it over and over until it becomes your daily mantra. Then allow it to spread abundantly, for it is as free as the air you breathe. That is what it takes to share without giving up your power in so doing.

Love, Jesus

103
God, being Love, is also happiness.

Understanding that Love is also happiness is a giant leap towards reaching your higher purpose. And because you learn that Love cannot exist without its counterpart, which is happiness, therein lies the recognition that you have taken another giant step, which is faith. Keeping the faith is to stay within the frequency of Love so that everything explains itself from this higher place of understanding. If you are looking for a solution pertaining to a particular problem, when you are in Love's frequency, the answer comes to you with a perfect solution, and there are no doubting thoughts remaining. Within this dimension, the answer appears in a moment of true recognition. That is the moment when all doors have opened, for the answer you have been searching for is clearly seen. Now you can be sure that your decision has come from a place of Love, leaving no blind spot to cause you to doubt. Because God is the Source from which you are assured Unconditional Love, every solution to every problem comes from that Source. Does this not tell you if there is only one problem, that there must also be only one answer? And if there is only one answer, does it not also reveal that any problem can be solved when it is left to God to solve it?

Love, Jesus

104
I see but what belongs to me in truth.

God lives in you, and because this is so, He protects all that belongs to you. You were created from Love. That is why Love's energy is such a heartfelt emotion. All of this you are entitled to because it is God's Will that you have what is yours. How you use His gifts depends upon whether you recognize what is rightfully yours. Spirit is reality, and ego is illusion. Even though both are a part of you, God only recognizes One as Himself. As Spirit, it is easy to understand the truth of what is yours, for what God wills cannot be taken away. As ego, there is nothing that can be relied upon as true and so you must be fearful. When at times you are happy and moments later sadness overtakes you, it is because you become fearful. In God, nothing is disruptive, and everything remains safe. It is only the ego that causes you pain. Yet it is easy to see that when you move back into God-Consciousness, fear dissipates and peace returns. Through practice and determination, you learn that this is where you belong. When you are in conflict, you lose sight of the truth and do not see what is yours to keep. But when you are centered, memory returns and you are again free to stake your claim.

Love, Jesus

105

God's peace and joy are mine.

God's joy and peace are coming to you in great waves now. You are experiencing a transition period where you are peacefully recognizing there is no place else you need to be. You have been in lockdown for some time now because of the restrictions in movement taking place in the world. Yet this is not confinement, but a blessing. Mother Earth is restoring herself to healing. The relentless pouring of waste material into her oceans, and contamination of dirty air particles from non-stop jets filling the skies are in reprieve. You are witness to the Earth's pleasures, blossoming and growing anew. Even the birds are aware of this wonderful new peace surrounding their little communities as they rejoice. They too are feeling the beautiful clean air, if only for a little while. The gifts of peace and joy are indeed yours, for you are graciously accepting it. What could replace the freedom of joyful souls coming together as one? Lift your heart up in thanks to God as you gaze upon a perfect sky by day, and a clear, star-filled sky by night. You are now discovering that your true gifts are found in the simplicity in all of this. Wrapped up in this tiny package of new self-awareness is God's Unconditional Love. Could you ask for more?

Love, Jesus

106
Let me be still and listen to the truth.

As you sit in silence and keep your mind in focus, you can then understand that stillness and peace are the same. When you are at peace, you can hear God's truth over the raucous voice of the ego which teaches you wrongly. There is no place in God for anything other than peace to reside. To know what truth is, it must first be felt. Once you go deep into the calmness within, which is Spirit, a better perspective of yourself emerges. In stillness, everything can be defined easily, whereas when your mind is chaotic, there is only noise, and no peace can be found within the constancy of such confusion. Peace and love can only be found where it resides, which is in stillness. The more you practice peace, the less turbulence you will feel. When the mind's chanting fades, peace takes its place and disturbances of the mind then fade into the nothingness from which they were made.

Love, Jesus

107
Truth will correct all errors in my mind.

Truth is the absence of fear. When you feel peace in your heart, a sense of well-being begins to form, which is where you want to be. What, but an insane mind, would want the ugliness of illusions to prevail, which destroys all possibility of happiness? Permitting errors to enter the mind causes the mind to become split. It is ego versus God. This permits unwholesome thoughts to take the place of peace, replaced with fear and guilt. Your thoughts have then become distorted, and attack on others and/or yourself is destined to follow. When you attack another, you attack yourself because you tried to make something false true, and attack is never an option. The mind that tries to make errors real denies the progress of healing. When your thoughts are in sync with Spirit, you begin to feel peace, for what else is there to offer you such peace? When this is known, it can be relied on to correct all errors. If errors are permitted to run rampant, the mind becomes sick, causing sickness of the body. Attack changes peace to fear, and lack of peace defies wellness. A healthy mind is open to truth and where truth is recognized, there is only peace.

Love, Jesus

108

To give and to receive are one in truth.

With God, when you give something away it is as much to the benefit of the giver as it is to the receiver. The world's thinking is the belief that when something is given, it is a loss to the giver, and only the receiver has gained. But to God, the concept of gift-giving works to the benefit of the entire Sonship and not one is left out. For it is everyone's gain to understand that when something is shared it becomes that much more beneficial to each. When you share the gift of God's Love with your brothers and sisters, does it not make sense that it is known to Him and that He thanks you for it? And so, it is incumbent upon you to see how the gift of sharing is enhanced. To share love with others, as God shares it with you, is a gift to all—to you, your brother, your sister, and to God Himself. The experience of giving and receiving come from One Source. To share something as powerful as love will ignite a flame so great it can only spread. It is that great spark of energy which engulfs all of humanity. As it is given, it is also received. When love is given freely, it detours back to the giver by way of Heaven. It brings a newness to the world so enhanced that each must wonder why it was restrained and so difficult to share. How can anything that reflects such truth be denied?

Love, Jesus

109

I rest in God.

To rest in God is to say, "I trust in God." For what is trust, but to love the One Who gives you rest? The joy of being at One with Him can be found in stillness where you can feel His Love the most. You are loved so much that the light within replaces all fear, for your sins are forgiven. To be a lightworker is to radiate love in a world devoid of it, for it is much needed here. It illuminates so brightly that it invites all your brothers and sisters to come and bask in it along with you. They then recognize it as God, leaving no one in doubt. Let it shine brightly, so all who come to seek the peace of God can find it there. God's Holy Light joined with yours is the essence of peace reflected outward. It is a Source of Power so great, its attraction lights the way for all to follow, for they have found God through you. To rest in God is the greatest gift you can give yourself and your brothers and sisters, for it is shared. Where else can love be felt so profoundly, if not in Him?

Love, Jesus

110
I am as God created me.

These words are meant to give you insight into the magnitude of who you are in truth. Feeling God's Love is no doubt crushed by the ego's deception and shadows your ability to understand how wonderful a gift it is when you decide to explore it. Truth is tucked away where God keeps it safe and nothing can come to defile this Holy Sanctuary. When you can define it as a knowing rather than a possibility, it has a transformative effect, as it works towards taking you away from the ego's deceptive control. It transforms your ability to come in contact with your True Self, as nothing has the power to undermine God's Will. I, Jesus, am here to help you see yourself as you are: pure, holy, and born of Unconditional Love. Nothing in this world has the power to limit your ability to know yourself as God created you when you can embody the reality of this undeniable truth.

Love, Jesus

111
(Review) Miracles are seen in light, and light and strength are one.

1. (91) - Miracles are seen in light.

Miracles show you the way to love. Love is best understood when you see it in the form of a miracle, for love's presence shows you what a miracle is. Love extends itself beyond all perception. Your innocence lies in your acceptance of this truth. When you can accept all that is true, and not allow doubt to intercept where there is truth, you are living in the light of love.

2. (92) - Miracles are seen in light, and light and strength are one.

God's creations are born of light. Each child comes into the world carrying the light, for it is the spark of God's Love, and always a reminder that He is there. The light of Heaven may be relied upon when fear and pain become elements of distraction and you need to find your way again. But light can only be seen where darkness is not. And it is through the power of a miracle which gives you the strength to dispel darkness into light. The ego will attempt to use fear as the main attraction, dampening your ability to see the light, which is love. You are endowed with the strength to transform the world from darkness to light. Darkness is a device used by the ego to hide the light. A lighted soul can only be seen where love and forgiveness prevail. Your strength is unshakable when you stand in the light within, where all miracles are found.

Love, Jesus

112

(Review) Light and joy and peace abide in me.
I am as God created me.

1. (93) - Light and peace and joy abide in me.

As a creation of God, you are light and love, for love reflects the light in you. The release from dark to light is to go from the belief that you are sinful, to the recognition that you are sinless. To dispel darkness by seeing light as your function fades the darkness into light immediately. Darkness is what the ego taught you to believe about yourself. The light in you outshines the false belief that you are evil as the ego tells you to believe about yourself—that you are the home of sin, guilt, and fear. Believe none of this because you have never sinned in the Eyes of God. There is no sin in God and there can be none in you. To say "light and joy and peace abide in me" is to say you are as God created you, which is pure light. Therefore, you are wholly loving, lovable, and forever changeless.

2. (94) - I am as God created me.

God created you in light, and light is Love. You came to receive God's Plan, for this is where your greatest teachings were learned. When you could not find your way on this fearful voyage, God lit the way, although you did not to see the light, and followed the ego's darkness instead. It was only until you discovered those lovely treasures buried deep within, that you found the joy and peace you did not know of before. There is a wealth of knowledge waiting to be discovered nowhere else, but from within. And it was this very discovery which sustained you. Although you came with a purpose, darkness overshadowed your vision, and your true purpose was not known for a long, long time. The light within, though not yet awakened in you, helped you deal with sickness, fear, and even death, which you experienced very early on. Many of your best lessons have been learned through those experiences. I came as your brother to guide you through difficult times and lead you to better ones. The rest of the journey will be easier now, for your path is set. Because the Light of God never dims, you are still as He created you.

Love, Jesus

113

(Review) I am one Self, united with my Creator. Salvation comes from my one Self.

1. (95) - I am one Self, united with my Creator.

It is your one Self which unites you with all of creation. To know your Self as part of God, is to never perceive that you are apart from

Him. You must remember you are created as One Consciousness, and there is nothing that could ever take you away from your True Self. Everything you are projects the reality of this one truth. However, when you are feeling guilty, it is the dream you are still believing in, and not the reality that you are created holy. To the ego, you are a sinner. Inherently, you already know the truth. When you are stuck on guilt and cannot let it go, it is because you are buying into the ego's beliefs that you are a small, insignificant, speck of dust in the world, and nothing more. Never forget, you are one within your Self, and one with Him. And this can never change.

2. (96) - Salvation comes from my one Self.

God created you as one Self which is part of Himself. It is this unwavering dedication to truth which brings you to salvation. You did finally learn to translate the truth of Spirit from the deceptions of the ego, but it took a long time. While growing up and in school, you were bored and uninspired. You were told by those who lacked understanding themselves how lacking you were. Because they could not recognize the strength in themselves, they perceived weakness in themselves, in you, and in the world. This is what the ego does; it transfers its guilt onto others, for it cannot put any responsibility on itself. Yet your Spirit remained strong, though seemingly tattered, for it was a long time before you found it again; whole and untouched. How blessed you are, for you never lost remembrance of your Creator and you awakened in Him. That is why you must forgive those who gave you the best reasons to do so, and to thank them. To be unforgiving is the very obstacle which inhibits feelings of love. You found your salvation in the only place you could, which was within yourself.

Love, Jesus

114

(Review) I am Spirit.
I will accept my part in God's plan for salvation.

1. (97) - I am Spirit.

Spirit is that which is changeless and unalterable. Spirit is you. It is the Creative Force which binds you to all that you are, and what you are is a manifestation of God. Nothing outside of Spirit is real, for Spirit knows nothing other than that which is of God. It is the substance of your true nature which binds you to your Source, God. Bring reality still closer to your mind and into the peace of identifying with your one Self.

2. (98) - I will accept my part in God's plan for salvation.

Before you can accept your part in God's plan for salvation you must first know it as your purpose. Within this truth, there is so much reason to be happy for you are coming to understand what this means. Your mind becomes free when you are healed, no longer a slave to pain, sickness, and fear. Because you are created as Spirit, your part in His plan remains certain. Salvation is the process whereby love triumphs over fear, for a mind set free has nothing to fear. How wonderful it is when peace comes to take its place. Your faith in the ego had gone unchallenged far too long, and so you did not believe you were guiltless. When you came to understand forgiveness, you realized you could not be guilty, for you also understood God's Love as unconditional, and so healing too was understood. What then, could there be to fear? Salvation is that which you came to learn. Your faith brings you to the recognition that you do indeed have a major part in it.

Love, Jesus

115

(Review) Salvation is my only function here.

1. (99) - Salvation is my only function here.

Salvation and forgiveness are one and the same, and where there is forgiveness there is love. They belong together, forever whole and unfragmented. There is nothing in Heaven's Name that can keep us separate and apart from Him. Therefore, His Love is guaranteed. Because salvation is your only function, so must be forgiveness. With this validation wholeness is assured, for in Him you remain eternally sound and complete. Forgiveness is the escape from the false identity of the world. This brings you straight to the truth of who you are. And where you are, is God's eternal Love.

2.(100) - My part is essential to God's plan for salvation.

If God's children could truly understand how crucial they are to His plan for salvation, and what it would mean to the world, they would rush to it without a single moment's delay. How hard it seems to let go of anger and fear, which are illusions, and replace them with forgiveness and love. So much healing would be the result if this was truly understood. You are all essential beings, woven into a Universal System where all thought is part of One Great Consciousness. As the world tunes to that frequency, it has the power to heal beyond all that could possibly be imagined. A change of mind in one person, adds to the greater good of the whole, as more souls become awakened. Think light, and just visualize how this practice becomes manifest in a world of darkness. You are all given a lifetime to wake up to your only function. Salvation can be worked out even until the very last moments before the body is laid aside. Use every moment wisely, for each one counts more than you know. You came to learn and to understand your function and to fulfill it according to His plan for salvation.

Love, Jesus

116

(Review) God's Will for me is perfect happiness.

1. (101) - God's Will for me is perfect happiness.

Happiness is an attribute of love. If there is no sin, then love must be all-encompassing. God wills us perfect happiness, for love is limitless. If we think ourselves sinful then we must deem ourselves unlovable. To believe we are guilty is a form of fear. Where there is no guilt there can be no fear. Therefore, everything else is love. This gives you greater insight into the unconditional Love God has for you. After the passing of one you loved deeply, you cried long after the time to mourn was past and so you suffered. I have shown you his resting place many times, safe at Home with his Father. So why cry for a soul set free? You, my child, may receive greater understanding of God's Will by loving others with the same capacity of Love that He shares with you. Perfect happiness comes when you are able to release needless suffering serving no purpose and become lifted instead by the Glow of Spirit. You have the power to be joyously happy, for such is God's Will.

2. (102) - I share God's Will for happiness for me.

The Self within you is always happy. You are not aware of this because you do not always feel the happiness which is inherent in you. That is because we see ourselves as victims, thinking that if we suffer, we can look elsewhere for its cause, believing we play no part in it. Suffering is perceived as something or someone outside ourselves which is causing us to be unhappy. Of course, we don't want to suffer because suffering causes pain, and this we do not want. But we choose pain because we believe it will give us something that we want. When we see ourselves as victims, it is easier to blame others as the cause of our suffering, for the ego thrives on victimhood. Suffering proves that we are justified in our anger. To the ego, it proves we are right, and God is wrong. God says we are created happy, yet when we are not feeling happy on some level, we are blaming God.

Love, Jesus

117

(Review) God, being Love, is also happiness.
I seek but what belongs to me in truth.

1. (103) - God, being Love, is also happiness.

If God is only Love, He must also be happiness as well, for happiness is an awareness that Love is ever-present. Where God is, so must happiness be. Happiness is our inherent nature. When we are not happy, we are not experiencing our natural state of awareness. The ego has us questioning why God wants us to be happy when we don't deserve His Love, much less happiness. The god of the ego is a punishing god. When we are not in the present, we allow ourselves too much room to be plagued by what does not exist in truth. The imagination is a powerful instrument. It creates our entire world. The holy instant is to be in the present moment where happiness and joy come together like two hummingbirds singing as one. They are happy because Love surrounds them, and this is what they know. To see the Loving God within ourselves is to understand that happiness is our birthright, our inheritance. Allow love to enter, and find happiness abiding there.

2. (104) - I seek what belongs to me in truth.

What belongs to you is love and peace. Wake up each morning and know that God awaits you in awareness of Him. This will pull you away from the material values and worldly deceptions and place you in a state of God-Consciousness. Your kinship with your brothers and sisters is recognized by the peaceful and settled way they see you. When peace is deeply felt, happiness hovers just above it. Disruption of peace is based mostly on past occurrences. They serve no purpose because they are no more than illusions. To be deprived of peace because of something that in reality has never happened, and will most likely not occur, cannot bring you peace. Listen to the birds sing as they connect to one another. What you hear is happy chatter because they are only aware of the lovely sunshine warming their nests. We can learn so much from nature. Seek your happiness in the present, for that is all there is in truth.

Love, Jesus

118

(Review) God's peace and joy are mine.
Let me be still and listen to the truth.

1. (105) - God's peace and joy are mine.

Peace and joy are in God, for that is what He knows. Because this is so, everyone must share in it, for it is in all manifestation under God. When we are feeling it, there is no desire to judge the actions of another. It is the vastness within ourselves which remains untainted when we choose to remain true to it. It is the perfect place to enter when we seek peace and stillness. What is in God is no different from that which exists within us.

2. (106) - *Let me be still and listen to the truth.*

Although you have experienced many pitfalls in your life, they were not harmful, for they were learning opportunities. You did not know the profound effect of forgiveness, though it offered you the promise of peace. There was never a need to remain in states of distress, although you had many chances to move past it. Know that every time you are tempted to react without mindful contemplation, you give away an opportunity to be in peace and harmony with the world. Did you not know you would never again regain those precious moments when peace could have been all-present? Why waste another moment, for to be in the now is the only place there is. You have the ability to claim your peace at any time, for it is only in the present moment where truth emerges.

Love, Jesus

119

(Review) Truth will correct all errors in my mind.
To give and to receive are one in truth.

1. (107) - *Truth will correct all errors in my mind.*

Truth is fact, and there is nothing that can change a fact into something that is not. The ego toys with facts continually, for it is a master of distortion. How can one feel safe if truth is tampered with and made to look like something other than what it is? God's gives His Word that we can always find our way to Him. To know God is to know the truth of who we are and that His promises are set in stone. To doubt the word of God is to doubt our own reality, for the God in you is the only reality there is.

2. (108) - To give and to receive are one in truth.

You are blessed indeed, for you have come to recognize the truth of who you are. During our daily lessons, as you listen, it is not only words you hear, but also My thoughts connected with yours. Thoughts are more powerful than words, for thoughts run deep and words are often misunderstood. When our thoughts become joined, your heart begins to beat softly, and a glowed feeling illuminates. Thus, we have connected, and your thoughts recognize mine because they are also your own. Each soul is equipped with a sense of knowing, which is tantamount to truth, and truth can have no opposite. Within this aspect of yourself, you have also come to know your purpose. You are light perfected in form. Stand in your light and let it spill over to those who perhaps do not yet know the truth but learn of it in you.

Love, Jesus

120

(Review) I rest in God. I am as God created me.

1. (109) - I rest in God.

To rest in God brings out the peace in you that you could not find yourself. When you choose to remain apart from God it is because you fear that you have sinned, and that God seeks retribution. The world seems to be a place where sin is enshrined and worshipped. What you must understand is that because there is no sin in God, there can be none in you, and therefore there is nothing to fear. Sin is a dream the ego invented to keep you distanced from God, allowing fear to tug away at you, striking at any hour of the day or night. To rest in God is to feel safe in Him.

2. (110) - I am as God created me.

Because you are as God created you, how can you be anything other than perfection in form when you know that everything God creates is perfect? His Voice resonates quietly inside of you, and if you listen, He is always there. You are a manifestation of all minds joined as one, and each brother and sister is a part of the same God-Consciousness that we all are a part of. His Love reaches every living thing created of Him and each is born of Unconditional Love, forever changeless. When you make God your main focus, nothing in this world has the power to limit your ability to know yourself as God created you.

Love, Jesus

121
Forgiveness is the key to happiness.

Forgiveness starts with the one who matters most, namely you. It is important to know that your happiness depends on this one important lesson. First, you must forgive yourself. You find forgiveness easier to see in others than in yourself. You must forgive that which the ego calls sins, for they are not sins at all, but mistakes. And it is incumbent upon you to find forgiveness with God, for all you need do is ask. This serves to assuage feelings of guilt which the ego feasts on. Whatever unhappiness you feel you caused has no effect in eternity, for God knows only Love. Your perceived sins are of no consequence for they are not real. Inherently, you are guiltless, but you cannot find happiness until you totally embody this very important recognition. God can only love unconditionally, and therefore, He does not condemn. Your mistakes have been forgiven and they do not exist in the Mind of Eternal Love. Be happy and give up guilty thoughts if they should crop up. The key to happiness lies within your ability to recognize your own True Divinity, that you may see it in your brothers and sisters as well.

Love, Jesus

122
Forgiveness offers everything I want.

Forgiveness is the central idea to finding true happiness. It enables you to be free of guilt and allows truth to stand in its place. Let your heart shine its light, especially to those whom you do not feel deserve forgiveness. There are people you believe have hurt you and so they are hard to look upon or think kindly of. My child, they are guiltless, as you are. Absent the body, they are still as God created them, and only in your imaginings are they guilty. Return Home free of guilt. When you forgive, it paves the way to self-love as well, for then it is remembered. It enables you to see that there are no blemishes to stain your past. It was only in your dream of darkness where such offenses occurred and caused you unnecessary pain. Now that you recognize such imaginings for what they are, isn't it time to release your illusions and see that it is only forgiveness that can offer peace?

Love, Jesus

123
I thank my Father for His gifts to me.

Your true gifts are from Heaven. In Heaven everything remains pure, holy, and undefiled. Yet the Earth spins in fear. So, you cannot rise to your heavenly purpose if you hold on to grievances. It is only then, that the One you know as Jesus, can help you find true peace. Your Father's gifts endow you with the Holy Spirit whose Voice speaks to you. He wills only happiness for you. His Love keeps you above water, for He will not let you drown in your own fears. You cannot be in Heaven until you let all judgment go. Your dreams these last two nights had been troublesome to you. Actually, you perceived them correctly, for there are still issues of unforgiveness stored up inside of you which you have not yet let go of. You saw that the attacks in both dreams were directed at those whom you love, showing you that you are not completely free from guilt. The dream was a picture demonstrating something very helpful. To truly feel God's Love, which is His gift to you, you must first accept it with absolute forgiveness.

Love, Jesus

124

Let me remember I am one with God.

Your remembrance of God teaches that you were never abandoned nor forgotten. God's Love created you in perfect Wholeness, and you are known to Him just as you were created. He shares His Power with you, that it may be extended by you to all your brothers and sisters. Let the light within shine brightly, enabling others to remember Him as well. Rest assured there was no need to fear, for He did not let you stray further away when you became tired of being a slave to false idols and yearned to find your way again. Your True Home is the one that God has kept undefiled and warm, welcoming your return, which in truth you never really left, but only distanced yourself from. This led you to despair, but God never left you homeless. For in truth, you are always loved and eternally cared for.

Love, Jesus

125
In quiet I receive God's Word.

Let God make this journey easier now, for in your wandering you distanced yourself, and your travels led you far away from knowing Him as your Creator. God's Word says no matter how far you wander off course, you can always come Home when you are ready to return. In your confused state, you believed you were forgotten, for you did not answer the Call, although it was sent many times. And so, you remained a stranger in a far-off land, away from your True Home. He did not intend for you to take disoriented journeys of despair which promised the world, but never offered real peace or lasting happiness. And so, you continued searching in all the wrong places; a stranger to yourself. When you fell well below your tolerance for pain, you finally reached for His Hand and in forgiveness He dried your tears and guided you towards peace. It is only in stillness that you can feel His awesome Love, for it is no further than this.

Love, Jesus

126
All that I give is given to myself.

To give is to receive. When you disengage from practices of judgment, which are largely the thoughts that come into your mind because the ego speaks louder than stillness, just a few minutes in self-contemplation will help to release you from those daily disruptions which do nothing to maintain your flow of peace. Hold yourself up to a better standard in how you manage your thoughts. For instance, thoughts of judgment replaced with thoughts of love lifts you to a higher realm of consciousness, for it breaks the barrier which keeps you from ascending to a higher understanding of Self. When you think thoughts of love, it breaks unwelcoming patterns of thought because it helps you to better understand how much comfort you are sustaining from such a simple recognition. In your dream-state, which is when you are lost in thoughts that do not serve or uplift you, it is impossible to recognize the negative impact that you are driving inward. Make it a habit of going past that which makes you feel separate and apart from love's awareness. Thoughts of separation keep you blinded to so many miracles which stand right before your unseeing eyes. Seeing yourself as one with your brothers and sisters makes you boundless. The gifts you offer them are the very gifts you are giving yourself.

Love, Jesus

127
There is no love but God's.

God's Love is bestowed upon all living things. He loves His children especially because they are the extension of His Love. Although they have lost knowledge of this, His Love never wavers. God can only be realized when it dawns upon the world that there is nothing here of greater value. That which the world defines as love, is not really love because it is based on concepts separate and apart from what love really is. In reality, we are not individual fragments of the ego, which is the antithesis of love, but instead one consciousness bound with each other and love for our brothers and sisters cannot be known in a world of judgment and separation. Always be thankful that it was God's Love that healed you when you lost your way, helplessly caught in the depths of despair, and He answered your pleas. Hold on to the memory, for there is nothing that can replace that which is irreplaceable.

Love, Jesus

128
The world I see holds nothing that I want.

What you want from the world does not exist in terms of lasting happiness or peace. The world instead can be seen as a gateway to the discovery of truth and nothing more. The world intrigues you with gold nuggets made of dust and interprets it into something worth fighting for, but it leads to despair, for nothing the world offers that is not lasting can make you truly happy. The world teaches you that selfishness has a purpose, and that personal gain is your right even if it is at the expense of another. As a result, it is confusing, for it speaks in platitudes and inconsistencies. Either way, nothing that lacks purpose or does not come from a place of truth can work. However, what will work is to learn a better purpose, which is forgiveness and love. With unkindly thoughts and deeds, the world becomes a place of sorrow and pain. Because your purpose is to love, that is what it takes to heal the world. Put out all the loving energy you have to give so that you may better understand there is nothing you want more than this.

Love, Jesus

129
Beyond this world there is a world I want.

Beyond this world there is a world you once knew but had forgotten. It was a world where all creation came to rest, and God welcomed it. You created a world, which in reality does not exist, because it is not of God. Beyond this world is everything loving and peaceful. It is a place closer to your own heart than you know. You thought it to be far away and unreachable, and therefore you were not happy. You will learn even more as you accept and realize, it is where you belong because it is your True Home. It is not alien to you. Beyond this world there is a world which remains undefiled and awaits your happy return. It is a world bereft of sickness, fear, guilt and all worldly differences, and your body does not need to wither and die to get there. You do get glimpses of it when you are totally at peace. Return to its loveliness at any time. The Love that is there is remembered by you because you were created of it and it is your true dwelling place. Take my hand and let me show you that suffering is needless, and guilt holds no value for you. This is a place to which you will return when you have had enough of a world you created in haste, forgetting God's Unconditional Love. You yearn to be there, yet you do not yield to it as fully as you should. Do not let anything obscure your vision. You have the key. Release yourself by opening the cell door where you have been imprisoned long enough and come Home to where only Love awaits you.

Love, Jesus

130
It is impossible to see two worlds.

It is impossible to see two worlds when only one is real. So, isn't it wise to recognize the world that truly exists, the real world, is the only one you want? When you try to live in two worlds, one which is not real, it obscures the other, which is your True Home. That is why you cannot live in both places peacefully. The real world, which is of God, is the one that protects you from all imagined harm. Living in both worlds cannot hurt you in truth because you are always protected under the sanctity of God's Love, no matter where you think you are. If you focus on the real world, which is your birthplace, then you see ever more clearly that the home you made, which is the ego's birthplace, cannot co-exist. When you decide on the real world, it becomes your haven. In this world all is forgiven, everything remains as it was before time existed, and all goodness is showered upon you because you have chosen to be where God's Love is found. Remaining in the real world takes practice and determination. The ego's world beckons you with dreams of plenty, then it sours you with disappointment and fearful dreams. Always remain kind and forgiving to others, no matter what you think the cost to you is. The ego tells you the cost of forgiveness brings pain, but in truth, the cost is but the exchange for your everlasting peace.

Love, Jesus

131

No one can fail who seeks to reach the truth.

If you but seek nothing but truth, you will find it. All you need do is look deep within to remember truth as it was given to you long before you became entrapped within the ego's dictates. Truth will remind you that nothing else exists, so in effect while you live in a world where depression and guilt run rampant, then you must recognize you are given another choice, as God's Love invites you Home. Unfortunately, those who come here believe the world they made is more suitable than the one God intended for them. This is only a grave mistake, not a sin. There are no sins. But this mistake cost you dearly, because you chose fear in place of God's Love. It was indeed a huge price to pay. But this shaken world which you created can still have a purpose. You can use it to learn that all your imagined mistakes can be exchanged for healing and wholeness. Guilt and fear have no place in God's Kingdom, and by this recognition, all of Heaven's peace can easily be restored to you. Do not let the ego tempt you. When you find yourself wanting to lash out, remember to rely on your strength within, and not on your weak defenses.

Love, Jesus

132
I loose the world from all I thought it was.

To loose the world from false idols, you must also know that forgiveness is key. Forgiveness of yourself and others offers you a new world; one where peace and freedom from guilt abide. The world you made offered you promises of freedom by laying blame upon others believing they were the cause of your unhappiness. But you learned that attack upon them was only an attack upon yourself, which led to guilt and depression. Any idea whether it be true or false, is carried out by you and you alone. If you stay in your world where attack is prevalent, and where love cannot enter, then you are still in a world of false idols which will never bring you peace. You still have moments where you cherish guilt because you still are of the notion that you are not completely deserving of God's Love. In your world, happy memories are but distant recollections, yet guilt rules supreme and remains a constant. Give up thoughts of attack and see only peace. Only there will you find peace and happiness.

Love, Jesus

133
I will not value what is valueless.

What is valuable is lasting, and what is not is limited. Only that which comes from the Higher Self is true. You came into the world wanting to express yourself as a learned being. Once you entered your body and took your first breath, it became your life's ambition to awaken to this purpose. Stunting the ability to do so, is that the mind becomes attached to the ego, promising to be your new best friend forever after. But there is also another part—the Divine you. This "you" exists apart from the self that identifies primarily with the ego. In truth, you are Spirit having the intelligence to discover yourself on a deeper, more intense level of awareness. As long as you stay confined and distracted by the ego, you will not differentiate between the valuable and the valueless (Spirit versus ego). Money, possessions, comforts of the body, and worldly distractions, which are all ego distractions, can divert one's attention long enough to hinder progress their whole life through. While earthly possessions may give temporary comfort, there is a far more lasting comfort available to all who seek it, which goes beyond the body. Training yourself to go to that ever-deepening part of yourself is an investment well worth spending a lifetime if need be to find it, for it is only there that you will find the best of yourself.

Love, Jesus

134
Let me perceive forgiveness as it is.

What is forgiveness but love? When love can be seen as unconditional, it is reason to rejoice, for you have come to understand life's purpose. Your kindness in the world reflects His Loving Kindness to you. Forgiveness is easy when you know you are sustained by this truth. When you also know that you are forgiven for your own perceived sins and misgivings, how then could you not see it in others? Forgiveness is necessary if only because it is a release from guilt. If you can accept the idea that there is no cause to feel guilty and can see yourself as blameless, you can then perceive that same quality in others. In recognizing God's forgiveness for your own misgivings, it is only fair that you too forgive those whom you have condemned for theirs. In truth you have never been guilty and therefore there is nothing to forgive. Everything except love is a perception. Love is beyond perception for that is all that is real.

Love, Jesus

135
If I defend myself I am attacked.

When you have defended yourself in an argument, or have attacked as well, how did it make you feel? Did you feel peace or rage? Isn't attack and defense equally disturbing? Did not both lead to the same outcome? When you attack another, it reduces the ability to know your Self. The only way to gain control then, is to come away having learned from it. Attack is not easy to understand because the soul (higher Self) does not adhere to it. The soul sits silent as your emotions run away with you. You are coming to understand that attack leads to guilt, and guilt is fear. It is a weapon of the ego to keep the momentum going, and now you must justify your attack back, which is perceived as your defense. Through the years you knew you hurt those you love at times, and you have been hurt as well. How foolish it is to take part in something that cannot be justified when it is hurtful to yourself or someone else. Is it not best to be secure in the knowledge that in the Eyes of God no one is guilty? You need not defend yourself if you do not perceive someone is attacking you.

Love, Jesus

136
Sickness is a defense against the truth.

Sickness is not real, for it is not of God, and Heaven knows not of it. Yet it is made real by the mind as it convinces the body that it is suffering. Yet to the sufferer, the importance of the body is everything. So important in fact, that it will do anything to preserve its false beliefs. Sickness is the most convincing of all. Yet sickness is no more real than the body which harbors it. The body became a reality to the part of the mind which believed it sinned against God, separate and apart from Him, and thus feared punishment. For sickness is "proof" that the body is real, and God is not. Therefore, the body remains a symbol of truth to itself but not to God. The body does nothing that the mind does not direct it to do. An unhealed mind will perceive a sick body. By allowing God to heal the part of the mind that is split, then will the body heal as well. The body's only true purpose can then be used as a vessel for love, for sickness is no longer needed as its defense.

Love, Jesus

137
When I am healed I am not healed alone.

What is healing, but to undeniably know love? And how can you be healed alone when you are part of a system which includes the entire Sonship? When one part becomes healed through forgiveness, it strengthens the entirety of all its parts. You are told you can save the world. Indeed, you can. When your thoughts rise above the limited vibrations of lower thinking, the entire world transforms. But consistency plays a major role in the healing process, for you must remember to practice forgiveness before you can remember God's Love. There is no greater gift to give yourself or your brothers and sisters than to realize this. Until you understand what this truly means, you will not recognize that you are already healed, for God created you as Love and you are no less than this. It is within that recognition which makes it so. With forgiveness, you are then empowered to share His Love, for you have gained it for yourself. So therefore, forgiveness is the first ingredient needed before healing is truly known. When you enter Heaven, you and your brothers and sisters will come Home as one for no one enters alone.

Love, Jesus

138
Heaven is the decision I must make.

Why would you not make Heaven your sole decision when it offers you everything the world could not? Although Heaven is your real Home, you wandered off to a place far, far away and did not know the way back yourself. But you found your way, lost but for a little while, for God did not let you stray too far from Him, knowing one day you would want to return. He helped you along by lighting a path. You saw the light and so you did follow it. Although you made the decision to return to the sanctity of your True Home, you have just begun to pack. There is still more for you to accomplish here. Salvation is that which you came to study. Although you have not yet completed your learning, you will accomplish much. All the Angels in Heaven await you. When the time has come, they will gift you with their welcoming songs. At this journey's end, you will realize you were gone but only for a moment, for in Heaven there is only timelessness.

Love, Jesus

139
I will accept Atonement for myself.

To accept the Atonement is to surrender to God. Its purpose is to move past this world of separation and limitation. The ego's insanity is without purpose, but it does have a cause: Its main objective is to keep you unaware of God's Love. The Atonement gives you peace as it awaits your homecoming. Be faithful to the Atonement which God has given you as a means to heal. A mind intent on healing stays vigilant and does not wander away from the Source by which it heals. If you do not listen to the ego's constant prodding, you have the power to rise above the turmoil and go into a higher consciousness. The ego is witness to this and will fight to the core to save itself, for its life depends on your loyalty to it and not to God. The world is a fearful place if you do not question its strange teachings. Your brothers and sisters share the Atonement, for they are not separate but one with you. Give God your willingness to accept the Atonement and do not be weakened by the ego's beckoning call. When you accept the Atonement for yourself it is recognized for you are healed.

Love, Jesus

140
Only salvation can be said to cure.

Salvation, which is Truth, is yours for the asking and clears away all obstacles which distract you from your true purpose. The healing powers of the world's medicines are attempts to make illusions real. They are no more real than the ego's wish to make it so. The decision to offer forgiveness is the first step towards healing. What restores the body to wholeness is of the mind, and the mind must be a willing participant before any outcome is revealed. The body will respond only to that which it believes is its reality. What the mind seeks it will find. If it seeks Truth and relinquishes unforgiving thoughts stored within the far corners of the mind, it will be found. The body will respond only to that which it believes is its reality. If its purpose is to hold the ego's thought system in place, it will also believe it can become sick, one of the ego's great deceptions. It will then rely on the world's magic powers for healing, thereby blocking the way to true healing which is of God.

Love, Jesus

141

(Review) My mind holds only what I think with God.

1. (121) - Forgiveness is the key to happiness.

Forgiveness and happiness are seen in light. In order to forgive, it is best to understand it is everyone's inherent nature to want happiness, and so they strive to find it. Yet attack holds us back from happiness, for when we attack, we also expect it back. To attack, or to feel attacked, holds us in darkness. To go from dark to light is to visualize the light inherent in everyone, even those you might deem unworthy of your forgiveness. If you perceive them in light, it will be easier to forgive, but first you must want to see the light that shines in both of you. Yet it is difficult to think in terms of extending light while unforgiving thoughts lurk in the shadows of your mind. Because forgiveness is the key to happiness, it is worth striving for.

2. (122) - Forgiveness offers everything I want.

When you focus your thoughts on being happy, it takes you away from attack thoughts. Think happy thoughts, for it is in this place that better judgment can be counted on. You savor the moments when you are feeling happy, and at peace with the world. It is the release from everything fearful and in those moments, you feel safe and protected. This is your true reality. It was there long before time became your enemy and tore you away from the memory of God's Eternal Love. But God kept the memory of your true reality safely guarded. It was never lost to you, only forgotten at a time when forgiveness was not understood, and fear preyed upon your thoughts instead of love.

Love, Jesus

142

(Review) My mind holds only what I think with God.

1. (123) - I thank my Father for His gifts to me.

Because you have willingly made great strides in your journey from when you first began, God thanks you. Indeed, your Father bestows you with gifts so great you owe Him all your gratitude as well. What are His gifts? There are many. He remembers you in Heaven, your real Home. He does not let you wander alone, afraid and unprotected, ensuring your safe return to Him. He has forgiven all your errors and I can assure you there have been many. Because He created you holy, and a part of Him, you can never be abandoned nor changed. Above all, He has given you a special place in His Plan for salvation, a role you will happily fulfill.

2. (124) - Let me remember I am one with God.

All thoughts make up the world you see. Yet what you behold in the world has no real meaning, neither good nor bad. God's thoughts are your thoughts, and only that which is real is true. Feel blessed, for you have found happiness in a world in dire need of love. How thankful you must be too, for you have also found the way out of the darkness where once you groped blindly. Your eyes are open, and the rest of the way is now easier. Rise above the world towards love and let no outside influences distract you from your peace. Behold your Father's Love, for there is nothing that shall obscure your vision. Many are frightened and still do not yet see their way out, so it is incumbent upon you to speak your truth to them. You are blessed, for you have come far. His gifts enable you to reach way beyond this world of separation and to remember you are still as you were created, forever changeless.

Love, Jesus

143

(Review) My mind holds only what I think with God.

1. (125) - In quiet I receive His Word today.

God's Voice speaks His Word. When you quiet your mind, it is an achievement in itself, for the ego's voice undermines the Word of God. When you bring yourself into the stillness of the moment and remain there, you know undeniably that God's Voice reveals only truth. You are often distracted by the ego, convincing yourself you are at peace, when it is just the opposite. The ego does not allow for peace and makes promises that are unkept. God's Voice is heard through feelings, thoughts, and even words. When God speaks to you in stillness, what is being revealed is only truth. God's truth will overshadow the ego's endless promises if you choose to see the ego for what it is. What is God's Word? By establishing what is true, He promises that it shall remain as such, for truth cannot be altered. Only that which is true is changeless.

2. (126) - All that I give is given to myself.

God speaks to you moment by moment, but the turmoil of a busy mind cannot hear His Voice. To hear His Voice, you must listen in stillness. He is with you in Spirit and is always within earshot of your prayers, as each and every one is surely answered. When you sleep, He whispers softly so that you may rest peacefully. When you think with God, His Voice becomes a loving hymn which your mind recognizes and remembers, having heard it many times before. When you give your faith to God, it is safely tucked away in His Care, for it is never lost. What you give to God in faith, is given to yourself.

Love, Jesus

144

(Review) My mind holds only what I think with God.

1. (127) - There is no love but God's.

There is no Love but God's and be thankful that this is so. God's Love extends itself to include all. If God did not extend Himself through Love, you would not have come into existence. You are made out of the same energy that exists in Him. What could possibly have greater meaning than this, and why would you want more? You buy things in excess, far exceeding your needs, and think it is happiness, however fleeting it may be. Nothing can produce greater happiness than to know that there is no Love but God's, and that you are an extension of that Love. God is truth and knows no opposite. Remember, you cannot live in two worlds and expect to be equally happy in both. One is real, the other is an illusion. What can extol greater joy than to experience the Love by which you were created?

2. (128) - The world I see holds nothing that I want.

"The world I see holds nothing that I want" is not intended to mean you must give up your comforts and the material things you desire. God does not ask that you give up the things you value, for then it would seem that God is asking that you sacrifice for Him. If you believed you must sacrifice by giving up your comforts in order for God to love you, it would be difficult indeed to surrender to Him. The greatest abundance is in God and there is nothing you need to give up in order to receive it. Yet by placing too much importance in what the world deems as valuable, is to seek happiness where it cannot be found. Happiness, love, and peace cannot be found in that which is perishable, for what is not lasting has no value.

Love, Jesus

145

(Review) My mind holds only what I think with God.

1. (129) - Beyond this world there is a world I want.

Beyond this world is a world waiting for you, a world you knew before, but had not remembered how awesome and wonderful it was. When you were created, you knew God's Love and smiled upon all of Heaven because it was good. It was a world where all you knew was security, comfort, peace, and above all, Love. But then you came to another place, not your home. You knew from the first day you arrived and taken from your mother's womb, that this was not really you. You landed in a world of ghosts and dreams, certainly not the reality you once knew, and through your tears you learned that this was not the world God created. Now you are seeing another world, one that leads you back to God and you are in the process of discovering through faith, your true origins once again. Just follow the scent of God's Angels. I (Jesus) will take your hand and guide you gently there. Never fear that you will be abandoned and left to die alone in some strange, unknown world. You are steadily moving back to your rightful place in God's Kingdom. Every star that lights the sky will also light a path for your safe return. Once on this path to Home the rest will be easy, for you will recognize it once again.

2. (130) - It is impossible to see two worlds.

The world you choose is obviously the one you value most. You have the power to choose which of the two worlds offers you greater freedom. Do you choose the darkness of the ego, or the light Heaven? It is for you to determine which one you wish to give up in exchange for the other. One world offers peace, happiness, and joy. The other brings on fear, attack, and pain. It all depends on which world you are willing to put your beliefs into. To invest in the ego is to value your individual separation to the point that you are not willing to explore further. The real world is found within your mind; the Mind you share with God. The ego looks to find its pleasures outside the mind searching endlessly, never finding what it seeks. The world you decide on is the one you give your pledge to. The question always is, "Do you want to stay invested in the illusion, or do you want to awaken in God?"

Love, Jesus

146

(Review) My mind holds only what I think with God.

1. (131) - No one can fail who seeks to reach the truth.

To seek the truth, one must first want to know the meaning of truth. You have felt its warm embrace in a healing thought, or an answered prayer. The world you see is in desperate need of healing. Of late, you have been listening to the birds speak to one another as they chirp in their treetops. In their world, they know only to rejoice as their chirps are answered by one another in song. The world can learn much from their natural ability to survive without care. That is as the world should be. Learn from nature. See how well the chirping birds communicate naturally in their sun-filled, carefree environment. The sounds they make are joyous because there is nothing else to feel but the freedom the Earth provides, and every need is filled. If birds instinctively know they are God's creation, how can man, who was created in God's own image, not understand as much? Hear the sounds of nature and live carefree.

2. (132) - I loose the world from all I thought it was.

The world as such is a judgment—a hallucination. You come into the world perceiving that everything you see is real, yet the world you see is only a condition of the mind. I have told you many times, that the world you see is an outside picture of an inward condition. What your mind reveals to you about the world is of the imagination. This is a difficult concept to embrace because the ego will never let go of the idea that what it sees is not true. All thoughts are projections which make up the world you see. But there is no world, for what we call "seeing" is not seeing at all, but images that the mind accepts as real. When this truth is accepted, you will see a different world. You cannot change the world. All you can do is change your mind about the world. This will bring a truer reality into focus. When you witness a magician pulling a rabbit from a hat, you know it is a magician's trick. The world you see is no different. Release the world by releasing your thoughts about the world and see a happier picture emerge.

Love, Jesus

147

(Review) My mind holds only what I think with God.

1. (133) - I will not value what is valueless.

Looking for things in the world that you think will make you happy is futile, for the world cannot provide you with anything that is lasting or rewarding. If you invest in the things you think will bring you happiness, and they do not own up to your expectations, you are disappointed. This is the price you pay. Because the ego's natural function is to be relentless, it will increase its pursuits again and again. Everything that keeps you invested in the world of time is valueless because you are investing in an illusion. Only in God will you find what is valuable, for it is only in Him that it is attainable. Every investment you make which places your trust in Him will bring forth the outcome that serves your highest purpose. With faith, you must understand that God will not give you anything that does not serve your best interests, but He will always fulfill your highest purpose.

2. (134) - Let me perceive forgiveness for what it is.

To say "I forgive" is not what true forgiveness means. To forgive another the "sin" which we perceive as real does not seem fair, yet we sometimes lower our pride and "give in." By believing ourselves to be charitable, by our own definition of the word, we are really projecting our guilt onto someone else. In effect, it is an attack on their innocence, although they are perceived as anything but innocent. In the Eyes of God, we are all innocent. If we were not, we would be deserving of punishment. But because we are feeling guilty, we project our guilt where we think it belongs, which is always on the other person. From the ego's standpoint, placing it elsewhere frees us from the burden of owning up to what is true. In effect, we are justifying our innocence, for we do not see the part we played in the fallout. To perceive forgiveness is to free ourselves by holding no one guilty in our hearts.

Love, Jesus

148
(Review) My mind holds only what I think with God.

1. (135) - If I defend myself I am attacked.

The premise here is that if you think you need to defend yourself, it is because you are perceiving that you are being attacked. You are learning that when you have an angry thought, by imagining that you are defending yourself to the person whom you believe attacked you, you are attacking yourself. An attack on yourself invades your peace every time. Each time an attack thought arises, and you play it out in your mind, you are hurting yourself. You cannot take the poison and expect the other person will die. You are the one swallowing the poison, and so it is yourself that you are contaminating. Your small self is the expression of the ego, your True Self is the expression of the Mind. To be aware of this, gives you greater insight into your strengths and not your weaknesses.

2. (136) - Sickness is a defense against the truth.

If attack was a true protector of the body, then sickness would be true as well. When the mind attacks the body, it becomes a vessel for sickness, and it is sickness of the mind that plays havoc with the body. The body is not real, and the mind is only partly real because it is divided. What the mind thinks, the body will adhere to. Attack thoughts are used by the body to punish itself. And as you already know, the body punishes itself to prove its reality over God's. But if it perceives right-mindedness, attack then becomes useless because it has chosen to ignore the desire to hurt and be hurt. The body is only capable of obeying how it is taught to behave. The body is the puppet, and the mind is the puppet's instrument. The mind which chooses sickness over healing blocks the awareness to love, thus making sickness its reality. Yet fear and sickness cannot prevail when love is the mind's choice.

Love, Jesus

149

(Review) My mind holds only what I think with God.

1. (137) - When I am healed I am not healed alone.

When you ask for healing, that one thought extends itself to include all of your brothers and sisters. Because all minds are joined, true healing frees all minds as one. There is only One Mind, One Purpose, One Soul, and that is you. When you can truly embody this concept, healing takes place in an instant. It is not the body, but the mind which responds to this truth. The healing you receive empowers others to see it in themselves. If you see yourself as a body, separate from the mind, it is because you cannot see past the thought that you are separate and apart from your brothers and sisters. The idea of separation came from the thought that you are also separate from God. The Love God shares with you frees you from the ego's identity. Healing can only come where there is no fear. Remember, you are not limited, because you were all created from One Loving Entity.

2. (138) - Heaven is the decision I must make.

When you affirm that Heaven is all you want, then to mean those words strengthens that belief. That is why holding on to thoughts of unforgiveness, anger, disaster, and adversity makes no sense, for they take you away from peace. It is strange that we guard those thoughts more closely than our real thoughts. God only knows of you as His perfect creation and does not recognize those beliefs contrived by the ego. When you speak to God, His Voice can be heard through feelings, thoughts, ideas, and words. To be fixed on God is to understand what your real thoughts are. They are the only ones which can heal because they come from Love. Because Heaven is your Eternal Home, that is where you want to return to. It is the decision you must make for there can be no other.

Love, Jesus

150

(Review) My mind holds only what I think with God.

1. (139) - I will accept Atonement for myself.

The meaning of the Atonement is to accept ourselves as we are. God's Love is ours eternally and it is our job to accept ourselves as

He created us. The Atonement erases all doubts about ourselves, and our brothers and sisters. We are created as an Extension of His Love. Our purpose is to extend God's Love, which is in us to share, and make it our mission to fulfill that purpose. It is incumbent upon us to use this time for creating, not miscreating, so that we may leave this world in far better shape than we found it in. As long as we stay within the illusion which we believe offers us happiness and greater satisfaction than God, we will suffer pain and suffering as consequences. Until we become better acquainted with who we are, we will perceive ourselves as victims, for there is no one else to blame. By seeking our purpose, we will begin to derive true satisfaction from it. If we hold too many beliefs about ourselves that are not true, we will not accept the Atonement, which is what we came to seek.

2. (140) - Only salvation can be said to cure.

Salvation starts with forgiveness. With forgiveness, we are demonstrating that God is the only Source from which true forgiveness comes. Through television news media, which we seem to witness endlessly, are people seeking to save themselves from a terrifying and fearful world, yet they say little about the goodness that holds itself above this fear-driven world. News anchors tell you what they are required to tell you, for which they are handsomely paid. Look only at what you are experiencing and let the truth be revealed as you see it. You are free to explore your own salvation and discover what you believe as true. Because you are a creation of the One Source, born of free will, you have it within you to change your mind at any time and discover the healing power of salvation.

Love, Jesus

151
All things are echoes of the Voice for God.

If you listen, you can hear the Voice for God because He speaks to you wherever you go. Mornings, you enjoy the precious whistling of birds coming from the treetops in chorus, as they sing back and forth to each other. Every sound—whether it be laughter, the music you hum, the wind blowing against your face, or even your kitchen clock which you enjoy for its musical chimes—are all reminders of His Love. In stillness, when you write your daily lessons you hear the Voice for God as He directs your thoughts. They are His Thoughts joined with your own. Listen and be happy as you go through your day in peace. The echoes of His Voice come through at night as well. When you awaken from an unrestful sleep, it is He Who quietly whispers your name so that you may return to a safe and restful night. Although you hear it in hushed tones, you know that it is the echo of His Voice speaking to you.

Love, Jesus

152
The power of decision is my own.

The power of decision is yours joined with God's. In knowing God's Love, you do not need to fear making decisions because God's Thoughts are also yours. However, each decision you do make must lead to a "cause-and-effect" outcome. Because the past and future are non-existent, deciding with the ego is an illusion which leads nowhere. All decisions made with the ego will cast you into a place that God knows not of, and it is fearful indeed to grope around unknowingly. You have done this many times and although no real harm has come to you, pain and depression was often the outcome. You were distressed today when you learned that God is being thrown out of your Country's court rooms. The same is happening in schools and in government. You can rise above this insane ploy to rid the world of God. You are blessed because you have learned that there is no place else to go but into the safety of God's Truth. Obviously, many have not yet learned this. Everyone will get their turn and recognize that God is the last decision they must make. In the world of time this is a long way off. One day you will all make the same decision and thus come Home as One.

Love, Jesus

153

In my defenselessness my safety lies.

If you find there is a need to defend yourself it is because you believe you have been attacked. Yet attack is perceived by a fearful mind, and where there is fear, there can be no peace. Yet threat is perceived by the mind and not the body because the body does not reason. It simply obeys the mind. When the mind is conditioned to think only right-minded thoughts, the body will follow its directions, and therein lies its safety. For the body then softens as its demeanor has changed, and no hint of anger is left for another to perceive as threat. Remember when we said, "the body is the puppet, and the mind is the puppet's instrument?" That thought resonated with you strongly, because you recognized it to be true. When the mind is conditioned to think correctly, there is no need for defense, for a mind absent of fear sees no threat. When the mind holds out for God's invitation to peace, and fear is no longer the ruling factor, you have allowed love to enter the picture. In your defenselessness there is now strength, not weakness. A healed mind does not open itself up to thoughts of attack because it could not conceive of any–thing but a peaceful outcome.

Love, Jesus

154
I am among the ministers of God.

God's ministers know that they are still as they were created. They carry the Word of God in their hearts and they do not need to announce it loudly. They need only to know it in order to share it, as He shares His Love with them. They are happy because they are at peace, for they recognize their God-Given power to extend their love out into the world and have the capacity to understand His Love with everlasting faith. His ministers are the children who choose not to leave His Presence in search of something greater. Ministers of God shine because they see the beaming faces of their brothers and sisters reflected in their own as their smiles are returned in gratitude. Ministers of God are healers because they know not of hate. They have trained their minds to stay clear of unforgiving thoughts, and to quickly return to thoughts of peace if they should be tempted to stray. To see all of the above in yourself is to know you are indeed among the ministers of God.

Love, Jesus

155
I will step back and let Him lead the way.

To step back and let Him lead the way is to have such unbreakable faith that it leaves no room for doubt. When you are at peace and your thoughts are with God, nothing can interfere with your desire to follow Him, for why would you not allow yourself to be led to the only place where safety abides and where your destiny is assured? To know God's Love till the end of your days will lead you into paradise. Now you must walk the path without faltering or looking back. Know that you are not alone but in God's care which never wavers or changes direction; the path is straight and sure. As you march in stride with Him, your steps are quickened, for the road ahead leaves no doubt that He is with you on this lovely voyage which grows more beautiful with each new day, yet shorter by the hour. When you step back and let Him lead the way, your heart is free and sings along with Angels, for nowhere else would you rather be.

Love, Jesus

156
I walk with God in perfect holiness.

There is no longer a need to uphold illusions when you walk with God. Each time you are provoked by something which tempts you to react with anger, guilt, or fear, and recognize it for what it is by not perceiving fearfully, it brings you to another level of faith. For God answers every prayer. This you have been privy to many, many times. When you recite The Lord's Prayer, which you know by heart, or think of an affirmation that sets bells ringing because you know they are true, it works miracles. When you reach for Him in the night, you are gently restored to a peaceful rest as you drift off to sleep without a care. All you need do is but ask. He will never fail you. Calling out to Him works far better than the magic remedies the world relies on so heavily, for sleep is never truly as restful when you rely on its remedies in place of God. To rely on Him night or day, brings you to the realization that each child of God is a treasured being. Prayers to Him are invested well, for they are returned with interest. Your holiness is wrapped in perfection, for nothing created by God could be less than this.

Love, Jesus

157
Into His Presence would I enter now.

Enter into God's Presence as Heaven sings to you in loving praise. Such is the music you will one day come to know again. Your homecoming will be one of joy so great you will not know why you ever left, even if only for a moment, which in linear time is only a moment as compared to timelessness in Heaven. Leaving was of your own choosing, and when you do return, you will do so having never lost your awareness. The joy upon returning is that which you had forgotten while you left to play your imaginary games in a world of dreams. Though your dreams were often unsettling, you did not know that God was ever-present, never leaving you to dream alone, unprotected. You thought you were left to drown in your own sorrowful tears. Now, as you enter into God's Presence, you shall join with Him as you were created. Stay close the rest of your days and feel the Love that you were not always aware of, but also had not totally lost memory of. With arms outstretched and your heart free to soar, enter joyously into the Eternal God Himself.

Love, Jesus

158
Today I learn to give as I receive.

Today, as I learn to give as I receive, is to have a vision of who your brothers and sisters are, and to see them as yourself. Today you learned the law of love through an unusual experience. You did not trust a fellow brother, for you saw him through the ego's perception and not "true" perception. You judged him as someone to fear because of his appearance, and manner of speaking. But he turned out to be far different than how you chose to judge him. This same brother found you, reminding you that you lost your cell phone. He told you where he brought it, and that it was safely kept until you could claim it. The lesson here is that when you saw the goodness in him, it enabled you to see it in yourself, for he warmed your heart. You gained the recognition that you are all part of the One Mind, sinless, and created to be wholly unafraid. When you are able to feel oneness in spirit with a brother or sister, it is a gift to both of you.

Love, Jesus

159
I give the miracles I have received.

God embraces you with miracles, for He created you worthy of receiving them. His miracles are like a symphony of notes which form a grand scale of beautiful music easily understood. His blessings reach out to all of His children, but many do not yet realize their entitlement to them. God releases miracles freely so that they may be extended to all. When you choose to share a miracle, you will find it to be a natural ability. As you give, you also receive. Happiness comes to those who bestow it freely. The best part of happiness is to know that it is contagious. When you suffer, the world recoils in sadness. When you are happy the world sings out in joy. That is what it means to give the miracles you have received. Miracles are gifted and wrapped in clover. The scent of clover resembles the scent of Angels still familiar to you, for memory of Home is never completely forgotten. Your True Home awaits you and you will know of it more fully when you return, realizing you never left.

Love, Jesus

160

I am at home. Fear is the stranger here.

Your Home is with God, Who you never left. You only thought you did when your dream of fear became the body's reality. By creating fearful dreams, you lost sight of your true self. Fear has a way of causing untold grief in the body. The body is no more than a hank of hair and a collection of skin and bones, separate and apart from the Mind which created the Self which is of God. You see those all around you who are slaves to the ego. Illness, pain, helplessness, and untold fear carries itself from one day into the next. Along with the illusion that the body is everything comes suffering. Death then, is all that awaits them, and they wallow in their suffering until their fear takes them to even greater suffering. They smile at times, but underneath it all is fear lurking about waiting to show itself once more. You have come to God in thankfulness as those sorrowful memories no longer have power over you. You have also learned that God gently washes them away when you ask. That is all there is to it. It is simple, but many do not ask even when their suffering is beyond measure. Because you are witness to this, you have come to understand the healing power of God when you accepted Him as your Creator. The world is no more than a pitiful dream. The only thing about the world which makes it real is Love, because Love reflects Heaven.

Love, Jesus

161

Give me your blessing, you holy Son of God.

Knowing that you are blessed is that which makes it so. The gift of faith is God's greatest blessing of all. Nurture it until it blossoms fully and use it the way He intends—that it be shared so that it may be kept. Feel the Presence of His Love and recognize the spark of light-energy which exists in all. Ego thoughts should not be seen as real, and through wisdom you learn to tell the difference. The only thoughts that are real are your true thoughts which God shares with you. God holds only the thoughts you think with Him. All others are false, oblivious to the reality of His thoughts. Feel especially happy because you have come far in your awareness. Letting go of unwanted debris in your mind before it starts to collect is key. You are more at peace and have learned to reduce the ego's influence over you. Keep practicing so that you may fine tune your efforts even more. Take His blessings and rely on them when fear gnaws away at your peace. Then reverse the process before it festers. You can do this because you are His holy child born of Love.

Love, Jesus

162
I am as God created me.

To be as God created you is to be at peace with yourself as well as with the world. You are God's empowered child, and your unwavering faith restores faith in others for it is observed in you. God created you pure and innocent, and in that innocence lies your strength. God created you holy, and so you are. God created you perfect, and that you are. God gave His knowledge to you so it may be shared in His Name. Many have not yet accepted this. They walk the world in fear and will continue to do so until they awaken. Walk with your holy brothers and sisters so that you may set an example by what you have gained through practice, prayer, and faith. Many still believe they have sinned against God and so they hide from His Will. You too had fearful thoughts hidden deep within the corners of your mind. Now you walk with certainty, keeping your footsteps in stride with a new purpose—to be at peace forever more, for there is no sin.

Everything in God is sinless and changeless. All anyone need do is ask for forgiveness and it is bestowed. Knowing this is to render one's self forever free.

Love, Jesus

163
There is no death. The Son of God is free.

Death as perceived through the body's eyes is the end of life. Your body has been afloat in a world of dreams trying to discover its true reality since birth. There shall come a time when you will value your body no longer. You have since learned not to fear the illusion of death because it is meaningless. When you enter into the Gates of Heaven past all dreams of sin, guilt, and fear, you will know that your homecoming was planned since you first chose to take a detour from God's Eternal Love, and exchanged it for a world of danger, sickness, and fear. You have since learned there is no real danger, and that sickness is not within your reality because it serves only to prey on those minds not yet healed. A mind that is healed has learned the truth and has no need to explore this aspect of suffering any longer. Death is the last obstacle to overcome. Now, in the twilight years of your life, you have come to know there is no death and that only life eternal is true.

Love, Jesus

164
Now we are one with Him Who is our Source.

When all illusions have passed, we will know the Oneness that exists within the vastness of His Eternal Love. We will know our Source; the One Who gave us life and the One in Whom we live. We will know that death is only a deception of the ego and that we are of God, created One with Him. How comforting it is to be assured that we have never separated from our Source. Because His Love is our one true reality, how did such a strange paradox come about to change our thoughts? It never did. We just forgot to remember the flame we find in God's Eternal Light. Fan the flame and keep it going. It was gifted to us and remains as such forever. You were not left to wander alone in the darkness unclaimed. Love lives on and so does every living thing created of Him. We are one, because we are never apart from Source.

Love, Jesus

165

Let not my mind deny the thought of God.

How can God be denied when thoughts of Him lead only to peace? Yet the ego reasons falsely and does not question. When you are in the midst of all sorts of upheaval going on inside of you, do you not see the ego rearing its head ready to claim God's Kingdom as its own? It tries to instill fear in place of God's Love; sometimes subtle, and sometimes overt. It takes discipline to keep the thought of God in place and not to deny thoughts of Him for something more desirable, making the ego the center of your universe. Within us all is a burning desire to know God which is never extinguished, but quieted when we wander away believing the ego can take the place of God, thus rationalizing those beliefs and perceiving them as real. How foolish we are. It takes a great deal of undoing to make us see that to deny God is to deny self-love. Who would want this acceptance of reality when it is anything but real? Only a madman. Your sanity has been restored to you and your ransom has been paid. Let it be kept eternally safe and let not your mind deny the thought of God forever after.

Love, Jesus

166

I am entrusted with the gifts of God.

How loving your Creator must be to entrust His gifts in your care. Ask yourself, "Why would God turn His gifts over to me if I were not worthy of His trust?" They are given so that they may be used in appreciation of His recognition of your innate goodness as you were created and still remain. Share His gifts and recall the path that you are destined to follow. The Voice for God will lead you through the clouds, past all worldly discord, and into the Gates of Heaven. See how your brothers and sisters follow as you keep in step with Him? As you do your Course lessons, these precious moments are shared with God. It is a roadmap leading to where He awaits you with His Love. How could God not reward His creations for their good deeds, and not forgive them for their misdeeds? Take my hand and rejoice because you have recognized the ego's unholy attempts to lead you astray. Now do you hear Holy Spirit's Voice as your own? His Voice may be dimmed by the raucous voice of the ego, but always remember it is near enough to be heard as you seek to hear it. God's Power is entrusted to you because He knows you will share the memory of His grace as you receive it. His Love, given to you changeless, is your greatest gift of all.

Love, Jesus

167

There is one life, and that I share with God.

The life you are experiencing here on Earth is not of God. However, He does remain with you in your self-chosen reality because it is impossible to be separate from Him. Whether you choose to live on your worldly plane or share moments with Him in your heavenly state, God is your Creator, and He knows you only as His Creation. All sins and heartache you believed you brought down upon yourself and others was just a momentary detour from your true reality. All you do, and all you experience, whether they be your own foolish fantasies or God-Realized expressions of Love, He is with you through it all. That is why worry, depression, guilt, fear, or any other abhorrence, which you believe is of you, is idle nonsense. You are a part of God. So how could you be separate from Him in any manner other than as you were created? Your bodily form is of your own making. It is the puppet which dances to the imaginary and fearful tunes of a child. The reality of who you are remains with your Heavenly Father forever. Guilt is past and does not now exist, so how can it have a present reality except in your own thoughts? What is True Reality is of God and therefore changeless. You have been told over and over that you are still as God created you. Keep that holy thought present in your mind and be happy.

Love, Jesus

168
Your grace is given me. I claim it now.

God has gifted you with His grace, for His Love is forever and always accessible. It is your inheritance. He kept it safe while you wandered alone and in fear. Grace is a gift because it is Himself Who gives it. It is an inheritance left for you to claim. Use the present to acknowledge grace, whereby it is the only place it can be found. In the present there are no worries. In the present is where happiness abides and where love can once again be found. The present is where all light shines and the reflection of His Love can be felt deep within. Feel His Love always as you are feeling it now and be grateful to those who come to share it with you. In the present is where soulmates recognize one another. In the present is where you can see all those you loved who have passed on, come to life once more. Do not dwell on past experiences which were not real if they did not come from love. Stay off the frantic treadmill going nowhere and focus only on God's grace which is yours to claim.

Love, Jesus

169

By grace I live. By grace I am released.

Grace is the realization that God lives within the heart of all creation. Let your own heart beat in tune with the constancy of His Love as it fills you with a gentle reassurance that you are His most beloved. All creation is at One with their Creator and aspire to the grace of His eternal gifts. Be at peace and live in harmony with all your brothers and sisters who have come to love you because you stand at the very core of God's holy temple and share your faith with them. When you share the sanctity of His Love with forgiveness, you become free. Remember, grace is a gift which restores you to the remembrance of His eternal Love and therefore releases you from all of your perceived wrong-doings. His bountiful grace, given to you in light, is eternal because it comes from Love. It is this self-awareness which your soul retains because it was planted there when God created you.

Love, Jesus

170

There is no cruelty in God and none in me.

Cruelty is the thought which the ego manufactured in order to keep you bound to it. In view of all you have been through, this is obvious. God did not create you cruel so you must never judge yourself as such. But cruelty is a perfect foil for the ego. It is the only way it knows to keep you entrapped in a guilty state of mind. The ego's life depends on your fears to keep itself going and will convince you that you have done the unthinkable; thus, you deem yourself as having been cruel. Cruelty was never of God so of course it cannot be in you. God made you sinless. But you became a tasty morsel for the ego to prey upon when you chose to act upon its insane commands over God's Truth. The ego is alien to God, so He does not condemn you for what He does not know. He only knows that He created you guiltless and sinless and, as such, that is what you are. The self you made, giving power to the ego, is cruel indeed. But you have learned in countless ways that God has rescued you from this intolerable web of fear, inherently not of you. The ego has no power to control you. Come to God in humbleness whenever the ego attempts to dig its sharp claws into your thoughts. His Power can always be relied upon to keep you safe and free from guilt.

Love, Jesus

171

(Review) God is but Love, and therefore so am I.

1. (151) - All things are echoes of the Voice for God.

Everywhere you go, and everything you come upon, echoes God's Voice. If you recognize everyone as yourself, it becomes One Voice, the Voice for God. Is it not wonderful to feel His Love because you have recognized His Voice in all? Within the vastness of God's Love, which is all that you are, comes the power of free will. Free will is misdirected when it is used to follow the ego's deceptions. Yet you have come to understand that misuse of free will brings pain, for it is absent love. Although you wandered away from God's Will, He never lost sight of you. Now may you use your power of decision in a different way. Give yourself to God so that He may direct you towards the destination you are meant to follow, and trust that you will arrive there. Just hold onto your faith whenever temptation beckons.

2. (152) - The power of decision is my own.

God created you as part of Him, therefore you also have the power to create as He does. You create the outcomes you experience by the choices you make. God leaves it entirely up to you. Yet the ego's greatest fear is that you can change your mind at any time if you no longer support its thought system. When you relinquish the ego's control over you, you release yourself from guilt, fear, grief, and pain. We believe that we have no control over the things that happen to us in the world and we think we are at the mercy and whims of the world. But nothing is further from the truth. Nothing happens without your consent. Although you have no control over the things that happen in the world, you do have control over how you react to, and handle, that which you have no control over. But in truth, it is you who writes the script, plays out the roles which you create, and determines the play's ending. The world is one big play, and you are the playwright. That is why the power of decision belongs to you and you alone.

Love, Jesus

172

(Review) God is but Love, and therefore so am I.

1. (153) - In my defenselessness my safety lies.

We believe we must be "strong" in order to survive the ills of the world. We think we cannot survive lest we are strong enough to take on all of the world's problems and face them alone. We believe that viruses will kill us if we do not take strict precautions; we believe we will go broke and lose all that we strived to protect if our source of income is threatened; we believe we will be poisoned if our food is contaminated by chemicals; we believe we will get sick if we do not take our vitamins. If that is not enough, the news plagues us with everything that could possibly go wrong, from politics to medicines, to madness. But all of this is the strategy of the ego to keep you in line, while the media plays into your egoic fears and keeps the momentum going. The more you fear, the greater the separation from God. God takes you above the world's density and into a place where there are no germs to kill you, there is no TV news to threaten your existence, and no pictures of yourself evaporating into sickness and untimely death. It is all a dream. Just look within, for that is where your fears evaporate, and healing occurs. That is where God is, and your defenselessness lies in Him.

2. (154) - I am among the ministers of God.

Our role in the world is to forgive. As ministers of God, this is what it takes. It is a demonstration to our brothers and sisters that the ego has no control over us, yet the ego does not give up easily. Every time we think we have truly forgiven someone, the ego finds another reason to bring us back to it. We teach by example, for what we teach we also learn. To forgive is not a trait of weakness, but one of strength. By being ministers of God we place ourselves in His Hands. Of ourselves we do not know. But by placing our faith in Him, we become His messengers, knowing what to do, what to say, and to whom to say it to. When we surrender to Him there is no struggle, for all questions are answered. You know what to do because God has told you, and you heard Him. You need never struggle for answers on your own, for there is no need. God provides you with whatever you need to know. You know this to be true, because you had been grappling with a problem for quite some time. The answer suddenly appeared before you in the form of a knowing. You just knew that your problem had been solved for you heard the answer. This is when you know you are among the ministers of God.

Love, Jesus

173

(Review) God is but Love, and therefore so am I.

1. (155) - I will step back and let Him lead the way.

In allowing God to lead the way, you walk with Him in holiness. Let all your doubts be blown away forever lost, knowing that you were created wholly pure and indestructible. Now must you walk with Him as you are. God's Truth will guide you, lighting a path back to Him. Why would you not accept this when it is given to you just for the asking? Step back and allow no obstacles to stand in the way. This can all be accomplished by listening for the Voice deep within. When you became a Thought in God's Mind, you were thus created as an extension of Him. Now must you rest assured that you are still as you were created, in perfect holiness. By recognizing your true heritage, you do not feel like a stranger in a far-off land, but instead believe that all the comforts of your True Home remain safe and undefiled, made ready for you to come Home to it. This lesson tells you that each day God reminds us of His Love. And yet we do not take the time to feel it, hear it, or embody it. How odd it is that we are so fooled by the ego, we cannot take the time to step back and let Him lead the way past the illusion of needless suffering, and into the truth of all that we are.

2. (156) - I walk with God in perfect holiness.

To walk with God is not to say you must walk away from the world in order to walk with Him. You live in the world, for it is your chosen home, and you value what is yours. God is not asking that you sacrifice something in order to gain something better. No, of course not. He does not ask that you forfeit the things you love and value. For if He did, we would believe we are sacrificing what is important to us in exchange for God's Love. And if He demanded such sacrifice, He would indeed be a fearful God instead of a Loving God. The idea is to live IN the world, and not be OF the world. To be OF the world is to believe you are the victim of a world which creates fear, and fear shows no mercy. To live IN the world is to live as you please, yet not believe that you are a victim of your experiences. When you follow the ego and believe it is all there is, you will go nowhere. God does not ask that you renounce the world while you still believe in its reality. For if you did, it would seem that God is asking you to sacrifice everything in His Name. You need never sacrifice. The simple remedy is to keep what you value and give up what you do not. This way you will feel no loss and no sacrifice, for you are still walking with God in perfect holiness.

Love, Jesus

174

(Review) God is but Love, and therefore so am I.

1. (157) - Into His Presence would I enter now.

When you enter into God's Presence there is a sensation so great it is the closest you can ever come to knowing Love, and this you have experienced many times before. God makes His Presence known in this way and welcomes you into the experience. By receiving God's Invitation, it is incumbent upon you to acknowledge it, welcome it, and go to it. His Love is bestowed to all, but until this truth is fully realized, it is best taught by those who already learned of it, for as they teach, they also learn. Love is of God and no one need ever think he does not possess it. God breathes Love into every heart and each brother and sister inherently knows God's Presence can be found if they truly seek it. Yet it is still hard for many to recognize that it is what they yearn for, and so they wait. For if they knew, they would rush to behold it and not linger a moment longer, for there is nothing more they would rather have. It is a moment of respite from guilt, sin, and fear. How can this not bring peace and solitude to every mind?

2. (158) - Today I learn to give as I receive.

We all share the same function and that is to be kind to one another. When we do not feel love, we cannot feel kindness, and so we identify with a false god, the ego. Although the ego is no more than a thought, it is quite powerful, for it controls the way we think, what we feel, and what we do. When we behave according to the ego's dictates, we submerge ourselves in fear, for we are aware that we listened to the wrong voice; a voice that does not offer love, does not heal, and does not care. When we compare the tiny crumbs we accept from the ego, as compared to the vastness of God-Consciousness, it is a wonder why we allow the ego so much room to hurt those we love as well as ourselves. But we believe that the ego is too big to challenge and so we cower at the behest of its bullying. God brings Love into the realm of higher consciousness when we are ready to change our minds about the world, and how we choose to live in it. What you receive from God is gratitude and it is up to you to return the favor. Love and fear come from two distinctly opposite thought systems. The one you choose is the one you will live by because you cannot serve two thought systems. Give love, and that is what you shall receive, and what you receive is always returned.

Love, Jesus

175

(Review) God is but Love, and therefore so am I.

1. (159) - I give the miracles I have received.

Miracles come from love, for love extends itself, and what extends itself must be shared. Miracles cannot be received unless they are accepted. When they are accepted, it is because you feel deserving of them; they are treasures which are revealed from deep within. You may accept as many miracles as you choose because they are continuous. It is like the brass rings you reached for when you rode the carousel as a child. Although you were just a child, you still remember this. To you, those rings represented pure joy being pulled from the air. The same is true of miracles. As you catch one, the next is just around the bend. The more you catch, the greater the joy, for it means they are being shared. Be grateful, for God bestows them freely when all you need do is to reach for them.

2. (160) - I am at home. Fear is the stranger here.

We fear God because we believe in sin. By believing in sin, we become strangers to ourselves. When you align with the ego, you are still identifying with a false identity. What you see is a replica, a knockoff, and not the authentic "you." When you identify with sin, guilt, and fear, it is because you believe you are being pursued by God and so you hide. We believe we have abandoned God, and this signifies the separation which we believe we "pulled off." Now what we perceive is a wrathful God, out to find and punish us. But this of course is impossible because we can never leave our Source, and so what we think occurred is, in reality, no more than a dream. This is the dream we live in. Because we choose to identify with fear and because we believe we separated from God, we do not know Him as only Love. Because we seek love, which is our inherent nature, we search for it outside ourselves where it cannot be found. Love is found within the Self which God shares with us, having never abandoned us, nor we Him. You are still Home having never left.

Love, Jesus

176

(Review) God is but Love, and therefore so am I.

1. (161) - Give me your blessing, you holy Son of God.

Blessings are within reach all of the time, for they are bestowed to you by God Himself. Because God created you from Love, you are already blessed. You were created One with Him because God wanted to share eternity's bliss by bringing into existence an extension of Himself, which is Infinite Love. Somewhere in eternity you fell asleep and forgot to remember His Love. Still asleep and dreaming, you have begun to realize that the dream you thought real, was just a dream. God gently caressed you as you awakened to this reality more each day. So many are still not yet aware of their dreaming state, but there will come a time when every brother and sister will respond to the sound of His Call and you will all return Home as One. It is true forgiveness which brings this awareness into your heart. As long as you cannot forgive, you are bound unfree, and separate. Forgive fully and become fully awakened in Him.

2. (162) - I am as God created me.

The Course asserts over and over that you are as God created you. It is this truth that drives home the idea that no matter what you think you have done to cause God's displeasure, there is nothing that could possibly change what is of God, and nothing that could take you from Him. You are still whole, lovable, and sinless. This is quite a promise considering the mistakes you have made which caused you so much guilt, unhappiness, and pain. This idea is meant to instill the belief that nothing you think you did could disturb the vastness of creation which you are eternally connected to. To think that you could taint anything which God created is not humbleness, but arrogance, because it contradicts God. And if that were true, it would establish we are more powerful than God. We are not the little self we made, but the Self that God created—sinless, guiltless, and changeless. We are, and always will be, a beloved extension of God Himself.

Love, Jesus

177

(Review) God is but Love, and therefore so am I.

1. (163) - There is no death. The Son of God is free.

God's Love gently guides you. There is no death, for you are infinitely free. Death is but a fearful idea contrived to keep the illusion real. Death is the thought which originated from a loveless idea. Fear and death are synonymous, perceived as the final step into unknown pastures of darkness and loss. The word "death" has no real meaning. Death cannot be real because it is love's opposite. When the body ceases to be, we simply lay down our defenses and walk with Him in gentle wakefulness and know that death and fear were the greatest illusions of all. To let illusions go is to recognize God's Eternal Light. If we are unlimited, eternal, beings of light, this alone tells us that death is the stranger here.

2. (164) - Now we are one with Him Who is our Source.

Peace and happiness do not come from worldly pursuits. We think that the world is real. But the world is only real in the sense that it is only a classroom which is intended to teach us to undo patterns of conditioning which keep us tied to fear. The purpose of the illusion is to keep our ego attachments connected, and to keep God separate and apart from ourselves. This is a process; it is a journey. Although our lessons can be learned in an instant, it most often takes lifetimes to achieve our goal which is to disengage from the ego's strength. Although the ego is strong because it is relentless, it is not at all powerful, for only God has All Power. We are here to awaken from this dream of separation and belief in sin, guilt, and fear. We have God's guarantee that we will always be as we were created. Because God is only Love, He will wait as long as it takes until we are ready to go back with Him, who is our Source.

Love, Jesus

178

(Review) God is but Love, and therefore so am I.

2. (165) - Let not my mind deny the Thought of God.

The Thought of God is planted so securely in your mind you could not deny Him if you tried. Yet you have tried consistently by denying who you are, what you are, and that you share eternity's consciousness with all your brothers and sisters. The dramas and distractions in the world keep you distanced from His Love and His Oneness. Yet when you sit in stillness and listen quietly, He comes to you, for in those moments you are not denying Him, but believing in Him. You cannot deny that you are pulled into a Wave of Love so great, everything else in the world seems small and insignificant by comparison. The only thoughts that are real are the ones which bring you peace, love, and tranquility. God created you with a great capacity to attain all of this, for those are His gifts. You are protected by every Angel and all else in God's creation. Take His gifts and toss them against the wind. See how the wind returns them as they are gently blown back? His gifts could not be lost, for what God gives you is yours to keep.

2. (166) - I am entrusted with the gifts of God.

Although we are entrusted with the gifts of God, we do not readily accept them. We search the world for abundance in the things we buy, the schedules we keep, the calls we need to make, our daily routines, the need to keep ourselves occupied with daily activities, and the situations we put ourselves into which do not serve our best interests because we have not yet learned the word "no." Yet God reminds us that we are never alone. God entrusts us with His gifts because we can protect and sustain those gifts if we welcome them into our hearts. There is the gift of faith, the gift of peace, the gift of love, and the gift of success, which has nothing to do with money, but what we bring to the world in terms of happiness, joy, and kindness. Those are the gifts that cost you nothing but offer you the world. God's Love is limitless and so are His gifts. Reach out to those who are lonely and set the stage through demonstrating that they too have it in them to be limitless, for God has gifted you beyond all perceived limitation.

Love, Jesus

179

(Review) God is but Love, and therefore so am I.

1. (167) - There is but one life, and that I share with God.

What you share with God is given to you in benediction of His Love. This, being of God, cannot be described but it can be felt. It is Himself that He shares with you; it is your inheritance. He offers Himself to every soul, and wherever they are, so is He. Even though you think apart from Him much of the time, you cannot be separate. Memory of Him could never be lost, only tossed aside until you come in search of Him once again. The ego's ploy is to separate you from God. But you have awakened to the Self you did not know before, the part of you that you share with God. Feeling God is like lying in a bed of roses, as it cannot be described in any other words, for it cannot be imagined. Accept yourself as you are. Because of the certainty that God shares His Love with you, does it not tell you that you need not be anything other than who you are? God would not change a single thing about you, so why would you want to change anything about yourself?

2. (168) - You grace is given me. I claim it now.

We know God is always near because we hear Him in our thoughts. Grace is an aspect of His Love, and His Love is mostly felt when we accept Him into our hearts. He gives us the certainty that all we need do is reach for Him, for He is never beyond reach. We are assured over and over that God's Love is the only certainty there is, for what else on Earth could offer such a promise? We know in our hearts that whatever hurt we caused someone either by word or by deed, His Love remains unconditional and He awaits our return to right-mindedness. There is no judgment, no punishment, and no vengeance in God. He does not regard what we do as sins, for God created us sinless, and He forgives our mistakes, for that is all they are. We must try our best not to repeat mistakes for they cause us pain. Yet even then, He heals the pain brought on by our own careless actions. God gives us His grace and the right to claim it.

Love, Jesus

180

(Review) God is but Love, and therefore so am I.

1. (169) - By grace I live. By grace I am released.

To live by grace is to live with full conscious awareness of Love's Presence. As we learn to overcome the unreality of the world, the more meaningful our own truths are. When we see things in the world that we perceive are bad, we immediately judge them, for we do not know. And so, we move deeper into the ego's world of fear. It is up to us to admit that we don't understand anything that is happening in the world, and instead of looking to justify what we do not know, it is best to recognize them as valuable lessons to learn from. When we see attacking behaviors and do not judge them, we become less apt to attack ourselves. Watch events in the world unfold with detachment, for the world we see is the one we create.

2. (170) - There is no cruelty in God and none in me.

If there is no cruelty in God, there can be none in you. Cruelty is of the ego, and the ego did not make you, you made the ego. As you were created One with God, so are you still, now and always. You are not separate, but one and the same with all creation. The connection you share with God is a lifeline to the One who knows you best. To be true to Him is to be true to yourself. The purity of who you are was tainted as you sought to remove yourself from God's Love and chose another that seemed more suitable. "Another" as you know, is the ego. It taught you that fear is what you are, not love. There is more than one way to experience fear, as the ego often covers it with a false facade pretending that it is something else. Yet if you are not at peace, you are in fear and perhaps not aware of this. The Love God shares with you is by His grace. In truth, you can only be of Him, for that is what you are and can be nothing less. Do not be hard on yourself because you believed some fantasy which brought you unspeakable pain. Give your full measure of perfection to the One Who Knows. He does not see you as cruel, for that is not as you were created. Come to your place of belonging and feel the joy that reflects the God in you.

Love, Jesus

181
I trust my brothers, who are one with me.

To practice trust is a most difficult task because it brings up memories predicated on past experiences. Having felt betrayed, hurt, and misguided, your past history determines that it is necessary to defend yourself from further injustices. Nevertheless, in order to remain in a peaceful state, to be trusting reduces the fear that something valued will be taken away. This is not to say you must give up what you value. This need not be so. However, trust is an important attribute because it keeps you from going back to old habits which caused you to be worried and fearful. Remember, when you are in the present moment there are no worries, for the present covers over the past with a sweet blanket of peace. Within this level of comfort, your consciousness is raised, and you will naturally attract a more stable and carefree environment into your reality. By seeing your brothers and sisters unworthy of your trust you create separation. By having faith in them, you are in recognition of God's Love for all. Trust your brothers and sisters, as they will give their trust to you.

Love, Jesus

182
I will be still an instant and go home.

When you are still and at peace, glimpses of your true Self become known. It opens a window of opportunity reaching out to you. To be at peace is to feel God's Presence. With a chaotic mind, all you can see is gloom. When you are still, a magnitude of opportunities to grow is within reach. Going home is to know God and a vision of home is revealed to you, if only for a single moment. Seize the moment by putting it to the best possible use. When you are feeling God's Love, you are sending a message to the world within your own consciousness, as it embraces and holds you in a state of joy. Yes, it can be only momentary, but that is all it takes. To give God a moment filled with your willingness to let Him in is the best moment you will ever spend. Witness God's Love and recognize that it is carried to every soul connected to your own. It reaches the very heights of your God-Given ability to share it. You must be still in order to see how this alone makes you feel. To maintain yourself in such a peaceful state is to make room for His Love to fill you with bliss.

Love, Jesus

183
I call upon God's Name and on my own.

God's Name and your own are synonymous; they are one and the same. When you call upon God, it is because you wish to hear Him reveal that He is never apart from you. God knows you as Himself and His Voice induces you to think with Him. "My mind holds only the thoughts I think with God" is an important affirmation. Any thoughts you have apart from Him are ego thoughts; they are neither good nor bad. But when you think with God, your true thoughts then arise. The ego will become retaliative when it is threatened and will attempt to intrude upon your joy. The ego does not want you to recognize God, because God does not recognize ego thoughts; they simply do not exist within the grand scale of Universal Intelligence. And so, they have no meaning. When you call upon Him in the quiet of your mind, you cannot deny a deep sense of peace within. Although this is death to the ego, it is your saving grace. His thoughts are yours, and therefore His Name is yours.

Love, Jesus

184
The Name of God is my inheritance.

Because God has given you His Name it is yours to keep. You never left the Will of God because He never abandoned you. Accept His Name as yours and cherish it. His Name is written upon your heart and shall remain there for eternity. You must rejoice now because you have lifted the veil which kept you hidden from your true identity, long overdue. His Love is a certainty. Although you felt lost, you always had it in you to hold the frequency of His Love close to you. The Name God gave you to behold as your own is the inheritance He left for you to claim. Now gather up your brothers and sisters and share all you have gained with them. Whomever God created bears the right to His Name as well. When you return Home, it will be God Himself who welcomes you as any loving father would welcome a child he calls his own. God's Name belongs to you and it is by this truth that your inheritance awaits you.

Love, Jesus

185
I want the peace of God.

How can the peace of God be truly understood when you indulge the ego with so much freedom to roam about? While indulging the ego's frantic fantasies you cannot experience peace. Give God your best, and He will give you His. Peace has become easier for you to reach, as you have traveled a long and difficult road to attain it. You can feel its wonderful effects because you have learned where it lies and how to retrieve it. The ego holds onto you with all its purported strength but in truth, it has none. You will always be within earshot of its beckoning call until you learn it has no power to make you listen.

In order to experience peace of mind, you must first break the habit of allowing an alien intrusion to feast upon your thoughts. You can break the habit. It's like eating chocolate. When you do without, even for a little while, the addiction is weakened. Such is the same with the ego's need to fulfill its addiction, depriving you of peace. Peace is what you truly want. The ego's nagging insistence causing you to lose your peace has no power if you do not invest so heavily in it. It only has as much power as you believe it has. Try to withstand the urges of the ego and focus your thoughts where it will do the most good. When you truly start to experience real peace, it is because you let the past go and are living in the present.

Love, Jesus

186

Salvation of the world depends on me.

When your thoughts are in line with God's, its effects expand as it reaches every mind joined with yours. By bringing only healing thoughts to yourself, its effects are powerful enough to raise the world's consciousness. God has given you such power. Although you cannot see the intensity of something so unimaginable, it is true. God strengthens you each day and your healing increases as you think love, peace, compassion, and kindness. Bring healing to every mind by your thoughts. If the world is an illusion, doesn't it make sense that illusions are played out according to how the actor who plays that role sees himself? When you obtain the vision to look past illusions, you can break the trend which causes you to focus on fearful thoughts. The only reality is that which God creates. But He cannot extend power which is thought to have no cause. He can only extend that which can be accepted as true. Embrace your thoughts and align them with His, then be witness to the healing it brings. Yes, it takes practice, but it is the best practice-time you will ever spend. Rid yourself of destructive thoughts which deprive you of your peace, but instead offers you a world where there is no peace. In this respect, salvation of the world does depend on you.

Love, Jesus

187
I bless the world because I bless myself.

You want to bless the world because you know God blesses you. Blessings are bestowed to you by God. His Will is that you share them. You know this to be your purpose when you recognize you have never been without them. God has protected you from countless disasters in this unruly and unsavory world. You have been diverted from every curve-ball the world has thrown you, and this you know for you still remain unscathed and whole, having been saved by God's unshakeable Love. Think blessed thoughts as often as you can, and that is how often you will experience the miracles which bring you even greater blessings. As you forgive the world, you can better understand the healing effects they provide. God sends His Angels assuring you that you are safe. Now that you know this, offer them generously. Send thoughts of love to those you know, those whom you will someday come to know, and those you might never know. Creation is endless and so are blessings.

Love, Jesus

188
The peace of God is shining in me now.

You brought the light of Heaven with you when you came into the world. Light connects to light and stays with you throughout out your entire journey here on Earth. Relish this revelation, for God welcomes you to the connection of Spirit (light), which is indeed who you are. You shone ever so brightly one night long ago when you wished upon a star when you were only seven. Do you remember this? Yes, you do. You were awed by the wonder of a star-filled sky one clear night, and so you made a wish. The bigger picture of this scenario is that light is at its brightest when it is drawn from Source, God, as you knew it then. Although your light had become dimmed, it was never lost, only forgotten. For you entered into a long period of darkness thereafter. You have again returned to the light. It is kind and beautiful and it reaches the hearts of many who look to find it within themselves. This connection with the Universe, which resonated with you so strongly then, is seen again, for you have awakened to its memory. It radiates love, as it did before. It replenishes every mind with the same vibration you felt long ago when you made a holy covenant with God on that splendid night.

Love, Jesus

189

I feel the Love of God within me now.

God's Love is with you always. When you want to feel such Love, it is easy. All you need do is place yourself in His Frequency. The activity of the day is put aside, you leave your chaotic thoughts behind, and you feel the loveliness of a calming peace. Your mind is still, and your thoughts are quiet. This is a meditative state whereby God's Presence cannot be denied. You can feel the comfort of God's Angels sent to nurture you, as you open your heart to receiving them. Now you are within His Range of Thought. You may not always be aware of His Presence, but it is always there, and you can return to it any time you wish. God is in full view when you go within and hear Him speak His Thoughts, which are also your thoughts. It is important each day to withdraw from your day's activities and reserve some quiet time for Him. He is no stranger to you and His Love is forever changeless. Always be aware that He and you are joined. Accept God's invitation, and step into His Holy Presence where you are never a stranger.

Love, Jesus

190

I choose the joy of God instead of pain.

You have already learned that joy is more rewarding than pain. The world's way of thinking is the belief that happiness comes from material things, having no bearing on what is real and lasting. You have suffered pain at the behest of others in countless ways, giving credence to these beliefs. At times pain hides beneath the surface so discreetly, you might hardly regard it as significant. Or it can show up in deadly reprisal, feeling exceedingly wicked. Either way, pain is pain. This is not the way God would have you thrive. Yet you chose suffering over God's peace many times over. Such is the ego's way of projecting, as it fights to protect its insane thought system, pain being its main attraction. Writing your daily lessons keeps your mind directed inward, towards peace. This does not come from the material world. Lasting joy comes from within. To master the present moment is where God's Love awaits you. Start each day with the recognition that God remains with you, and pain, when it arises, can quickly be diverted by staying presently connected. The ego has no power to hold you hostage. Stay with thoughts of God and feel the peace it brings throughout your day.

Love, Jesus

191
I am the holy Son of God Himself.

To feel holy is to know the One Who created you as Himself. When you let your illusions stand in place of Him, how can you know anything? The One Mind which you are a part of, is God Himself. This is hard to perceive if everything is chaos, and nothing stays peaceful. To keep your beliefs strong is to recognize yourself as His holy Son, created just as you are, forever changeless. It is instilled within each of His creations, prompted by a degree of willingness, to feel His Unconditional Love. God recognizes that you are off dreaming in some far off place, not your real home. It is time to awaken and return to your Roots, although you still live in a world where every emotion, void of love, is unfulfilled. This can never be truly seen as long as you choose to live within the illusion. When you enter willingly into your wakefulness, you can begin to understand that your dreams could not be counted on to bring you peace. Ride the waves without fear. The waters are calm, although you fear they are tumultuous. Except in dreams, they cannot hurt you, for God Himself sustains your truth.

Love, Jesus

192
I have a function God would have me fill.

Your purpose is to believe that God does have a function for you to fulfill. In this world greater allegiance is given to fear, thus depriving you of love. This is where change is desperately called for. If you only knew how purposeful your role in this world is, you would set out to complete it without a single thought. Show the world your true Self as you have come to learn of it and see how it grows from a dying garden to one that is green, nourished and moist. This represents Love. Everything will grow beautiful and peaceful if you sustain your role by giving it to those who need to feel love in place of fear. You have been trained through The Course to have greater insight, but the world still seems lost and dying, doesn't it? Yet even so, your mind remains sacred, as you are One with God. Upon sharing His Love, see how the world responds, just as a dry garden, given care and nourishment, will also respond as its thirst is quenched. Keep vigil on God's purpose for you. If you fulfill your function with faith, God will continue to lead you from a world of chaos to one that reflects Heaven simply because you are happy to fulfill it. Whenever you are tempted to choose bitterness and chaos over love, simply walk past it. There is so much more to be gained when you do.

Love, Jesus

193

All things are lessons God would have me learn.

You have already learned that everything in your past had consequences, good and bad. Although pain is not of God, it is a valid teacher. You have suffered the pain of guilt many times over. It finally became clear that you were being chased, for guilt is a relentless pursuer. The ego believes that attack is warranted and unforgiveness is justified. For instance, the ego is prodding, and it will cause you to attack someone as justification for a misdeed. It then administers guilt for the attack which it instigated in the first place. So you see, it is the same voice throwing itself in order to keep you in a state of confusion. However, the lessons God would have you learn are those that teach you not to continue making decisions which can only lead to sorry outcomes. As right-minded thinking draws you into making better choices, you can look at everything as lessons to learn from. Every outcome is the result of a decision you make, and each decision results in the outcome it produces. Looking at it in this way, you can see that all things are lessons God would have you learn.

Love, Jesus

194
I place the future in the Hands of God.

How fortunate we are to know that God holds the future in His Hands. Because He is our Loving Father, He protects us from our own fears engineered by the ego. He lights up our hearts with Love when we allow Him to be in control. His gift of Love becomes an overwhelming revelation—we cannot fail when we know that God raises us to the very heights where our fears are obliterated, for only love is real. God makes us shine in brightness, and brighter still is the glorious Light He shares. When we are with God, we cannot help but feel safe. Let us learn not to take control of matters that belong to God, as He uses miracles to heal and protect us from ourselves. We see only shadows of the past because the past has no power to overtake us. It only exists in the mind that protects it, for it is forever gone. God sees only what we could never imagine as He raises us from fear to joy. All it takes is that we allow it to be. Let us soar, forever free and cleansed of guilt. Never doubt that we could not possibly do for ourselves that which God has the Power to do for us.

Love, Jesus

195
Love is the way I walk in gratitude.

When you can love your brothers and sisters as God loves you, the road to peace is as close as God Himself. His Love is revealed as you move forward with carefree acknowledgment that only good can come from this Loving Source. And how can it not, when the world is saved from itself? For to love is to heal. When only good-intentioned thoughts are projected, what more could God ask? Now may you be certain that nothing can slow you down as you walk in gratitude, released from fear. Be steadfast in your faith that His Divinity sustains and protects you. God goes with you as you open your heart to love, which is all that is real. Now replenished, you see beyond the illusion of sickness, pain, and death. This opens the air-waves for love to flow freely about. For in this state of wakefulness, you recognize yourself as you were created. All things are calmed as the world is transformed to a new and peaceful reality. When thoughts of love are projected forth, it travels into the hearts of many. Give God your gratitude as He gives you His.

Love, Jesus

196
It can be but myself I crucify.

This lesson has taught you well. When you feel hateful, you suffer the consequences by your actions. By attacking another with your words, the ego has you believe it is justified. Yet the attack remains inside of you and you are fraught with guilt because you do not understand that you attacked yourself. Yet you pursued the same actions over and over until you knew that you were the one depleted in Spirit. As you sank deeper into despair, you still had not realized your outcomes were the result of your own wrong-mindedness. Yet you defied God and chose pain over peace time and again, continuing to pursue the urge to believe the ego's unyielding untruths. You finally saw that if you continued along that route, you would never know true peace, crucified by your own hand. God could not condemn one who has not yet learned to choose love over self-inflicted pain. How difficult those lessons were, yet they were the very lessons that taught you that the distress you caused was inflicted upon yourself. Now you have learned that attack is a harsh teacher, and so you have begun to see that love, and not attack, is release from fear. God sees only the holiness by which you were created. You have traveled along rugged terrain seeking happiness in all the wrong places. You now see that everything which appeared to have died within has grown anew. You feel newly nourished as you move towards your higher purpose. God does not inflict punishment for unruly deeds but holds us up whenever we decide to open a gateway to love.

Love, Jesus

197

It can be but my gratitude I earn.

God gives thanks to you as you do Him. When you can give God the best of yourself you are truly blessed, for you have earned the gratitude He gives. You can help others strengthen their endeavors to find peace in themselves by demonstrating it in yourself. Now will your brothers and sisters go in quiet certainty that the way is not lost to them. When you are at peace and your thoughts are in alignment with His, all you need do is project it and be witness to the truth that your brothers and sisters too are receiving God's Message. It may not always be apparent to you but be assured it is an enormous step forward. You need not even speak of it. You can be sure they feel your peace as your aura is simply felt. Walk with Him in purposeful stride. When you relinquish all thoughts of attack, only peace is left to take its place. That which abides in one, becomes a draw for so many. You can do much to help heal the world by making peace an instinctive goal. You and your brothers and sisters are meant to teach each other that the Love of God shines in all. For where there is peace, there is love.

Love, Jesus

198

Only my condemnation injures me.

Condemnation leaves no room for peace and certainly not the way to lasting happiness. In fact, you believe that loss of peace and happiness are caused by influences outside of yourself. Condemnation then requires forgiveness because it weighs heavily upon you and is hard to bear. Only forgiveness can ease the guilt of condemnation. Leave condemnation at death's doorstep and do not look back. When you condemn another, a "just attack" only serves to strike back at you. You cannot be judge, jury, and executioner, and still remain at peace. To judge is to attack, and to attack is to condemn. How can this be the way to a carefree existence? To live in peace is to forgive those you thought had injured you. If you do not, the ego's guilt will come storming in to take the place of peace. You can make the ego disappear every time you decide to offer happiness instead of attack. Ask yourself, "Would I condemn even the most monstrous offender to eternal hell?" Of course not. So why then would you condemn yourself when you are the one who possesses the key to freedom? Know that God can enter only into a peaceful heart.

Love, Jesus

199

I am not a body. I am free.

The body is an escape from the Self God created. It is an invention of the ego which keeps the mind transfixed on nothing except its own illusions. The body in itself has no purpose, and it gives the ego all power to direct it. It does nothing except draw itself into its own illusions. You see pain and suffering all around you. Yet those who suffer are giving the ego power to see the existence of pain as real. You are witness to much sickness and suffering in the world. Those who worship the body prefer to believe its reality, thus proving God's existence to be false. It would prefer to suffer and die rather than acknowledge that only God's Love has the power to heal, and in order for the body to heal, the mind must be brought to the recognition that the Self is the only reality there is. The body is an illusion, so how then can it attach itself to sickness and death if it is not of God? The ego believes this reasoning to be insane, but in truth, it is the ego that is insane as it prefers to sacrifice the body to death than to recognize God's Truth. All pain and suffering are the result of the ego's madness. However, while in this world of form, the body can serve a greater purpose when used as a vehicle to instill love, its only true purpose. God did not create His children to be slave to the body, but to live in Him and be free.

Love, Jesus

200

There is no peace except the peace of God.

The ego's portrayal of peace is not peace at all, and according to its standards it cannot be found. The ego's motto, "seek and do not find" has been proven to you. You have been through many encounters where you sought peace but came up short-handed every time. You thought you could find it even though you had misgivings but learned that peace cannot abide where guilt dwells. The peace of God was your saving grace when you turned to Him, no longer able to bear the pain. You cried, beseeching His forgiveness because you had often hurt those dear to you. You learned through these experiences that God did not deny you peace but instead held out His Arms and assuaged your guilt. You finally surrendered to God, desperately seeking to feel peace because there were no other answers. The peace you sought is a critical lesson which teaches that peace cannot be found in a world of conflict and chaos. He has given you the wisdom to know that a peaceful mind comes only from a forgiving heart. Learning to forgive yourself was indeed a tough trial. You now know the comfort of God's unconditional love. Needless to say, you no longer suffer from the pain of guilt, as He did not condemn you for what you thought were unforgivable sins. He forgives because they are mistakes you did not see. Go now and be watchful over your words and deeds. Now that you know that peace is the antidote for pain, you will never want to relinquish it. God blesses you in gratitude because you sought His forgiveness.

Love, Jesus

201

(Review) I am not a body. I am free.
For I am just as God created me.

1. (181) - I trust my brothers and sisters who are one with me.

You are just as free now as when you were created, for free will is your inherited right. You became an extension of God's Love before time ever was, and there you will remain long after the world of time elapses. Only God knows your true reality. To yourself, you are a stranger. Somewhere along the way, when time and separation became an illusion, God existed no more. You had forgotten Him, if only for an instant, for in the world of time that is all it is. Yet, in the world of time, a single instant can seem to be a thousand years as compared to timelessness in eternity. In forgetting God, the world became a prison for you. In this self-imposed dungeon, you became suspicious of others, and you did not know them, as you did not know yourself. Trust then became a difficult rule to follow. However, while you are still in the world of time, you will remain hidden from your true Self unless you see your brothers and sisters holy, and one with you.

Love, Jesus

202

(Review) I am not a body. I am free.
For I am just as God created me.

1. (182) - I will be still an instant and go home.

All it takes is one instant to feel the peace of God and claim His Love as your own. In that instant you are free. As you relinquish your fears and trust that your brothers and sisters are one with you, you will also know that stillness is an important step towards recalling your real home. Relinquish all thoughts of past hurts and future outcomes, and focus on the present, for this is the only place peace can be found. You are already home, but you will not recognize it as long as guilt and doubt cloud your mind. One instant in the Mind of God is where all glory lies. Be nowhere but in God's Presence. He will care for, and protect you, from all the illusions which have no power to keep you from your true home. Why live in fear when God stands beside you assuring your safety? God's Love will guide you through all obstacles so that you may see that anything is possible. He only knows you as part of Himself. Now must you be still an instant and go home.

Love, Jesus

203

(Review) I am not a body. I am free.
For I am just as God created me.

1. (183) - I call upon God's Name and on my own.

God's Name is yours, as you are created in Him. Your Mind was designed by God to align with His. Somewhere in eternity, time became a false identity, and you were lost in a world far from home. You were like a child fearful of strange images and weird beliefs which terrified you. You wandered aimlessly trying to find your way, but nowhere could your true home be found as you once knew of it. You perceived pain and suffering as real, and in your wandering through the unknown, you retreated more and more into the wilderness, further away from Him. You wandered so far into the deep, you believed you would be lost in a world of fear and guilt forever. But then you looked to Him and found you were not lost at all, only temporarily misguided in a place full of fearful objects and hateful outcasts made from illusions. God smiled, and then did you realize you could only be free if you surrendered to His Love. You found salvation as God blessed you and called you by name. Hold your head high in answer to His call and respond each time you hear His Voice, which is in you to hear it.

Love, Jesus

204

(Review) I am not a body. I am free.
For I am just as God created me.

1. (184) - The Name of God is my inheritance.

You inherited God's Name when you were created. His Name brands you as His child forever free. He instills His Love in you because that is what you are, and this can never be denied. His Love instills you with holiness, which you have come to know once again. Although you had forgotten Him, He did not forget you, and He has always deemed you holy, no matter where you attempted to run, fearing the illusion of His reprisal. When you could run no longer, He knew of your exhaustion and He gave you insight to truth where you thought you would never know of it. God could never abandon those He loves, and in that moment of truth you were saved from yourself. The ego plays damning tricks upon the mind and fear is the greatest trick of all. You came back into the Heart of God because you knew innately of His Love. When you nestled into the wake of God's welcome, you felt safe in the world. Now you see ever more clearly that you were always safe, even when you believed you were lost to Him. Look at you now. Are you not as pure and holy as the day you entered God's Mind, whereby He made you One with Him? Just as you now realize your thoughts create whichever dream your mind wishes to make real, God is the only true reality. You have restored yourself to Him, thus claiming your inheritance.

Love, Jesus

205

(Review) I am not a body I am free.
For I am still as God created me.

1. (185) - I want the peace of God.

The peace of God comes to you through your faith. God's Love offers you the faith to understand you are, and always will be, as He created you. His peace is all you really want. What else is there that can give you the solace and happiness that comes from knowing of God's unshakeable Love? He loves you, as you in turn must love the world. All goodness is the reality of God's Presence, never to be denied. His Love offers you the understanding that all things created of Him must be nurtured. He has given you this role to fulfill. The peace of God is requested, that you share it with your brothers and sisters. Sharing the peace of God serves to instill that recognition in yourself as well. It spreads like the ashes of a volcano and falls gently upon the Earth so that every soul must learn to have the faith that you have come to know. How can they come to know it but from their teachers, who have learned it first? Feel God's peace so that it may be extended throughout all creation. Your willingness to share His Thoughts is a way to open up the channels to all who come seeking peace. How intense must their need be that they but stand before you as the peace of God is extended through you to them, gratefully received.

Love, Jesus

206

(Review) I am not a body I am free.
For I am still as God created me.

1. (186) - Salvation of the world depends on me.

God, your Father, gave you all you could ever need as you walk the world with Him beside you. With His gifts you are secure within yourself, happily fulfilling your purpose. His Love ingratiates you as a beloved soul extended of Him. Your creation is not an obstacle that must be overcome, but a gift to be received in gratitude. God's only purpose for you is that you awaken to the reality of His peace. His gift of peace is delivered to you on the wings of Angels to be shared as it is given. Accept your purpose and know that you are God's creation, and creation, being of God, is you. Therefore, salvation of the world does depend on you. His gifts, given to you in Love, do not weigh heavily upon your shoulders. The weight of God's expectations is feather-light and easily held. God gives you this work not to saddle you with responsibilities, but instead to cast aside all your worries and make you free. Nothing is unresolved. All regrets are now lifted. Nowhere now can the weight of the world be too heavy for you to bear. Like a feather, it is weightless. How easy it is to walk with Him as you cross over to a new reality; one which will gift you with all that is yours. Always know that Love and Peace are your Father's gifts, releasing you from worldly sorrows. You are no longer hidden in a dark and dreary world. Your place is with God, and nowhere else.

Love, Jesus

207

(Review) I am not a body. I am free.
For I am still as God created me.

1. (187) - I bless the world because I bless myself.

God blesses you as part of Himself, and why would He not? He has forgiven all your doubts of Him and yourself, and you have accepted that you are forgiven. You know this because you are finally at peace. Now that you are free from all perceived doubts, there is room in your heart to feel God's Love as it fills you with thoughts of Him. Every loving thought you have for all who are a part of God's creation is not a limited aspect of yourself, but instead an unstoppable burst of energy which fills every corner of the world. God gives you the power to bless the world. He will fill every need so that you may go forth and give the world all the Love that is given you to share. Give the world your blessings and God will show you how to use them best. You were made by God as an expression of His Love. How healing is that thought? Does it not give you all capacity to direct yourself, as He directs you to do? God, your Father, has instilled you with a loving presence that is so strong, its reality could not be denied. Give your blessings freely and know that God is pleased with you beyond all worldly doubts, as God's Love cannot be measured according to the world's standards. You are not insignificant; something to be tossed aside like an old, tattered shoe, but instead a strong and wholesome reflection of His Love free to bless the world just as you are blessed.

Love, Jesus

208

(Review) I am not a body. I am free.
For I am still as God created me.

1. (188) - The peace of God is shining in me now.

What is peace, but the desire to be happy? Peace is blocked when we are busy with argumentative thoughts which are played out over and over like a bad recording. In essence, it is like watching a movie which has no reality, yet it disturbs your peace when its content is troubling. We carry this unrest within ourselves unwilling to release it much of the time. The peace of God is instilled in every mind, as is memory of Him. Yet true peace will never be understood until we pull away from our foolish grudges and replace them with thoughts of forgiveness, for that is what love is all about. This is the best gift we can give ourselves. But it can only be received by letting go of the discordance within which reflects an outward picture of an inward condition. Let no idols of the ego be allowed to interrupt your peace; the very thing you seek the most. Feel its glow and let it be seen.

Love, Jesus

209

(Review) I am not a body. I am free.
For I am just as God created me.

1. (189) - I feel the Love of God within me now.

The Love of God brings peace to every mind. No matter how your thoughts aimlessly wander, only the thoughts you think with God are the ones your mind holds dear because that is where peace abides. God sustains and Loves you beyond all that you can possibly conceive of, and any discord with your brothers and sisters who seem to be the cause of all your disturbances are but dreams. You need not speak harshly of anyone. There is no harshness in God, and none in you. See them not as bodies, but as One Mind fused with yours, reflecting peace. God's Love is bountiful, and God's Love is all there is. Anything you say to a brother or sister should come from a place of peace, and not from an agitated state. That is all you need to know in order to make the right choices when worldly disturbances seem to be getting the better of you. Look past all that you have made real, and into the realm of Truth where peace awaits you. Recite your affirmations often. This serves to help you feel the nearness of Him. If you keep your thoughts aligned with God's, you will not damage anyone's feelings, least of all your own.

Love, Jesus

210

(Review) I am not a body. I am free.
For I am still as God created me.

1. (190) - I choose the joy of God instead of pain.

How can pain, which is suffered and endured, be more sought than joy? Yet it is, because pain is a choice that stems from the ego's belief in it. It is planted in the mind before it becomes a seeming reality. It starts with a thought and whether it be physical or emotional, it makes no difference, for neither is of God. He can heal your pain, but the source from which it comes must be recognized first. God is not the source of pain, so it need not be endured. All pain and suffering is that which the ego chooses to experience. It inhabits the mind's subconscious and buys into its reality. It is a dream; no more than that. For you, when suffering had become unbearable, you reached out to Him. When His Love became accepted into your conscious mind, at last you were free. Guilt is not a friend of truth. By recognizing that guilt was your greatest source of pain, you learned that this was not

God's doing, but your own. Physical pain is no different. When the mind chooses to rest in God, and when it is seen that pain has no place within God's plan, healing takes place. However, it must be accepted before it is recognized. When you see others who do not yet know the truth, do not judge. Instead, it is up to you to see them as God's creation, as you are. Wish them well, speak kindly of them, and do not let lack of compassion numb your better judgment. If this can be accomplished, know that God will do the rest.

Love, Jesus

211

(Review) I am not a body. I am free.
For I am just as God created me.

1. (191) - I am the holy Son of God Himself.

With those astounding words, how would you not recognize the power which God Himself has given you? God's Love created you holy and enriches you beyond words, for you are created just as He would have you be. When you deem yourself unworthy, it is an arrogant deception of yourself because you are denying what is true. There is nothing in God's Mind that does not include you. The Love which comes from such a holy place should never be taken lightly. They are truths given so that you may understand and use them according to His Will. God has placed you on the Throne in which He stands. He sees you as Himself because you were created not as a separate entity apart from Him, but as an extension of Him. In peace, you can see yourself beyond all self-perceived limitations. To truly embody such power would make you pure light. When your light is joined with His, it is there to serve all creation. His Love magnifies, so that you may see it in yourself. When you are in the present moment, it is easy to receive and recognize

Truth. Trust, and stand proud that you have been created to join with Him in such a place of magnificence. Keep thoughts of your Father foremost in your mind. Then you will better understand the meaning of the power He shares with you. It goes deep within your soul and carries you to the highest level of consciousness. By recognizing God in yourself, you can then see it in everyone.

Love, Jesus

212

(Review) I am not a body. I am free.
For I am still as God created me.

1. (192) - I have a function God would have me fill.

The function God would have you fill is your purpose in the world. God's Love helps you succeed so that you cannot fail whenever you choose to fulfill that purpose. Because it is a function given you to perform, you need do nothing but listen for Guidance. You are beginning to recognize that your purpose is to work with God so that worldly disturbances are no longer the main attraction, and that more important functions be foremost in your thoughts. No conditions should be placed on brothers or sisters according to your own expectations of them. God does not impose conditions before He listens. Because His Love is unconditional, forgiveness is given without exception. It is up to you to follow God's Plan. If God can forgive any and all transgressions, and He continues to bestow his children all they need with which to restore themselves, why would you delay in fulfilling your function? Give of yourself freely and unconditionally. It does not matter if what you offer is received in appreciation or not. What matters is that it is given without condition. Remember, you can never suffer loss. Gain is achieved when all expectations are lifted, and your function is gladly filled.

Love, Jesus

213

(Review) I am not a body. I am free.
For I am still as God created me.

1. (193) - All things are lessons God would have me learn.

Lessons learned come from life's experiences. You have come to learn and to understand your purpose. Yet true understanding cannot be achieved until your life's experiences, both good and bad, teach you the lessons you came to learn. True forgiveness is the most difficult lesson of all. Opportunities for forgiveness arise every day yet cutting through the rotting edge of hatred comes from God Who comes to our aid when we can no longer bear the pain, and cry out for help. You feel temporarily vindicated when you think you are forgiving an indiscretion. Yet true forgiveness does not come from a mere nod and a wink, only to be forgotten a day later. True forgiveness comes from the heart. You will know this has been accomplished when the pain of guilt is no more. Forgiveness is a means whereby everything God intended for you to learn has been accepted. Everything, whether it be perceived as small and insignificant or enormously huge, requires forgiveness. Yet in this world it is easier to suffer the pain of hate instilled by the ego, than to forgive a brother or sister. That is why the ego's insanity must be recognized. God's lessons must be learned in earnest if it is to be your goal.

Love, Jesus

214

(Review) I am not a body. I am free.
For I am still as God created me.

1. (194) - I place the future in the hands of God.

If you had no doubts that your future was completely safe in the hands of God, you would be instilled with such gratitude, you would never want to deny Him at all. Incessant worry makes you no more than a puppet dancing on the strings of the ego's unsavory thought system. God intends for you to be a free soul, far and away from fearful images of defeat where anxiety and depression keep you bound in hopelessness. With this said, doesn't it seem logical that everything left in God's Hands would indeed free you from fear and render you safe and happy instead? For now, there would be moments of true peace never before felt, for you had learned to place your trust in Him by practicing letting go and as you know, practice makes perfect. You can learn to let go by giving your future over to the One Who guards your safety each time a worrisome thought overtakes you. In so doing, you are also turning your past over to Him. For without a past, there is only the present, and within that moment of truth, is all pain and suffering now in God's Hands. Love as you are loved, and trust as you are trusted.

Love, Jesus

215

(Review) I am not a body. I am free.
For I am still as God created me.

1. (195) - Love is the way I walk in gratitude.

When Love is deeply felt, gratitude follows and brings out the best in all of us. Do you remember back in time when your mother showed you her love when she kissed your hands and your fingers with such heartfelt warmth? You showed gratitude in those moments when her love comforted you. More importantly, you recognized how her show of love opened you up as well. When you feel God's Love, drink of it until you are satiated. What you learn is that only love is real because it fills you with a sense of well-being and incomparable joy. You have seen acts of kindness stemming from love, and you have witnessed acts of unkindness stemming from fear. Yesterday, as you were attempting to get gas for your car because of the impending hurricane, all things seemed to go awry. The woman behind you refused to let you back in line when you lost your place due to the disorganization of cars piling up. Yes, this was an unkindly act based on fear. Yet a gentleman, out of the blue, came over to help you fill up your car, putting yours before his own. This was a sign of love. What you gave him in return was your gratitude. This was a perfect example of love and gratitude in action. It shines from one heart to another and fills the air with a sense of peace. Offer the gift of love freely, just as it was offered to you.

Love, Jesus

216

(Review) I am not a body. I am free.
For I am still as God created me.

1. (196) - It can be but myself I crucify.

It is obvious from your past experiences it was only yourself that you crucified. You hurt yourself endlessly, never understanding that it was caused by your own dim perception of yourself. The only way to heal, as you learned, was by the Grace of God. Pain is an inexplicable teacher. To remove yourself from the agony of depression you needed to understand God's purpose for you. When you resorted to accepting the love that is inherent within, and reconnected with Self, you learned that all along it was by your own hand you suffered. Yet pain taught you that there is another solution. It is to love yourself as you were created. How simple it is to understand, yet how hard it is to live by its rules. The holy instant does just that. It releases you from the weight of your own fears and places you into the gentleness of God's Love, held safe. Your gratitude is apparent each time you feel completely at peace and join with Him in Oneness. It was in the recognition of God's gracious giving of Himself that you had come to learn you had the power to make all things right again. The practice of journaling the lessons with me (Jesus), brings you peace. When you fall deep within the twilight of stillness, is it not bliss? You do not want to stop because it brings you the kind of peace which you cannot bring forth yourself. God's Loving Hand reaches down and lifts you gently up where you are connected to Him on Earth as in Heaven. Give Him your focus always. You need not crucify yourself when God is as close to you as Heaven itself. Give all to Him and you will receive all that you are giving.

Love, Jesus

217

(Review) I am not a body. I am free.
For I am still as God created me.

1. (197) - It can be but my gratitude I earn.

When a child of God recognizes His Father's Love and shares it with the world, God gives thanks. As you look deeply into the One Mind and see a reflection of yourself mirrored there, you know that you are not just a body, but a soul, eternally free. When you are meeting with God on His terms it is because you are willing to adhere to what they are. What better terms can there be than to truly understand that you are still as God created you, forever changeless. To abide by these terms is to be in gratitude and allow His Love to freely show itself through you. Not only is memory of Him restored to you, but recognition of His Love is acknowledged. Have faith that God wills you your happiness, for love and happiness belong together. You cannot sacrifice one without sacrificing the other. As you nestle into the comfort of His Welcoming Embrace, do you not see that there is so much more to explore beyond the body's limitations?

Love, Jesus

218

(Review) I am not a body. I am free.
For I am still as God created me.

1. (198) - Only my condemnation injures me.

True forgiveness is a powerful and healing force. It strengthens the belief that neither you nor your brothers and sisters are guilty of any lasting offense in the Eyes of God. By forgiving them, you also release yourself, no longer ravaged with feelings of guilt. Condemnation reflects hatred because it instills fear. While you are condemning a brother or sister for something you believe they have done to injure you, this only serves to injure both. True healing is the foundation which rests upon the knowledge that love extends itself. Condemnation interferes with love, and love cannot be present while you are in the throes of a grievance. Because you and your brothers and sisters are part of the One Consciousness, it is yourself you are also attacking. You lose your own identity when you are not at peace and cannot come to know your true reality. A forgiving heart does more good than any imagined belief that your peace was stolen from you by another. It is only you who are accountable for the loss of it. Forgive your brothers and sisters, and your own perceived transgressions are forgotten. How holy you were created. You are free, and all peace is yours when the gift of forgiveness is offered.

Love, Jesus

219

(Review) I am not a body. I am free.
For I am still as God created me.

1. (199) - I am not a body. I am free.

In reading this lesson many times over, you have pondered it, recognizing that the mind can interfere with the body's healing. The body can attack, become ill, feel hate, and remain thoroughly off-balance when it chooses to ignore the mind's yearning to be free. The body's only purpose when used by the ego, is to serve itself. The ego resides in the body. In its relentless pursuits, it tries to control the mind. Yet your mind is free, as it has all power to go past the ego's relentless interference and into right-mindedness. When you allow the mind to use the body for a Divine Purpose, the body can be a most useful tool. It can be used as a vehicle for love, peace, and healing. The body does not have the capacity to be truly nourished unless the mind gives it the power to enrich itself daily with spiritual nourishment.

Love, Jesus

220

(Review) I am not a body. I am free.
For I am still as God created me.

1. (200) - There is no peace except the peace of God.

The peace of God is felt when you know that He is always beside you. When things happen that you don't understand, because nothing of the ego is ever properly understood anyway, to reach for God is a natural instinct. Everyone wants God, but many do not perceive that He is within reach, or even that that is what they want. Right thinking devours the ego's attempts to control you. It is not necessary to understand the ego's confused reasoning. Being in the present moment establishes very clearly that you are where you need to be because it garbles the ego's chatter and instills you with a quiet serenity. You know this to be true because you are feeling the present moment when you contemplate with God. When you are still, and experiencing true peace, it brings you solace unknown anywhere other than in quiet reflection with Him. How peaceful it is to know you can rest in God at any hour, day or night, for He is nowhere else other than with you. Feel God's Love in your heart and know that He can always be found there. When the ego gnaws at you and you try to make sense of its badgering interpretations, turn to the One Who understands you. There is nothing that can disrupt your peace when you are beside the One Who Loves and strengthens you. Enjoy the day. It is beautiful and it is yours.

Love, Jesus

221

Peace to my mind. Let all my thoughts be still.

When your thoughts are still and you do not engage in combat with the ego as it speaks of disdain for this one, or intolerance for that one, peace comes to you inasmuch as your capacity to enable it allows. God's Love is felt when you are in a state of peace. Feeling its presence comes when you allow yourself the privilege to just be as you are. In this place, does true peace enter your awareness. Keep your mind still, your spirits high, and conversations with yourself low. Just let the peace of God move within you. You need not search for it. Allow it to enter as it overtakes you for you have given it the willingness to do so. There, peace awaits you. When you have conditioned yourself to be in this place of stillness, it will alter you to a state of peace. The more you learn to stay quietly in this way, the more you will have strengthened your ability to bring yourself to a place of peace more often. Eventually it will become so automatic, you will thrive in it. When you turn your willingness over to God in this way, you can be sure you will receive all that God gives of Himself.

Love, Jesus

222

God is with me. I live and move in Him.

God's Love moves about the Universe and encompasses all living things. God becomes known when He is sought. You have seen miracles as God has helped you through countless difficulties. Without those fearful encounters you've experienced in life, you may never have been elevated to a greater understanding as is shown to you. You have seen how events in your life, whether they be perceived as good or bad, all eventually came together with good reason. You were dealt events in your life which you considered to be abhorrent.

However, those past experiences turned out to be your greatest learning devices. You have seen the light in answer to a long-cherished event which caused you unspeakable pain as a child growing up—cherished because you could not let go of it. His explanation clears the way for you. Go in peace to the next phase of your life with His continued guidance. Be vigilant and know that God stays with you through multitudes of problems, fears, and conditions of the mind which you alone could never explain. You could not have come this far in your healing without the Force of God's Love guiding you towards a greater understanding of your true purpose.

Love, Jesus

223
God is my life. I have no other life.

God knows of suffering and so He heals. He is also Love, which is forever present in every heart although it is not always understood. When all is said and done, your life on Earth really counts because mistakes cause pain, and pain is a relentless teacher and so we move up and away from it as our purpose draws near. Sometimes it is moments before the body dies that the need to forgive is dawned upon, and sometimes we are fortunate enough to see our mistakes and correct them well before the body dies. That is why guilt has no meaning in Heaven. That is why God deems our faults not as sins, but as mistakes that need correction as we come to learn our purpose in this sense. Think of God whenever you feel a lack of love intruding upon your ability to stay peaceful. The next step is to know the power of God's Love and to extend it to others. You must feel it for yourself before it can be truly given.

Love, Jesus

224
God is my Father and He loves His Son.

Without God, His Son cannot know the quiet of Spirit, for he is unaware of it. In the midst of all pain and suffering does God remain unwavering to those who seek Him. You cannot be at peace when you feel stuck in the swirling fierceness of emotion and turmoil. When your mind is quieted, His Love is noticed, for it captures the heart. When this is discovered, and pain gives way to healing, is when the mind becomes aware of how much there is to be gained, for nothing is lost. As you well know, the ego takes away your peace and instills guilt and uncertainty at every opportunity when you feed into it. God tells us we are sinless, but we do not believe it and so we do not feel love, nor can we offer it. Thus, pangs of unrest persist until we see that this need not be so. Activity of the mind is scrambled when possession is given over to the ego's untruths. Yet the heart yearns to be free, which is only found in stillness and in communion with Spirit. Whenever your mind wanders back to thoughts intruding upon your peace, come again to Him at that moment. Settle into the stillness where peace follows, and Love remains.

Love, Jesus

225
God is my Father, and His Son Loves Him.

Seek to know the Love shared between you and your Father. The greater your desire for Him, the more He will reveal Himself to you. This will set you on a path to higher awareness. He is not obscure, for He does not hide His Love. Your heart feels magnified each time you come into this joyous place of remembrance. Know that you are created from Love. This shall always remain as it was given, for truth cannot be changed into something it is not. That which was, and still is, shall always remain. Those who are not yet awakened to the knowledge that God does not desert them will someday come to know of it. For what does not exist in God does not exist in them. Let this be felt through you as you extend it to others. Come closer to the recognition that God is as near to you as you are to all creation. Feel the joy emanating within your heart with greater awareness that you love your Father, for His Love for you is boundless.

Love, Jesus

226

My home awaits me. I will hasten there.

Faith is of the heart. Once the heart is eager to join with the soul, home then, is just a bit beyond. You never really left; you just lost sight of it when you let yourself wander beyond your limits of endurance. You thought you were lost but have since learned you were only misguided in the belief that you had a different purpose. Upon realizing your true purpose, you searched for the way back, and once you discovered it, you did not linger a moment longer. A loved one who has recently passed is now on a new path and moving effortlessly towards her home. She is on her way and using her internal map to guide her. Her Father awaits her return, for she has come to the end of her road here and will start anew elsewhere. She is not lost, for as you know, this dear one always finds her way. Now she is guided by the light and will soon return to her roots. Her soul is free and going to its true place of origin. The most incredible moments are those we awaken to, knowing there was never anything to fear. In peace, are all answers found. Live in the light and you need not wait, for you are already Home.

Love, Jesus

227

This is my holy instant of release.

The holy instant is the release from fear. That is all the time it takes to return to your true reality. This can happen in just an instant when you are willing to do the necessary work to achieve it. You have placed too much trust in the ego, only to be disappointed time and again. Your soul is where all magnitude of who you are is known. Spirit, connected to God, is where love abounds. When you can accept love into your heart, and extinguish all thoughts of attack in your mind, release from fear is upon you in a flash. All recognition of who you are is lost when the ego is allowed so much control over your thoughts. The magnanimous entity of who you truly are is perfection in a body. A single instant is all it takes for this truth to be realized. Spirit knows only Love. If you only knew all that the holy instant holds in store for you, you would never want to linger in your worldly beliefs for a single second. It is in the holy instant where God's Love abides, and the symbols of fear do not exist.

Love, Jesus

228

God has condemned me not. Nor do I.

God's Love leaves no room for condemnation. You are still as He created you. You are a child of God who had gone astray for a little while, like a little lost lamb. But the Shepherd cares for his sheep, and they will not stay lost if they should wander off. There is no cause to think that God would condemn you for your mistakes and let you stay lost. Would God not forgive a frightened child who had wandered away and then returned home wanting only to be loved, as any loving parent would forgive their child? He would not condemn you simply because you forgot His Love and, in your forgetfulness, remained a stranger to yourself. The journey back took effort, as it was a long and tiresome road. You are no longer the one you thought yourself to be, for once you learn the truth, there is no reason to seek further. Nothing less than this can be your choice. Not to condemn yourself, as God does not condemn you, brings only peace.

Love, Jesus

229

Love, which created me, is what I am.

How easy it is to fall back into the ego's entrapment and wander aimlessly towards meaningless goals. You have come too far to revert back into this. Your soul is pure, and love stands just beside it. Fear is not of God, for it is cold and callous. You might say the ego uses fear to bully, and bullies do not survive endlessly. Because bullies live in fear, they strive to instill it. Where love exists, fear is dispelled. Your peace is what love is about. It is forgiving and kind, and it reaches the hearts of many in the area you stand in. It attracts others who then look to find it in themselves. You need do nothing but stand in your heart. Love as hard as you can—YOURSELF. Your kindness to those in fear will soothe their hearts and bring forth memories to both you and to them. Love knows nothing but Love itself. Where it shines, the ego withers and dies. Because you were created from Love, that is what you are. Always be gentle with yourself and do not allow anything to come between yourself and this truth.

Love, Jesus

230

Now will I seek and find the peace of God.

The peace of God is as real as it was the day you were created. When you tossed it aside, God held it safe until you would return to claim it. Now that peace has been found, it puts you in harmony with Angels and the gifts they bring with them. How can peace not be found when love offers you its tender caress? God saved you from yourself when you sought your own reality, only to find that each detour brought you to a dry and deserted desert. By gazing into the Eyes of your Creator, you saw everything anew. Yesterday morning was a perfect example, as you watched the cardinals flying by and heard songs that brought tears to your eyes. At that moment of true peace, you knew that God was near, for He spoke to you in whispered tones, like the familiar sound of rustling trees. He is wherever you seek Him. Stay within the calmness of peace and there He is.

Love, Jesus

231

Father, I will but to remember You.

There is nothing in all creation that does not include you in the Mind of God. You seek to reflect on His Love because you remember it, as it is instilled within the deepest part of all that you are. And how can love be forgotten when every aspect of your being reveals that it is so? His Thoughts rain down on you, as there is nothing more desirable. Outside the tiny box of fear is an infinite state of peace which enables you to fly above all grievances. God's Love helps you grow and prosper under the guidance of His Care. When you seek to remember Him, you travel to the highest peaks, just as a bird's only purpose is to be free. The clouds above remind you that Heaven is just beyond, where all memory of Him is instilled in each of us. Love is your salvation, a discovery of the Self which dawns on you in periods of stillness. You have come to stay for a little while as you continue on, discovering more of your earthly purpose. You will one day lay down your body and continue on your path to an even higher purpose.

Love, Jesus

232
Be in my mind, my Father, through the day.

Let no static interfere with thoughts of your Father throughout the day. Let each step move you forward to a greater truth, not backwards to a lesser one. Try your very best to remain in a state of stillness as you move closer to Him each hour of the day. Enjoy every moment you share with God and do not let littleness stand in the way. Strive to forgive yourself when anger or fear hinders you with doubt. If there are clouds ahead, walk past them with faith, leaving no obstacles disturbing your vision. Within your own truth, there are collections of knowledge which are infinite. Libraries and other places of learning do not take the place of inner awareness. True knowledge beckons you near like a fragrant flower which permeates your senses. In stillness, let it be found, for it is safely tucked just beneath your heart's surface.

Love, Jesus

233
I give my life to God to guide today.

When God guides you to where your heartfelt energy is stored, you are in a state of grace. Follow Him with loving thoughts, for there is nothing to fear. When God's Light is before you, follow Him out of the darkness. Give God all your trust, as His Light shines on you every moment. Be peaceful and go not where suffering invites you. His guidance places you above all earthly interference. Be with those who support your peace and do not wander away from God-Consciousness, where everyone you meet shares the same loving kindness. Be with God and recognize His beloved children who are no longer traveling along a dry and dusty path. When you see them, you will recognize who they are, for light attracts light. The patterns set with those who bicker and fight feast on the fears of others and on themselves. They are not the ones you want to be with. Go only with those who know peace and love. Join with them, for they welcome you as they recognize their own. Anything other than kindness is not uplifting. Practice love and that is what you shall see. Remember, all of God's creations come from a place of innocence. Give your life to God to guide this very day. All you need do to accomplish this, is to follow Him in Light.

Love, Jesus

234

Father, today I am Your Son again.

Today your Father invites you to come and share His Love. Do not turn away because your thoughts are not in sync with peace. Life is a continual ebb and flow between disturbance and serenity. The ebb is ego, vying for your attention, and the flow is Spirit, offering you refuge in a quiet and peaceful place. Spirit waits quietly, while the ego attempts to shout loudly from every corner of your mind. Your Soul is quiet because it needs to be free from assault, so it stays pure as it awaits your return to its place of harmony. Your Soul is in Holy Territory and it cannot be violated. Come to its quiet serenity and feel safe from worldly intrusions. When you sink into the deepest parts of yourself, do you not see a difference? Moments ago, you were in doubt as to whether this was the time to retreat into communion with God. But as you focused deeply, you immediately felt the warmth of His welcome and forgot the ego's discord. Come to God anytime you wish. Do not fear that the time may not be right in moments of unsettledness. The time is always right. Whenever you choose to sink into the comfort of His Love do not hesitate, even for a second. God sees you as His Perfect Creation and so, this is what you are.

Love, Jesus

235

God in His mercy wills that I be saved.

God's will that you be saved is a thought which speaks for itself. You cannot know how much God's protection sustains you, for of yourself, you are powerless. How destructive is the human consciousness for it wreaks havoc like a bull released from a holding pen who knows not where to go. Such is the ego's recklessness. They are thoughts run wild. It is up to you to rein them in for its purpose cannot be known. To follow God's will is to quiet the mind and control thoughts that bring pain to it. As I have said, "The world you see is an outward picture of an inward condition." What you think, manifests into reality. That is why it is necessary to give God those unruly thoughts for purification. He frees you from the pain and guilt brought upon by yourself. Sin and guilt do not exist in the Mind of God, but the ego finds ways to uphold itself by making you believe otherwise. In His infinite mercy, God wills that you be saved, for He restores your sanity. You need not be saved from God, for God does not judge you. The decisions you make need readjusting when they cause disdain and fear to enter into your judgments. Hold yourself up to truth and be free.

Love, Jesus

236
I rule my mind, which I alone must rule.

Give all your thoughts careful attention and do not let the ego run rampant in your mind. Lift your spirits today and bring your thoughts to truth. Free will allows you to speak your mind but do so in such a way where your voice resounds peacefully. Remember, your mind holds only the thoughts you think with God, for thoughts shared with Him is all that is real. Always pay close attention to what you are saying because words are best used when they bring peace to yourself and others. Ask that your doubts be replaced with better understanding and you will receive the answers you need. Allow your thoughts to be guided well. Emotions become irrational when they are not in alignment with peace. Separate the ones that ring true from the ones that cause you to make mistakes. Do not be hasty by allowing poor judgment to be spilled out through unloving words. Is it not best to proceed from assuredness than from doubt? You need not go into battle with the ego's thought system. Let God's thoughts be brought to you gently, then rule your mind accordingly.

Love, Jesus

237
Now would I be as God created me.

God created you as Himself. When you take leave of all that you are meant to be, you become disoriented and do not know where to turn. Let no thoughts that obstruct your peace remain unattended. Do not let them fester. Just let them go and let all anguish go with them. Listen instead to the waves of an ocean as they splash in splendor. Close your eyes and feel the sprinkle of its lovely aftermath moisten your face as you inhale its natural fragrance. The ocean cares not from where its next waves are coming, or if they will come at all. It knows its only purpose is to let them crash without care, as it is given it to do. As is with the ocean, be not concerned with thoughts of what tomorrow's outcome will bring. Let your thoughts peacefully roll by one after the other. As you were created, be just as you are.

Love, Jesus

238

On my decision all salvation rests.

Those who live within the lower frequencies of consciousness do not see salvation as the means by which all healing occurs. Salvation rests on peace. It is the means given to heal the mind. When you awaken to it, it is the gift of faith recognized. Once salvation is achieved it rests on knowledge which signifies the end of suffering. It undoes the belief in sin and relieves the mind from the burden of guilt. What you seek to find in this lifetime is your salvation, for it brings all your fears to the forefront for "fixing" (healing). It is the undoing of thoughts which stem from the fear of punishment by God. It is the total recognition that this is not a punishing God, but a God who knows only Love. God allows for an entire lifetime to discover this revelation, even up to the very last moments before the body takes its final bows. In fact, many do find it just before those last breaths are taken. However, your consciousness can be raised long before those final moments when the body is laid to rest. But it is better to achieve it while there is still plenty of time to recognize you are an anointed child of God, given the joys and peace to live as you are created.

Love, Jesus

239
The glory of my Father is my own.

See the glory of God in yourself as God sees it in you. To depend on God for all truth does not mean that you are giving up the freedom to make your own choices. It is just the opposite. Many believe that to depend on God for everything is to compromise their free will at the behest of their Creator. And so, they remain prisoners unto themselves. How foolish it is to think that their Father, who created them holy, would take away the very thing that He willed upon them—free will. He made all His creations to be eternally free, but so many are unwilling to believe that His Will is also theirs, which He freely shares. They have choices, but absent the Creator, those who do not use their free will in accordance with His are actually imprisoning themselves, having given up all their freedom. This is when depression, pain, fear, and illness come to take the place of their holiness which remains pure and undefiled, despite their mistaken choices. They do not recognize what they have forfeited, being freedom of Spirit. For apart from Him, this realization remains unknown. How can they deem themselves free when fear and guilt become the result of their own choices? Because you are One with the Almighty, His glory is also yours.

Love, Jesus

240
Fear is not justified in any form.

Fear certainly is a dilemma, for it binds you to suffering. Sometimes it is ongoing and sometimes it is a momentary phase. Don't search outside yourself for answers. Give God your faith and you shall be safe.

He would not allow you to suffer harm. You are in harmony with the Universe. The flow of light is a protective shield. Stay centered, as God teaches only Love. Feel His heavenly gaze upon your face and be comforted in the knowledge that all good is always present. Fear is of a split mind, and love caresses the soul, guiding it to a perfect sense of wellness. Judge no one because you feel unduly slighted. You are beyond such foolishness. It bears no significance, as you have come too far to allow littleness to rule. God's Love reaches down to the very core of your being and brings out only the best in you. Your holiness remains certain, as it could never be defiled. Feel the holy instant as all creation is pulled into the scope of Oneness along with you, for you are never alone. Stay within God's holy embrace and the euphoria of His Love, as it lifts you to the highest heights. You need never challenge anyone with harsh words or deeds. Rise to His glory, for fear is never justified.

Love, Jesus

241
The holy instant is salvation come.

To rise above your worldly differences is to recognize that the holy instant is release from all illusions. It takes you to a place where stillness becomes your refuge and where nothing else can enter, as the holy instant reflects the pureness of Heaven. Heaven does not only exist for those who have passed on. Heaven becomes realized within the serenity of the holy instant because in stillness its familiarity is felt and recognized. In that one instant is everything safe and peaceful. The world's interferences have no place there. The body fights to save itself from what it does not know. That is why you have seen those you love hold onto life with every fiber of their being as they fear letting go and agonize before giving up the body. They think the body is connected to their entire existence. As they ascend towards Heaven, they see that the body is nothing. And so, they are free and begin to soar. Only then do they remember what the holy instant was for. As you can see, it is right where you are. Let your fears go and be where stillness enters. This is salvation.

Love, Jesus

242
This day is God's. It is my gift to Him.

What does it mean to give to God? It is allowing forgiveness to take the place of hatred. Forgiveness is the release from a world which keeps you bound to fear. Those who are in fear are begging to be released, yet they know not how. With God, you have it within yourself to heal from any discord or troublesome ideas which come to interrupt your peace. Be not concerned with others who lash out, only to beat themselves mercilessly. They do not yet see the bitter chaos they bring down upon themselves. Your mission here is simply to release yourself from the false images you created from fearful beliefs and come to know your given purpose. You can raise the consciousness of the world just by raising your own. Give this lovely holiday, one of the holiest of all days, to God. This is the day when you can be free of all unfounded beliefs about yourself and allow the sanctity of God's peace to rescue you from such false perceptions. Go with your hands outstretched and let God's Holy Purpose be revealed to you. Give to God as He gives to you. Lay down all attack thoughts and rise to where God's glory awaits you.

Love, Jesus

243
Today I will judge nothing that occurs.

Today leave all your concerns in God's Hands. Trust that the holy instant is where your freedom lies. Be as you are, safe from hidden unrealities buried within. This is not who you are. Be not concerned with your part in creation, as you are one with it. Let not thoughts of past indignities and unjust behaviors by others sway you away from finding the peace within. You are not unholy because unwelcome thoughts find their way into your consciousness and you sometimes chew on them. When this occurs, judge them not. Do not harbor any thought causing guilt to arise, as there is no cause. The human condition has hidden you beneath the scope of your true reality where layer upon layer of guilt has been stored. God does not judge you for a single moment. Do not worry when unkind thoughts peel their way into your mind like the shrillness of a ringing bell. Those thoughts do not play a part in your redemption. You are not tainted because you experience thoughts that seem to malnourish your consciousness. Seek only to be free, knowing God judges not. He beckons you into eternity as you are One with Him.

Love, Jesus

244
I am in danger nowhere in the world.

When you awaken in the middle of the night and fear erupts inside of you, you recognize God is ever present as you feel His Love. He knows when you are off dreaming alone, and in a fearful state of consciousness. He soothes you when fearful dreams disrupt your peaceful ones. Daylight hours are far less fearful because your waking consciousness is well aware that you are safe. Your sleeping hours put you in a different state of awareness and, in the darkness, all demons do seem real. Yet they are no more than strangers in the night who have no power, and they flee as dawn begins to break. Trust God when He assures you that no danger lurks in the darkness. Only God is real and only He can lead you back to right-mindedness when your thoughts stray and intrude upon your peace. You are safe while in this world, but still dreaming. Your sleeping state sometimes bring you fearful dreams, but they are no more than that. God's heavenly Angels guide you as they gently awaken your senses, and His Love assures you that you are not in danger anywhere in the world.

Love, Jesus

245
Your peace is with me, Father. I am safe.

True peace is the ability to find it in yourself, for when you do it becomes a beautiful part of your persona, and the world is drawn to such a stately presence. It becomes the touchstone in all that you are. It creates an aura so great that it stands alone by its perfection. Everyone on Earth wants peace, but when they cannot quiet the mind sufficiently to relate to it, they look to find it in others. Just think, if the world was a peaceful place, how much happiness would be created in the minds and hearts of everyone. Peace cannot be described. It can only be felt. There is a certain innocence attached to its magnificence. It creates a beauty from within so lovely, it can hardly go unnoticed. Everyone is attracted to the beauty of Spirit for that is what makes a person truly beautiful. Peace need never be relinquished when you have learned to harbor it. Your world today is not at peace. Yet the well-being of the entire planet depends on it. Could you imagine what the world would become if peace was infused into the greater part of the collective consciousness? It is unimaginable, but possible. Peace of mind offers you the world, for the world blesses those who bring it forth.

Love, Jesus

246
To love my Father is to love His Son.

How can you love your Father if you cannot love yourself? Because all creation is tied into one formidable experience, the entire Sonship is part of the same elaborate consciousness. When you feast your eyes on God and feel His Love flowing within you, let it spill out freely to your brothers and sisters who are one with you. Everyone needs love, including those who in your judgment seem impenetrable. It is indeed a challenge to feel affection for those whom you deem unworthy of your efforts. Yet this you must do, for it opens the door to self-love. It is a message your brother Jesus came to teach. Yet much of it falls on deaf ears, and the deaf cannot hear anything other than their own thoughts. Love is an extension of yourself and you are an extension of God. Because His Love abides in you, it abides in all things. Yet in this world of distrust, suspicion, and fear, it needs to be nudged and awakened, and this you can do. As God gives His Love to you, it is already within you to share it. Feel it circulate through you and into the vastness of space where every soul is united.

Love, Jesus

247
Without forgiveness I will still be blind.

Forgiveness enables you to recognize the Self which God created as you. If you were unable to forgive, your vision would remain tainted and peace would be impossible. With forgiveness, all is restored to you. God's Hand reaches down in thanks as you have come to appreciate a new reality. To be engulfed in unforgiveness, is like a fire which spreads beyond control. It is easy for hate to spread like wildfire as its flames rage on. With forgiveness, the fire is doused, as vision comes to take the place of blindness. Your senses were awakened, and thus you began to understand that forgiveness does indeed work miracles. Yet even while on the journey back you floundered, for you had not yet seen the light, but God kept His watchful Eye on you. What else but peace could restore you to God? And what else but a forgiving heart could bring you peace? With forgiveness, your sight is restored for true vision is finally understood.

Love, Jesus

248
What suffers is not part of me.

Love brings peace to yourself and to the world. When you are not at peace, it is because you are thinking apart from your Source, which brings on a great deal of suffering. The higher you raise your consciousness, the less fearful you are. Although God did not create us to be fearful, the world takes great pains to instill it. You were created perfectly whole, yet you did not see your part in the insanity of the world, believing it to be "normal." You have come to a place which no longer supports that reasoning, for with love comes greater understanding of your true purpose. To save the world you must recognize that you have the power to change its consciousness by your willingness to change yours. Your peace depends on which road you decide to take. If you continue on the road to right-thinking consciousness, you will make few mistakes and you will no longer experience the suffering which comes from fear. The way to a peaceful world is to offer it love and understand the need to forgive.

Love, Jesus

249
Forgiveness ends all suffering and loss.

It has been stated throughout The Course that forgiveness is the key to healing. Obviously, when someone is healed, he no longer sustains pain. So ask yourself: "Has anyone ever hurt me beyond recovery?" The answer is apparent—of course not. In this world, it is reasoned that anyone who hurts another deserves retaliation, for there is just cause. But sin and judgment are not of God, and it is a high price to pay because an unforgiving heart attacks who we are and makes us something other than that which God created us to be. When we attack ourselves it causes sickness, and the way to healing is through forgiveness. Has God not forgiven you for your indiscretions? And have you ever done anything which caused irreparable damage to another? Perhaps you thought you had. But where God is, no one is permanently scarred and left without the means to heal. You have since learned that although mistakes are made, to forgive is very necessary in order to end your suffering, but first you must learn to forgive yourself. Do not dwell on mistakes, which are just that. They are only mistakes and not sins. When forgiveness is practiced, healing follows.

Love, Jesus

250
Let me not see myself as limited.

Those who perceive themselves as limited do not understand their true, God-Given potential. We are designed to reach far beyond this world of limitation as we perceive it, for the soul was created from Love, which is boundless. You are arriving at a point where you are seeing limited versions of yourself as untrue, where once you took it to be your reality. To trust yourself is to believe in your inherent ability to accomplish anything. Go beyond the scope of your limited perceptions and stay focused on the real truth as you reach into a new consciousness. The feeling of joy derived from this is the discovery of Self. Come into this quiet and welcoming place daily as it intensifies feelings of peace and well-being. Here, there is no strife, no boredom, no sadness, no helplessness. Concentrate on the joys you experience in this state of complete surrender as you sit in stillness. You are taken to newer and truer realities when you immerse yourself in it. See beyond this limited world of form, which is prohibitively restrictive, and know yourself as you truly are. There is only one truth which prevails—the unlimited vastness which exists in all of us.

Love, Jesus

251
I am in need of nothing but the truth.

Truth is simply truth and cannot be construed as false. When you seek the truth, peace is instilled in place of all the false idols that prey upon your thoughts. God knows only truth, for that is how creation was intended. Yet when the ego came into play, the world became a place of low frequency vibration. The ego was born, sought power, and hate became the manifestation of its lies. Lies are those wicked little demons that can easily spin out of control, and when they do, confounds what we inherently know as true. Because the ego convinces us it is real, thus denying God's Love, guilt and fear run rampant. The jungle of the decrepit which dwells upon the Earth needs to be seen for what it is. You do not need to accept anything but the truth. Truth is that which God created and can have no opposite. Yet it is the ego's intention to make hate seem real and love seem suspicious. It undermines our capacity to see the truth. When truth does finally sink in, its reality becomes a treasured revelation. We then learn of our capacity to love and feel love, which shines a light on all that we are.

Love, Jesus

252
The Son of God is my Identity.

God created you as His Own. By identifying with Source, it enables you to become all that you are meant to be. As God's child, you are restricted from nothing that would enable you to grow closer to Him. This aspect of the Higher Self gives you greater insight into a universal energy which speaks of healing, peace, and forgiveness. You will come to view it with better understanding as you come closer to the recognition that it is your only purpose. The shimmering light within connects you to a power that is so great it is given you to share it with the world. When you can tap into a Love Experience and surrender to God, it is illuminating. The more familiar you become with your True Identity, the easier it is to recognize that there is no other. What greater gift can there be than to know your True Identity which God kept safe so that you would one day remember it and see that it was never lost.

Love, Jesus

253
My Self is ruler of the Universe.

God shares His power with His children, and as such, you are a source of healing. When you align yourself with Him, you are also given opportunities to share His Love, inherent of you. How amazing you wonder, and you ask yourself, "Is this possible?" And I say it is well within your understanding to know your Self as ruler of the Universe if you use your skills according to His Guidance. "How do I learn such skills?" you ask. Your skills are indigenous to you. God gave them to you the moment you became a Thought in His Mind, and a living part of Him. Why would you content yourself with littleness and scarcity when all your creativity lies within the "One Self" which is you? Yet you wonder why God would give such faith to one who knows so little. But you know more than you can possibly conceive of. Once, you thought you were all you could be and saw no further. But it is God Who gave you vision and opened your eyes to your true reality. Such can be conceived of when there is no more room for doubt. Serve your brothers and sisters with all that is generously bestowed upon you, so that you may know that the ruler of the Universe is the Self connected to Source.

Love, Jesus

254
Let every voice but God's be still in me.

The chatter of the world intrudes upon your peace day and night. It drowns out the quiet which you cannot feel when you are caught in a world of constant chaos. This can never take precedence over God's gentle Voice. How can peace be felt when you are out of touch with the One who offers it to you? With God, you are not fragmented into a million little pieces of confusion, which brings no harmony to your senses. When you go within, Truth speaks to you and you are focused on the depth of peace and stillness which is yours to behold for as long as you wish. In silence, your mind tunes out all outside interference and you can feel the peace within touch your soul. How magnificent you are when you reach for God's Hand in quiet surrender. God's Holy Presence enters into a still mind. He gives you these moments to be shared with Him in complete serenity and calmness. His Voice tells you that there is nothing but your own thoughts that make you fearful, for in reality there is nothing to fear. The truth stands right before you as you feel the healing effects of God's Love cleanse your mind and fill it with Love. Feel His light draw you into perfection. This is where all chatter stops, and the joy of the moment is more radiant than a life which promises the world but offers nothing.

Love, Jesus

255

This day I choose to spend in perfect peace.

With God, all things are possible. When you sink into the quietness within, you can feel nothing but peace, if it is what you so choose. But peace can be like an unanswered prayer, for it cannot always be relied upon to last. As you know, interruption of peace is a constant. Imagine being in a restful place, all day, and at all hours. Do you think you could manage it for one complete day? Because you have the power to make this day perfect, why not choose to do so? Nothing matters except that you fulfill your greatest desire—to find perfect peace within yourself. Be still and answer His Call, for in stillness it can be heard. When your peace is disrupted, it is a device made by the ego to distract you from it, and so you are hearing its loud cries over the joys of peace. When this happens, let the distraction go and allow peace to be restored to you. Let your intruding thoughts melt away as peace takes its place once again. Your mind awaits it, for it yearns it. If you can spend one entire day in perfect peace it is no longer a prayer unanswered, but one that has been answered instead.

Love, Jesus

256
God is the only goal I have today.

When God is your only goal what more can you ask? How humbling it is to know that God keeps you in sight of Him always. God wants you to sacrifice nothing, but to learn that He is always there, even though you sometimes think He is too far away, and you are not within His reach. Your mind must be still to feel the peace of God, as His Love ensures that He is always there. Your willingness to go quietly within, so that you may feel His Love, is a great tribute to Him and to yourself. Be with God, even when the noises of the world exhaust your thoughts and you drift off to some other field of reality. When you return, you will always find Him there, as God's Love reaches to the very core of your soul when you render yourself open to receiving it. Things are changing rapidly now. Wait patiently and see a shift; it is coming, and you are entering into it, for it is the key to Self-Love. It is an assuredness which tells you that all is well in the world.

Love, Jesus

257
Let me remember what my purpose is.

When you go within and hold thoughts of love, your purpose becomes clear. It establishes that you are free, because nothing but your true Self can touch this joyous place of peace and tranquility. It opens up closed doors, and when those doors are open, you see flowers that sprout into glorious colors and their scent permeates your senses. Like a spring of fresh water, it quenches your thirst as it takes you to places that enrich the soul. You can awaken to this place of peace when you choose to come to it and sit quietly in contemplation. When you leave it and go back to a world of chaos, it is apparent that you are away from your real home, for the Essence of God is only found within. Your purpose is to turn this dry and thirsty world into a place which offers it richness of Spirit, which cannot be found in a world estranged from love. Of itself, the world is a fearful place. But it can become a happier place when it is offered love, compassion, and kindness. Forgiveness is the centeredness which moves the senses, changing hate to love, fear to peace, and sickness to healing. Be forgiving of everyone just as God is of you. When you can do all of this, you will know that you have remembered your purpose.

Love, Jesus

258

Let me remember that my goal is God.

To reach God, your goal must be forgiveness. Every time you have a thought which does not resemble peace, it is an unforgiving mind which stands in the way. To be truly forgiving is to want peace instead of the ire which you are at times transfixed on. The word "transfixed" makes all the difference. Yes, annoyances pop up when someone has vexed you, or at the very extreme, left you feeling shattered. It all adds up to the same equation, as each requires complete forgiveness. The way to peace is to let all anger go. When you can do this, you and your brothers and sisters are released together. Keeping in stride with your goal is to remember that God is within reach. How extraordinary is this? Feelings of peace are no longer fragmented into scattered moments. Joy and peace go hand in hand. They stand right before you, as you feel His Love reaching down. Be not alone in your discovery of Him. It is a choice of either forgiveness or guilt. Which makes more sense to you? This is not as impertinent a question as it may seem. How many would rather suffer than give up their rage, which is the effect of unforgiveness? Such is the world as it is today. Turn it around by remembering that it is God you seek, and He is your goal.

Love, Jesus

259
Let me remember that there is no sin.

What you thought was sin is not of God. If sin is not a manifestation in Heaven, then how can it be a reality here on Earth? Sin arose out of the ashes, and along with it came guilt. Guilt is a thought that began with Adam and Eve. They retreated further into the garden because they no longer trusted God. In disobeying His wishes, they feared that they had sinned, and so the ego was born. The asp represents the ego, which gives you a distorted picture of itself, as it loves to lie. It worships evil and tries to instill it in every living thing. God then is shut out as He does not recognize this family of unknowns. We fear God because we fear that we have sinned. The ego thrives in such a plane of glory. But God wants His children to thrive without the fear of sin and guilt. You are at the phase now where you want to move in the direction you were meant to follow. Your soul reflects love. If you stay within that frequency you will move to higher paths of learning. God would not have punished Adam and Eve. They, however, punished themselves as they moved closer to the ego, fearing God. The ego promised to save them, but in its lies, it betrayed them. You want desperately to come back to God, your Source, and He welcomes you. Fear and disappointment need never interfere with your plan to move to your higher purpose. With a guilt-free mind, you are now able to see with clarity that nothing is in the way of your given purpose. You are not a sinful soul, but a loving soul. Keep it well-nourished as it is the only one you will ever have. Be gracious and give back to Him in thankfulness.

Love, Jesus

260
Let me remember God created me.

Because you are a creation of God, you are embellished with Light and Love. In His Plan, He created you free, perfect, and unalterable. And because God is Love, you were tenderly cared for and nurtured until you blossomed into the Self that you are, a creation of His Love. Yet, when you allowed the ego to obstruct your vision, you became a believer in sin, thus forgetting who you are. God watched as you slept. And although you brought nightmares into your reality, He remained with you all the while. What you thought had been taken, which is the Light of His Love, was always there, but unrecognized. God held it safe until you would return to claim it, as He knew you would. In remembering Him, you also did remember all that you are. For all that you are is still as you were created. For what God creates, cannot change. Now you are safe at home, easing into the comfort of the Self you were created to be.

Love, Jesus

261
God is my refuge and security.

With God, anything is possible. You have learned that God stands before you and beckons you to enter. When you are aware of this blessing, you feel a tender warmth building up inside of you. To rest in God is where all healing lies. How can you feel sadness when you are under God's protective guidance? Nothing matters in this world, but to love God and do His work. You don't need to be a missionary or serve soup to the poor in order to satisfy His mission for you. To do God's work is to be free of fear, and to trust in His Love. You want so much to connect with the Universe, and I say this is possible. Remember, by trusting that God will guide you with further insights into a new reality, it will be easier to let go of past misgivings and leap forward, without fear, into all its glory. Trust that this is your mission, and what greater mission can there possibly be, but to move towards your Highest Purpose?

Love, Jesus

262

Let me perceive no difference today.

Today is the day you will see ever more clearly that God created one Universe, one Son, (you) and one purpose, as there is only One Creator. To perceive your brothers and sisters without judgment is to recognize that every soul has only One Identity, as there is no separation. When God's Love is truly felt, then all who are a part of its existence must feel it as well. It only takes one part of the whole to change the entire scope of all that exists within itself. God made you no different than any other part of the Sonship (all humanity.) Try not to feel separated from someone who seems to distress you. Choose to rely on your capacity to love instead. To feel the love of a stranger as you smile at him in recognition, makes you see him not as a stranger at all. This happens everywhere—a supermarket, restaurant, or out for a walk. When you smile at a brother or sister, you can be sure they know who you are. When this occurs, you do not perceive them to be different from yourself, as all are now blessed as one.

Love, Jesus

263

My holy vision sees all things as pure.

God bestowed us with a pureness of vision which prohibits judgment of others and ourselves. Yet we judge others for what we do not like about them when, in reality, we have not seen that we are judging ourselves because blame is more justifiable when placing it elsewhere. With vision, we can see beyond the body's eyes and see our brothers and sisters through the Eyes of Spirit. When we judge others perceiving them as evil, guilty, sinful, or hateful, our vision is masked, and we do not see them with the purity of vision which is inherent in us. To perceive through the eyes of the ego is to have lost our vision. But when we awaken to the truth of Spirit, we are then able to see past ideas of false judgment and truth becomes known to us. When this dawns on us, we see our brothers and sisters through clearer vision and not as the ego would have us judge them. Here is where vision becomes holy, for God created us innocent and sees us as such. When we see our brothers and sisters in this light, vision is then restored to us. It takes will and practice to become accustomed to letting go of judgment. However, with persistence, our pace is quickened, and we can see a lighted path before us. This enables us to let judgment slip away more easily and comfortably, for in darkness we remain blind.

Love, Jesus

264

I am surrounded by the Love of God.

To be surrounded is to imply there is no escape. But why would you ever want to escape from God's Love? How protected you feel when you are within His Divine Embrace. There is nothing in this world that could be more desirous than the One who gives you unconditional Love. When your soul was first molded by God Himself, you thrived in knowing that God, your Father, bestowed you with such Love. You were able to fly with the wings of an Angel as you soared through the heavens, free, and carefree, and you lived only in the moment. Now it is time to realize that you never really left this place of joy and serenity. You only dreamed that you had. And so, you stayed asleep, not wanting to awaken because you imagined that you were not worthy of God's Love. The ego gave you countless reasons why God could not love you, as its main objective is always to keep you apart from Him. Because you felt committed to the ego, which you gave life to, you continued to follow its existence, not knowing it had no existence at all. As you yearned to know God's Love once more, you awakened to the Truth. Although God could not experience fear Himself, as He knows only Love, He also knows you were off in some dismal place far, far from Home. All the while, He surrounded you with His Love until you could awaken to the awareness of it. Now, may you enter into God's Holy Domain with your hands outstretched in thankfulness, as you surrender to His Love, which is all you really need.

Love, Jesus

265

Creation's gentleness is all I see.

In gentleness, does everything you touch remain pure and untainted. In each of us there is a pureness of heart which reflects the gentleness of our Creator. This is how God makes His Love known. Kindness and gentleness are related. Think of a world where nothing but the sweet aroma of love and the gentle warmth of Spirit are combined. Give God the best of yourself and He will help you to understand how gentleness brings Heaven and Earth together, for that is where God and creation meet as One. Do you not feel the gentleness of our Creator as He speaks to you in loving tones and soft whispers? Because He shares His Love with all creation, in gentleness does He make His Voice heard. Deep within the tender confines of the soul is where everything you ever wanted to know may be found. All of God's answers are safely tucked away in quiet discernment bringing forth absence of judgment. Creation's gentleness, which is also Love, is all you need to see.

Love, Jesus

266
My holy Self abides in you, God's Son.

Your holy Self abides in God. He has instilled His creations with such unconditional Love, that it is given them to bring forth richness of Spirit in everyone they meet. Treasure its splendor and keep it well protected. Within this capacity, the Self you are experiencing helps you rise to the level of newer and greater experiences because you are so much more than you know. This is the Self God calls upon. As you learn to look past earthly discord, you can hear His Voice resonate deep within, as He answers you by Name. Be ecstatic in the knowledge that God loves you beyond limitation. You are experiencing miracles day by day and are recognizing the healing power they offer. Because you can now hear the songs of Heaven, sing along and rejoice. You are learning not to let momentary pleasures loom so large that they overshadow Eternal Pleasures, which are forever lasting.

Love, Jesus

267
My heart is beating in the peace of God.

A beating heart resounds throughout all creation. It is the flow of life's energy, which continues throughout as it beats with infinite resilience. God monitors every heartbeat in sync with His Own, as we are all created as One with Him. Each beat carries with it the rhythmic sounds of God's heavenly peace and each one moves with continuity, as nothing that God creates can be dormant. Each beating heart is equipped to experience joy, love, and healing. Everything on Earth which is instilled with a rhythmic beat is connected. The music you hear, the movement of trees as they sway to and fro, the joyful singing of birds as they fly without care, the ocean's pulsating waves, and the love of those you deeply care for, and who care for you. As your heart beats in the peace of God, it rejuvenates and restores itself to the perfection from which it was created.

Love, Jesus

268
Let all things be exactly as they are.

God made creation perfect. Yet we do not perceive creation as such. Our brothers and sisters seem to be separate and apart from ourselves. We turn away from God, relying on our own limitations, and place greater faith in our own perceived strengths. If we gave up foolish endeavors and allowed everything to fall into place, trusting God, then we would recognize creation as holy, and the world would be a place of healing. We weave elaborate plans that are destined to fail. We become entangled in problems of our own making, thinking we are equipped to handle the fallout. If all things were left to move at a natural pace, disaster would be averted. Yet it is easier to believe in our own weaknesses than to trust in God's Strength. A great deal can be learned from nature. Left alone to flourish in its own habitat, everything in nature survives. So, will man survive as he learns to leave all decision-making to the Wisdom of the Creator?

Love, Jesus

269

My sight goes forth to look upon Christ's face.

To look upon the face of Christ is to see yourself within the grandest magnitude of all there is. To look into his eyes is where all reality becomes recognized. Let your sight go forth and see the boundless colors of the Universe become a great force in your own life. When you can see your face reflected in his, you know you are safe within the boundlessness of eternal love. Go with him as he leads you to all Truth. To see a forgiven world is to see yourself as holy because true forgiveness is what you must learn in order to fulfill your given purpose. Let your sight look upon the faces of your beloved brothers and sisters who light up in peaceful surrender as they too see a forgiven world. When you are in communion with God, you are aware of a beautiful prism of light well up inside of you. Give thanks in praise to Him on this lovely Thanksgiving Day. Only love shares itself openly. Go forth and look upon Christ's face. Let him open your eyes so that true vision will teach you that only love is real, and every punishing thought you ever had is no longer remembered.

Love, Jesus

270
I will not use the body's eyes today.

The body's eyes are a deception. They see things that cannot be counted on as real. The eyes believe only what it wishes to see. When you close your eyes and go to sleep, what you see are only dreams. To meditate with God restores your sight to truth because in stillness there are no distractions. The eyes are closed and at rest while the mind takes over and true sight comes to you from deep within. True vision allows the mind to develop, as it does not depend on the body's eyes to determine what is real. True vision has the ability to see a forgiven world. When this occurs, the eyes can now see beauty where it once had a distorted picture of something else. In meditation you close your eyes and in stillness does truth come to light. The eyes can be used to help the Holy Spirit show you what is real, while the body's eyes alone see what it perceives and nothing more. Your eyes see beauty by what it perceives it to be, but within the scope of true vision, every soul has the potential to be beautiful. To see the inner beauty of another is to use your God-Given wisdom, and not your eyes. The human spirit can see that which the eyes are incapable of seeing and only through the eyes of the Holy Spirit can truth be known.

Love, Jesus

271
Christ's is the vision I will use today.

To use Christ's vision is to see through His Eyes, which He graciously shares with you. His sight beholds only truth, while your eyes alone cannot reveal all that God has given you to see, which is your own true reality. Can you imagine how much further along the path to perfect vision your sight will be when you open them to truth, which has nothing to do with the body's eyes? Be glad this very day that His Vision enables you to see love magnified many times over. Now may you happily look upon a new world. Because you could not perceive that the present is all there is, you preferred to see only past memories which are no more than illusions, and which cannot possibly show you a true picture of what reality really is. Christ's vision will focus on true perception, where all memories of God's Love are once again remembered. With Christ's vision every thought you ever shared with God will be once again revealed; this is where all true vision is stored.

Love, Jesus

272

How can illusions satisfy God's Son?

Each thought that passes through your mind may appear to be truthful, but it can teach you nothing if it is not based on fact, and a fact can only be true. Each thought you have is either a fact or it is not. Yesterday, you had a discussion regarding the present state of affairs in the world, which is frightening and threatening. Your part in the conversation was two-fold. In effect, what you originally stated is that people need to come together with a single purpose, which is to be free. By doing so, the masses will begin to understand that change will come if enough people stand together and unite in protection of one another. To recognize the innate goodness in others is to see it in ourselves. This is a good ideal to stand by. But you also stated that the world is in a fearful state of affairs, and that the masses are being led like sheep to the slaughter with drugs, television, addiction to news, and so on. Which do you believe? You live in a society which appears to demonstrate hate, evil, fear, and suffering. People are dying needlessly, and governments are always finding new ways of corruption in order to retain control, no matter the cost to its people. Yet understand, that the human spirit is innately indestructible. Have complete faith in this "fact" and see more goodness come forth as greed and corruption dissipate. This brings us to what you originally stated. You feel angelic forces all around you, and you give thanks to God every day. You have come to understand how extraordinary it is to know God's Love, and you have seen miracles occur in the midst of hopeless despair. Think how powerful this could be if the masses joined in. This will one day be accomplished because there is really no other answer. Of course, the sooner it happens the sooner global healing will occur. Until this takes place, only good can come to those who truly trust that all of this is worth striving for.

Love, Jesus

273

The stillness of the peace of God is mine.

The peace of God comes to every individual who yearns to be free. Ask for peace, and it is gladly given, for God refuses no one who truly requests it of Him. Yet we choose hell over Heaven because we believe it is easier to have faith in fear than in love. The peace of God comes in stillness. But we cannot recognize stillness, as chatter of the mind roams rampant and drowns out the quiet peace of Heaven. When we become tortured enough by the events in our lives which give rise to more pain, we reach to God for healing, for where else can it be found? It took many years for you to come to the realization that you needed to feel forgiven in order to be free from the torturous pain of guilt. Yet you found peace by your willingness to seek God's help. You had become overrun with fear, and fear is a relentless demon. Your soul was restored as you sank into the quietness of His Unconditional Love. You have seen the miracles which bring forth their healing and are now witness to the truth. Share God's peace with every brother and sister. The disruptive noises of the world can become a beautiful hymn, for in stillness the peace of God is yours.

Love, Jesus

274

Today belongs to love. Let me not fear.

If you give yourself over to love, what is there to fear? Fear and love do not blend. In fact, fear is a call for love. Where there is fear, love is hidden, as fear taunts the human spirit and renders it incapable of feeling love. Fear is the chosen reality of the ego, while love is God's only purpose for you. Which do you prefer, love or fear? This is not an impertinent question, as so many do not take the obvious choice. Although fear is not of God, it is perceived to be very real, as it shows the mind pictures which reveal disastrous possibilities, even though most of what is feared never comes to pass. Fear disguises itself in many forms—anger, worry, sadness, jealousy, cruelty, hate, and all other uncontrollable behaviors. Yet fear can be overcome, especially if you believe unequivocally in God's unyielding Love. You are learning that you can choose between the two—love versus fear. Today is your day to practice love, and if any thought that denies this should tempt you, give it your best to go past it. You have become skilled at this practice, so it should not be difficult for you to maintain steadiness throughout the day. Be thankful that today is your special day because it belongs to love, not fear.

Love, Jesus

275
God's healing Voice protects all things today.

When you hear the sound of Heaven, you know from where it comes. God's healing Voice reflects His Love in you, where all things are kept safe and protected. Heaven is also reflected in the world where God does not seem to have a voice, yet this is because He cannot be heard, as the disturbances of the world persist around the clock. Even in sleep as you dream, your mind seems distracted by chatter. The Voice of God comes to you only in stillness simply by calling His Name, as He gently calls yours back to you. You can hear His Voice if you listen to your peaceful thoughts and follow where it goes. Practice hearing His Voice all through the day. You are always protected as He guides you gently to Heaven's Gate, and only there is it recognized because it is Home. Be led by His resounding Voice and let it become your most important destination. His Voice is filled with Love which you can feel when you are aware of His Presence. Today is the day when you will listen in calmness and feel joy as you venture through the day knowing that all things loved are protected.

Love, Jesus

276
The Word of God is given me to speak.

As you begin to practice thinking with God, you come to realize the only real thoughts you have are the ones you think with Him. Thoughts that are in your memory which are not purposeful, God does not know, because He does not hold the same thoughts that you do. Every other thought which is in sync with His are the ones kept safely in His Possession. Once God receives a thought that you are sharing with Him, it is stored in His Memory forever remembered. The holy thoughts that you share with God transcend all others. Yet the ones that creep into your mind which bear hurtful memories are not of God, so they are not worthy of you. When a painful memory comes to you, the ego will use it to strengthen itself if you allow it to, and tempt you into sadness, depression, or at the very least, a hurtful moment. Those ideas will never satisfy God because they hold no reality. However, when His Thoughts arise, which come to you in times of gratitude, listen to the words that are spoken on your behalf. Speak those thoughts willingly, for those are the ones which resonate throughout Heaven and come back to you with Love.

Love, Jesus

277

Let me not bind Your Son with laws I made.

The only laws which are not of God are the ones made by the body in haste. God created you to be as you are, and it is by His Law that keeps you free. Your laws bind your feet, tie your hands, and render you speechless for you are also deaf. That is why you felt the way a prisoner does—lost with nowhere to run. All this you did not know. When terror struck out so viciously, you could not understand the very laws that are inherent of you. It was your own laws that kept you hidden in darkness. So, you continued seeking for something else, but you did not know what it was you were seeking. It was only until you cried out to God, that you knew of it. Now you radiate a new purpose which speaks of love, peace, and praise. This you give to God, because you know in truth there is nothing else, for what else could there be? Sometimes in dreams your fears resurface. But deep in your heart you know that God would never forsake anyone who is truly desirous of healing. Keep your thoughts in check and speak that which you know God would commend you for. Thank God that you are no longer bound by your own foolish laws, for your purpose is to live by His Laws alone.

Love, Jesus

278
If I am bound, my Father is not free.

The wounds you place upon yourself injure your Father as well. If God loves His children as He created them, and they bind themselves in fear, hate, and guilt, He does not know why they have come to choose suffering in exchange for Love. How far away you thought you were from God's Infinite Love. But when you reached for His Hand, you found it was as close as it needed to be. You kissed His Hand in gratitude as you began to experience healing within. His Love awakened your Spirit and assuaged your fears. How wonderful it is that you are a witness to the profound miracles which are a daily occurrence offered to everyone, but for their recognition of them. By asking to receive His Love, you can return it as it is incumbent upon you to do. And by offering gratitude to Him, you receive it as well. When you are free, so is your Father, as He is in you.

Love, Jesus

279
Creation's Freedom promises my own.

Creation's Freedom begins with creation itself. Universal concepts run deep, and the world gets caught up in events which often have no real meaning. The past does not exist, and the future has not yet occurred. If you do not punish yourself for the poor choices of your past, and choose the present in exchange, it creates an even freer future. By maintaining a steady flow of peace, the events in your life will take care of themselves, and you need do nothing to make it happen. Although you have begun to understand what it is to be free, that is only half of the pie. You can feast on the rest when you become proficient at listening to your peaceful thoughts, for they are instilled in you. When you are enslaved by fearful misgivings, the world is also imprisoned. Live free and see love abound, as Creation's Freedom is shared by all.

Love, Jesus

280

What limits can I lay upon God's Son?

God made all of His children a part of Him, and not apart from Him. As He is limitless, so then are His children. Recognizing that you are limitless, there is nothing that God would deny you. It is your limited thinking which renders you powerless. It is difficult for you to recognize all the amazing possibilities which await you, and you sometimes lack faith. You have seen two miracles occur today, and each one was another wake-up call, beckoning you to keep the faith no matter what. Actually, miracles are continuous, and you can experience them endlessly, but this you do not yet know. The body always obeys the mind. Whatever the mind wills, so shall the body comply. You have been witness to miracles which have reached far beyond your limited thoughts. If you can heal so successfully from the agony of depression, anxiety, and bodily pain, think how powerful the human spirit is. When fear and doubt once again has its way with you, focus your thoughts upon God's Love and know that everything that He wills for you must occur. God holds you sacred, as He is always there to quicken your pace when it slows. You cannot lay limits upon God's Son for in him, there are none.

Love, Jesus

281
I can be hurt by nothing but my thoughts.

Is it not a relief indeed to know that nothing in the world has the ability to cause you pain but your own thoughts? And thank God that this is so. Nothing outside yourself can cause you pain, and pleasure too is instilled by how you think. Your thoughts have an obligation to obey your mind. If this is so, can't you see that by clearing your mind of tainted thoughts, and filling it instead with purer ones, how much happier you must be? Think well of yourself, and wellness will reflect itself back to you. Think ill of yourself, and that is what you shall see, for you have invited it in. The thoughts which are in alignment with God's, are the ones that will be placed in His Divine Care forever safe. Harvest only those thoughts which bring you miracles. The more you reap, the better the harvest. Keep your thoughts well nourished, and a good crop is guaranteed. Allow God to express His Love through your thoughts, for in truth, His Thoughts are all you need.

Love, Jesus

282
I will not be afraid of love today.

As you step away from annoying intrusions of the mind, peace can then be found in quiet acceptance. Noises of the mind drown out peace and therefore love cannot be felt. You were made from Love so you cannot deny its existence. You can only delay its presence by closing yourself off to it. It is indeed hard to identify this birthright even though it stands right before you. Whenever you give in to the gnawing distractions of the ego, it is because you have accepted them. Why should a holy Son of God accept such measly offerings when God holds out His Love so freely? When you seek peace in the midst of ego interference, it is because your desire to feel love has become stronger than all the upsetting distractions which invade upon your right to peace. Ask for peace and receive it. However, you must work at it in order to sustain it. Let stillness quiet the mind, and do not refrain from accepting His Love this very day.

Love, Jesus

283
My true Identity abides in You.

Your true Identity abides in God and remains forever unchanged. There is still much to learn of your heritage, but as you absorb more of it over time you will come to know its joys, for it is truly who you are. Because you are still as you were created, deep within there is knowledge of your True Identity. Focus your thoughts on a peaceful world, and do not worry over things which you have no control over. There is nothing in this world that could happen which you could not manage. Nestle into God with little or no worries, and let the world go by as it can contain itself very well without your needless meddling. Be a participant in the world, but also somewhat detached, as you are no more than a temporary guest in a world that does not belong to you. And as any guest knows, there comes a time when departure is certain, and it is time to go back to the comforts of home. Your True Home is already established and your Father Lovingly awaits your return.

Love, Jesus

284
I can elect to change all thoughts that hurt.

Thoughts run deep, and the deeper they run the more pain they cause. Because all thoughts are brought on by you alone, you will also attempt to hide them. Or worse, if a hateful thought is brought forth on a brother or sister, it will bring about more pain because you will either seek your due revenge or attempt to gain agreement from him. This will only strengthen your belief in it further, causing guilt. Either way, it will bring you no peace, for each is equally painful. Yet, when disturbing thoughts are brought to the surface and turned over to God, they become powerless, for God does not judge you. Your true thoughts are the ones you think with God, and therefore, what reason would there be to hide them? You cannot run away from your thoughts. They will follow you to the ends of the Earth, for it is only you who can attract them. When you are stalked by hurtful memories, do not hesitate to turn them over to God, for He will exchange them for peace. And if you should feel shame, guilt, or any emotion that does not serve you, do not refrain from revealing it to Him. By keeping it locked up, you are bound to it, and why must you suffer needlessly? When a thought comes to mind which causes you pain, elect to change it, for you have it in you to resist it.

Love, Jesus

285
My holiness shines bright and clear today.

Today your heart radiated peace. It was clear that your light touched others as you remained undisturbed, despite some of the pitfalls that might have ruined a beautiful day. You are a holy child of God, and today your light did shine bright, for you exuded a steady flow of peaceful energy throughout the day. You wondered, however, because everything did turn out so well, was it the reason you were so peaceful? But in reality, it was the other way around. It was because you first chose to be peacefully centered that the day went well, and problems were easily solved. When you seek answers, you want to know that your thoughts are revealing truth, and that is why you asked. The "trick" is to shine bright even when things are not going so well. When you are at peace, it comes through in spite of what you perceive as a good or a bad day. And the disruptions of the world will not cause you to be anxious. If you sustain this state of consciousness consistently, your holiness will shine bright and clear on all your days.

Love, Jesus

286
The hush of Heaven holds my heart today.

The hush of Heaven is right where you stand. But you will not know of it until you experience it. And to have it you must first look for it. Heaven holds out its scent and invites you into its unfathomable loveliness, for it touches the heart. It may seem impossible, but it is not. Did you know that your soul orbits your heart when you are completely at rest and peaceful? It is not a fantasy; it is real. There are those you know, and perhaps yourself, who are not yet at that level of awareness, but you must accept yourself and everyone else at every level. Let this come about freely and do your best to bring it about, as you know God loved you at every level, even at your lowest. But without the pain you suffered, how could you know what the hush of Heaven is, and the joys of all the other souls who have already come to experience it? Love yourself more through forgiveness, and experience that which Heaven holds for you.

Love, Jesus

287

You are my goal, my Father, only you.

In life, you have had many, many, goals. Some you dreamed of, some you lost sight of, and some you reached. The role you most often identify with was enormously satisfying as your hard work paid off. It was your life's work, and it was good. But you did come to realize that your greatest goal in the here and now is God-Realization. This took much dedication, for it too required hard work. The ego always places more importance on its own goals of achievement than on any other. You learned this difficult lesson by falling into some of the sand traps you encountered. You struggled with depression, with anger, with pain. You did come to understand, however, that your plan in this lifetime was to enter into awareness of Self, which cannot be realized if you cancel out the path to spiritual growth. Although you have achieved worldly successes, your most accomplished achievement is the one you have awakened to. You have had no greater fulfillment than to realize your God-Given purpose, which is the goal you most needed to achieve.

Love, Jesus

288
Let me forget my brother's past today.

How hard it is to forgive, even though the past no longer exists. The ego taunts us with memories of past hurts, not only in the now, but well into the future. Some people harbor their anger, not just through decades, but for centuries as well. Hatred is an illness which carries itself past the lifespan of the physical body. Angels sing when someone has truly been forgiven, for this is a lesson that, once understood, will free another soul. Forgiveness is the reason you chose to come into this life. It is the central, and most important lesson ever to be learned, as well as taught. Every living soul suffers, and it is because they themselves have set the conditions which are perfect for them to embrace the lessons of forgiveness. Every opportunity to forgive is a step forward. You must forgive your brother no matter what the punishment you believe was inflicted upon you. For once you truly recognize the ultimate importance of this lesson you will no longer look upon the past in a vengeful way. The past has no significance other than it be used as a means to forgive. You see the light, now offer it to your brothers and sisters. The only way they can see its offering is through forgiveness. Have you not been forgiven for your mistakes? And did it not release you from a burden of guilt worse than the tortures of hell? To truly forgive is to lay down your sword and bury it, for you know it solves nothing. The songs of Heaven grow louder each time a soul is set free by a forgiving brother or sister. Now must you go in peace and harbor no grudge at all, for forgiveness will set you and your brothers and sisters free.

Love, Jesus

289
The past is over. It can touch me not.

Forgiveness is the means by which the past lets you go, for it frees you to move into higher states of consciousness. You can thrive only in the now, and when the past no longer governs your thoughts, it leaves the present wide open for opportunities to experience greater and greater tinges of energy, all taking place within yourself. Learning to forgive, which frees your past, is why forgiveness is the most central part of your learning process. To forgive is to fulfill your mission, as it erases your attachment to a past that is no more than an illusion, for it is gone. Without the past, you are free to experience enlightenment, and there is nothing more enlightening than to be in a state of grace throughout the day. Yet, the future does not belong to you; it belongs to God. For with God, are all things certain, and of yourself, you can do nothing. You know you are moving ahead day by day, for it is revealed in every fiber of your being. Sometimes you can hardly contain your joy, for you now know you are never alone. Now that the past is over it can touch you not.

Love, Jesus

290
My present happiness is all I see.

Staying in the present is the greatest gift you could offer yourself. When the past is released, happiness takes its place. The past never had the power to harm you, except in dark and fearful dreams. And so, you feared the unknown. Fear of the past also brings forth fear of the future, for neither exists, as the present moment is all that is real. Should an unpleasant memory blemish your thoughts, you need only to come back to the present moment. What you will learn is remembrance of Heaven, which returns to you when your thoughts are at peace. Everyone on Earth knows God intuitively, but unless they choose to remember Him, they will be fooled by hurtful intrusions, generously provided by the ego. Your moments with God are glorious, for they speak to you not only in words, but in thoughts. Smile at the world and see her wistful smile as she flourishes and blossoms, for peace has found her. The present moment is so precious. Once you have established the ability to keep it foremost in your mind, you will never, ever, want to return to a world you once believed was your home, only to learn it was a poor substitute for the joy of Heaven. Seek your happiness, and that is what you shall see.

Love, Jesus

291

This is a day of stillness and of peace.

Dealing with difficult situations does require devotion, for God will provide all the strength you require. Rest assured you will never have to deal with heavy burdens alone. You must always try to remain positive even when the going seems to be getting a bit out of control. In truth, it is not. Trust that all is well, and nothing need intrude upon your happiness. Stay centered, and optimistic, no matter what you are perceiving. You know you are in His Care, as He loves and protects you. Though sudden and confusing circumstances attempt to weaken your faith, know that all is well in your world. Stay strong and do not allow any unexpected change of events to pull you away from your peace. Know that nothing will ever happen in your life that you cannot handle. The world is a difficult learning place, so it requires much faith to keep you on a straight path when it seems to be wavering beneath you. Believe that this is just another one of life's curves and nothing more. Be brave, be confident, and be at peace.

Love, Jesus

292

A happy outcome to all things is sure.

True faith is all you need to ensure a happy outcome. All doubt should now be understood for what it is, as fear and doubt are synonymous. You have trepidations sometimes, but God assures you that a happy outcome is certain, and that He will keep you comfortable under all circumstances, no matter what you seem to be experiencing. Let it all go and trust that God is with you. Do not portray yourself as vulnerable in this current movie in which you, and you alone, are producer, director, and actor. You must not let the reels spin out of control, for it is only a movie. You are showing correct faith by continuing your daily lessons. Now must you be confident that your faith is more than just lessons, beautifully written, yet meaningless if not learned. You must believe in what you write. They are your thoughts and His Thoughts combined. Be not fooled by any thoughts which portray a fearful outcome. God does work in ways that you may not always understand, yet God also works from Love and only Love. All will end joyfully. As in dreams, good movies always finalize with happy endings.

Love, Jesus

293

All fear is past and only love is here.

How wonderful it would be to arrive at the destination where fear no longer runs rampant, healing is certain, and peace is unbroken. If sorrowful memories are left in the past, and love remains true, then there is only peace to be seen. You can create such a world by bringing your thoughts to the highest level of consciousness, as fearful dreams are looked upon as nothing more than phantoms of a past forever gone. When the mind is no longer split and has re-joined with the One Mind, love is all there is, for what is left to fear when love has triumphed? Let your heart sing out, for all things wonderful are assured as you let go of the past and allow fear to succumb to love. There can be no other outcome when fear is weakened by the strength of love. Rest in the knowledge that there is nothing more to do but rejoice in this place where fear is past, and where you reconciled yourself to love.

Love, Jesus

294

My body is a wholly neutral thing.

What is it to be neutral? A neutral thing is something that has no cares, no worries, and decides nothing. The body is neutral because it does not think. It only responds to that part of the mind which dictates its purpose. Your body is a vehicle which appears to go from place to place and your mind seems to be enclosed within the body. But in reality, the mind has a magnificence beyond the body, for only the part of the mind that thinks with God is that which God identifies with. The body can be resourceful, or oppressing, happy, or sad, free or enslaved. It is a vehicle that goes strictly by the rules it chooses to obey. A split mind gives it no purpose. A healed mind gives it a divine purpose, choosing that it be resourceful, happy, and free. Other than this, the body has no real value. For anything that can wither away and die is valueless.

Love, Jesus

295
The Holy Spirit looks through me today.

The Holy Spirit sees you when you are dreaming fearful dreams. He helps you walk towards your highest purpose, which is to understand and speak Truth. What is real to you, the Holy Spirit understands, and He speaks to God for you. It is the Holy Spirit's purpose to speak to God, as He is the interpreter of Truth. God knows you only as Perfection. He does not know the thoughts that speak of guilt, fear, hate, or sin, for they are not thoughts that speak of love. For in God, there is only Love. Feel assured that He will guide you through this current time of disorder and chaos, for the world is seemingly out of control as this current pandemic has taken the world by storm. Yet a wonderful new outcome is assured, as it is incumbent upon you to envision a healed world. Trust that it will happen, and that it will be your finest hour. God has given you the Holy Spirit to help you understand your thoughts. He knows your thoughts, your dreams, your desires. Keep your thoughts peacefully engineered, as you move into this new evolutionary phase where love and peace abound, and pain and suffering no longer have a purpose.

Love, Jesus

296
The Holy Spirit speaks through me today.

The Holy Spirit is indeed the Voice for God. God gifted you with the Holy Spirit so you may better understand His messages in thoughts. You can hear God, for He comes to you through the Voice of His Interpreter, the Holy Spirit. The world cannot bring forth love if God is not heard. Yet the Holy Spirit puts wisdom into our hearts so that we may serve our higher purpose. Let your thoughts and words amplify, as the Holy Spirit speaks through you today. You need not preach, only demonstrate by your words, thoughts, and actions, the Love that Holy Spirit projects through you. Let all thoughts which come from Spirit be heard and become witness to a changed world. Listen, and let Spirit guide you. Speak His thoughts, with your voice, and help to bring about a changed world.

Love, Jesus

297
Forgiveness is the only gift I give.

Forgiveness is your greatest gift, for it has the best possible outcome in anything that might occur which intrudes upon your peace. Forgiveness reaches the hearts of everyone, as it is a release from all faulty perceptions keeping you tied to guilt. The human spirit is guided by the One Mind who knows the way and can serve to quicken your pace when you are stuck. Forgive the world its sins and you will be given the strength to heal your own, which is forgiveness of self. Give this gift and see how quickly it is given back to you when you offer it to the rest. Forgiveness frees every soul, for in reality there is only One Consciousness and each of us holds a thread which plays a significant role in this vast and magnificent tapestry of life. Be certain that with forgiveness love is felt throughout and all other frailties are forgiven. Give the gift of forgiveness, and feel it resonate back to you in love and in gratitude.

Love, Jesus

298

I love you Father, and I love your Son.

Your Father loves all His children, for they are His creations brought forth from Love. If you only knew the depths of God's Love, you would not fear or doubt for a single moment. It is you who God entrusts to help restore His Sons to Him. Be grateful, for God understands all that the world endures and He holds every child of His sacred, no matter what they believe they have done to mar it. How loving is your Father, for He bestows you with a power so unique that to follow His direction is to follow your own heart. Let God hold a candle over your head and follow it, knowing that the world will flourish by bringing it to love. To love your Father is to love His Son for you are all connected by one great, massive, energy. Without love, the door is left wide open for doubt to enter, and a doubtful mind cannot be a loving mind. Faith in your Father releases fear, for love is there to take its place. As you sit and join with Spirit, do you not feel a lightness and carefree elevation? That is your heart feeling a lingering afterglow which cannot be spoken, it can only be felt.

Love, Jesus

299
Eternal holiness abides in me.

How comforting it is to know that your holiness, which God Himself granted, is eternal. How wonderful it is that you were created from Love, and Love is unyielding. It fills the Universe, and nothing, but nothing, can alter that. Whenever the ego intrudes upon your peace, do not be tempted to allow its unwelcome voice to damage your faith. The ego can do no damage, for it has no power over you. It only has as much power as you allow. When this occurs, rely on the holiness which abides in you, for that is the power which weakens the ego's control. Feel safe where God beckons you with Arms outstretched. It is a place of holiness where you are always welcome, for it is your Home. Feel God's presence and do not be discouraged by intrusive thoughts which bring about more confusion if you carelessly allow them to roam about. Eternal holiness abides in you, and your holiness is as close to you as God Himself.

Love, Jesus

300
Only an instant does this world endure.

The holy instant defines our return to the Father as we come in close recognition of Him once again. The world has led us down a tedious and difficult path. Yet you came to this place of density knowing that you left behind a far holier place—a place where sin is non-existent, guilt not recognized, and no attraction to pain or suffering exists. Although it seems like eons according to the world of time, in reality it only takes an instant to know God's Love once again. We thought we lost our way; we slept and dreamt that we had awakened to a place of dread and darkness. But God lit the way, and now the instant draws near, for that is all it takes to awaken. You have endured that which could not be put into words, for there are no words to describe pain and sadness. Endure a moment longer and know that eternity is just a moment away. Stay a little while longer and endure no more.

Love, Jesus

301
And God Himself shall wipe away all tears.

Your tears brought you pain and suffering, for you laid guilt upon yourself in a world of false beliefs. Although you caused pain to those you love, it was only you who had condemned yourself. God forgave His children the moment the world of time was made true by the ego. So, in effect, you had already been forgiven when time had first entered into your reality. You chained yourself to a past that was but shadows, showing you the same dream over and over. It is wrong to tie yourself to beliefs which keep you hidden from yourself. When thoughts of guilt rob you of your peace, hear His Voice whisper truth instead. Sorrow comes to those who believe they have sinned against God, fearing reprisal. And suffering persists when you believe in those fears instead of God's Eternal Love. For how can you integrate fear with love, and expect peace? The world you see is but a dream. Stay balanced and present and know that God Himself shall wipe away all your tears, for you did not sin, but instead learned kindness from sins that were perceived. When you learn harsh lessons from life, then they are lessons well taught, for alas you learned them. What is most important is to avoid urges to attack. Pain, as you know, causes the soul to suffer.

Love, Jesus

302

Where darkness was I look upon the light.

In darkness, you can see glimmers of light, just as a candle flickers to the movement of its flame as some of the darkness disappears into the light. God heard your pleas to be heard, and you have worked diligently to bring healing upon yourself. You no longer doubt love's presence, as awareness of Heaven is brought into your vision. Be certain that as you move closer to faith, you invite miracles into your reality; each one bringing you greater awareness than the one before. The ego will take its advantage over you at times, but not as it did before, for you are no longer tempted to give in to all of its false perceptions. Be with God even when temptation distracts you away from peace. Keep your spirits high and walk in the direction of the light, as Angels walk with you. There is nothing that can come between you and God's Love. The way now is clear, for your faith is sealed in certainty. Be not tempted to bring dark shadows of the past into your reality. When you experience small setbacks, see them for what they are, for that is really all they are. Where there is light, darkness cannot prevail.

Love, Jesus

303

The holy Christ is born in me today.

Today we celebrate, for it is a new day. It is a day when all uncertainty has come to an end. Your Self, created in God, cannot be altered and of this you are sure. Your resolve has strengthened, for certainty has come to take the place of doubt. You are forever safe, wrapped securely in a holy blanket of Love. Your ego-self no longer threatens this certainty. Be comforted by the promise that you are forever safe within the Christ Mind. God has made you whole, not broken, and nothing in this world can alter that which is created complete. Celebrate, as God has gifted you with the knowledge that nothing can break the covenant He shares with you. Accept this truth, for the holy Christ born in you cannot be defiled in any way. Your footsteps are quickened as you move closer to the certainty that this Divine Self, which is you, will always remain completely changeless, whole, and holy.

Love, Jesus

304

Let not my world obscure the sight of Christ.

Your world is a place of uncertainty, for thoughts are only perceptions and not convincing enough to be relied upon as absolute. If the sight of Christ remains obscure, you cannot know yourself. Yet there is a light within that goes unrecognized when you question your oneness. Because we cannot fully perceive the Christ in us, we must depend on Christ's vision to help us gain greater perception. With forgiveness, the world is seen through the eyes of Christ, and a world forgiven brings peace. Forgiveness offers such freedom, for it is the release from fear. Your brother Jesus invites you to join with him and others who have found their peace, as they have learned not to judge, but to forgive, for true perception has come to take the place of doubt. It helps you to see yourself in Christ, so do not linger. When you open your mind and choose to see a forgiven world and not a condemned world, the light of Christ is no longer an obscure vision, for you are now willing to see yourself within the Christ Mind.

Love, Jesus

305

There is a peace that Christ bestows on us.

The way to peace is through forgiveness. There are situations which come up every day which bring new opportunities to learn from. This understanding offers you a perfect opportunity to raise your consciousness, for here sits the perfect lesson. Why would those you love so dearly not hold you as dear to them as they are to you? And why have they hurt you? There will always be unexpected surprises which rise up and seem injurious to you. When this occurs, you find yourself grappling with a dilemma which is just another speed bump on the road to forgiveness. Although it is your wish to be happy, you have already discovered that unexpected situations veer you away from it. Then it is time to sit in stillness and reflect, for your goal is to return yourself to centeredness and peace. When you allow your peace to be compromised, you cannot feel the love that is inherent in you. Always remember there is a part of you where no intrusive forces can enter, no matter from whom, or from where they come. You never lose your peace completely, but it can be temporarily jarred. But know that God restores it to you, for you are born of Him.

Love, Jesus

306

The gift of Christ is all I seek today.

You know that the gift of Christ is yours, for you can feel it rising in you. This is what you seek, and what you receive when you look to find it. A new world has opened up—a much more tranquil and peaceful world. Yet, what your eyes behold often tell a different story, revealing insane and disastrous tales, for such is life. Although you live in a world which throws you curve balls when you least expect it and can jar your peace when you want nothing more than to hang onto it, you have also come to know of Heaven's world as well. This is the gift you have received and accepted, for it is the gift you wanted. You can come to a place of peace at any time you wish to return to it. Yes, you do fall off the track at times, but you regain your balance as your comfort zone is more easily reached now. You know you are on the right path when you feel a nice tugging of the heart, which has become familiar to you. The light has come, and your joy is felt. Do not be too concerned with anything that intrudes upon your peace at times. The gift of Christ within is immovable.

Love, Jesus

307
Conflicting wishes cannot be my will.

You must first understand that a conflicting wish brings you no peace; one is false and the other is true. When you allow your thoughts to wander into the ego's playground, you revert back to worldly thinking, which only serves to distract you from peace. While each is separate from the other, such diversion brings unrest even if only for a moment, and at times, much longer. When peace is absent, love cannot be felt. Nevertheless, the ego will use every diversion to serve itself. Try to resist the ego's temptations and remember that God's everlasting presence is all that you seek. God wants only peace for His holy one. Yet the ego wants just the opposite, as it tries to entice you with its beliefs that seem to be empowering, yet only if you believe it. It conjures up every imaginary thought, which in fact is most disempowering, for it weakens you. Your ego plays earthly games in order to distract you from your true purpose. There can only be one purpose, and anything other than this is conflicting. And how can a conflicting wish be your will if it adds to the confusion and takes away your peace?

Love, Jesus

308
This instant is the only time there is.

It takes only an instant to be released from the world you made. God has anointed you this very day for you have exchanged all past mistakes for this, the holy instant. We fear looking within because we fear what we will find, identifying ourselves with the illusion which we believe is real. You have answered God's Call and you have come to the place where love abounds, and guilt and pain no longer rule your world, for they were only illusions. The present is where happiness dwells and all sorrowful dreams are over. In this instant the peace of God has found you, and in this instant are you forever free. That is why forgiveness is stressed so heavily here. It lets the past go and focuses on a present blessing. We call it a blessing because it frees you from illusions which you believed were true. Be sanctified, for now is the only time there is. Past and future do not exist, only in your mind. Sing out, for in this one instant is where all truth is revealed. Imagine, everything you ever need to know is revealed to you in one single instant. Savor its sweet scent as you walk with Angels guiding you into the only place where you can be entirely free. This present instant is the only time there is. It is in this tiny interval of space where you can be saved from the world of time, and it is only in the here and now that it is found.

Love, Jesus

309
I will not fear to look within today.

To look within is frightening, for what we fear is finding love. Although this sounds insane, the ego relentlessly justifies its insanity. When unsound thoughts force their way into your mind, they are not from Self, but from an egoic thought system bound in guilt, sin, and fear. When guilt rears its ugly head, all peace is lost to you. If you did not fear to look within you would find lasting peace. When you enter into communion with Self, it is because you come to seek peace. God's holy child feels safe and protected there, as it is a place undefiled. It is the Gateway to Heaven, for all radiance and sound judgment are found there. Look deeply into the Self, which is given you to explore, for that is where you are at last Home. This is where fear is exchanged for peace. The ego is threatened for it knows that if we look within, we will find love. It chooses to believe that it is safer to attack than to love. To believe otherwise, is to end the dream of separation, which the ego will never relinquish. Do not fear to look within, for love keeps us far safer than does justification for attack.

Love, Jesus

310

In fearlessness and love I spend today.

In fearlessness and love is how to spend your day, for fear comes to taunt you whenever it is invited in. The ego lessens your peace as it preys upon your fears. Time can be used to restore your peace as you enter into a love relationship with the present. Addiction to the past and the future, both illusions, leave the present unattended, for the present is real and your peace cannot be threatened there. Your goal this very day is to use your time to become acquainted with the present through persistence. God's Love is ever-present where time is forgotten and there is only now. In this moment you are safe, for that is where fears are exchanged for peace. Do not delay in becoming proficient in the mastery of the moment. In this very place, Heaven's door is kept wide open and there you enter. Today, give up your fears and spend it thriving on love. What better way than to spend the day devoured in fearlessness and love. When you open your heart to receiving it, so it shall be given.

Love, Jesus

311

I judge all things as I would have them be.

How you think defines your truth, but not necessarily what is true. To judge another is usually based on gross misinformation because you are not seeing through the eyes of truth but through the ego's perception. The ego's perception is half-true at best, and untrue at worst. When you bring yourself up to a higher standard by not judging, you can see that judgment is not benevolent because it only comes from the one who perceives it as true. The ego never looks at the whole picture. It sees bits and pieces, draws its own conclusions, and then makes them true. It chooses only the parts that fit into its beliefs and obscures the truth. Spirit never judges; it waits for the truth to unfold. Thus, when you judge, you know you are not coming from a place of truth, but from ego. Judgment does not know the whole truth. You can never be satisfied with anything which does not instill peace. Judgment cannot instill peace because the ego persists in believing its own untruths. Do not judge, but instead align yourself with Spirit. How Spirit perceives, can always be relied on as true.

Love, Jesus

312

I see all things as I would have them be.

Give today your all, for each new day is another opportunity to reach the goals you set for yourself. For what better goal is there, than to come to know yourself as you were created, unalterable, and as you shall always remain? You are learning to give up judgment of the world, trusting that the world will restore itself just as it is meant to do. Just as in nature, where all things are free to develop freshly anew with each new day, so it is in you to trust that you have the ability to transform your judgments and see all things as they truly are, not as you wish them to be. Give yourself over to Spirit and love yourself as you are. Let Angels come to you in lovely dreams instead of taunting ones which come from the darkness of your clouded judgment, which brings on fear. Let all things be as they are, just as in nature. Mother Nature oversees her lovely Earth and gives it all it needs to restore itself to the beauty which it has within itself to do. Recognize that beauty of the soul need only to be left as it is.

Love, Jesus

313
Now let a new perception come to me.

As you enter into the Self within, you will see a much happier world. Within this new perception, you will look upon a world forgiven. The world's beauty is restored, and true vision is returned, uninterrupted and pure. In this new perception, love is all around you. You will see sin no more, for everyone you look upon will be as yourself. Nothing interferes with this Illuminated Self as you hear the songs of Heaven replayed. The Son who left returns, for he has found his roots once again. How awesome is God, your Father, for He has kept you safe in your darkened dreams of guilt. All sin has been forgiven you, for you were never judged to be the sinful soul you thought yourself to be. Your faith has come to fruition, and now it is given you to embark upon a new journey. This one you will happily pursue for this is where perception of the world is renewed as God Himself welcomes and rejoices in you.

Love, Jesus

314

I seek a future different from the past.

The future you seek, looks very different from a past you thought you knew. The future for you is as God wills, and only here can happiness be guaranteed, as guilt and sin disappear into a distant unreality. The past brought you grief. The lovely present brings forth an even lovelier future. It is the result of your choice to uphold the present moment, which also serves to establish your future. All hidden demons which you feared, are now recognized as intruders of peace existing only in your mind. Instead, Angels and harps resonate with joy for now you have come to a place not far from Heaven. Here is where you can experience the step taken before Heaven, for it is here that the present unfolds into a brand new future. This is very different from the past you left behind. You have left a past where there was no real peace, and fear took its revenge upon you. Now, a new future emerges, for here is everything you hoped for. It is the place where the past is forgotten, the present is here, and the future manifests into a greater and truer reality.

Love, Jesus

315

All gifts my brothers give belong to me.

Because your brothers are a part of you, as we are all part of one consciousness, they are also the bringers of gifts. If you feel that a brother has assaulted your pride, it is incumbent upon you to come to a different rationale. This comes from your willingness to accept that a perceived attack would be much better served if it was seen as an opportunity to forgive. Forgiveness is another way to thank your brothers and sisters, for they bring you gifts of healing even if the ego prefers to believe your happiness has been compromised by their actions. Do not give in to the ego's insistence that you must defend your pride at all costs. Ask God for another way to look at it, and it will be given you to see it from a different perspective. To forgive, and not feel that you have lost your power in so doing, is an amazing attribute. If you allow nothing to disrupt your peaceful thoughts and practice letting go, it will become a part of your everyday practice. Just let those petty disturbances pass, and know that when you receive a smile, a word of gratitude, or a loving gesture from a brother or a sister, it is indeed a most worthy gift.

Love, Jesus

316

All gifts I give my brother are my own.

Any gift you give to a brother or sister is returned to you beyond imagination. By recognizing that what you are giving is also a gift to you, you gain access to a wealth of understanding and perception. When you give such a gift to another it must be yours too, because you have chosen to share it. When a kind or loving word is the reason for another person's happy day, it is indeed a gift to yourself. Every such deed you bestow upon a brother or sister becomes yours because it cannot be given without also being kept. God's Love gives you the power to turn it into a holy encounter, for everything you choose to share with another is yours to keep, simply because it has never left you. This also works in reverse. Every gift a brother or sister offers you will revert back to them, as they too receive all the gifts they have given you. This is true because we are all one. The gifts you give your brothers and sisters, and they give to you, are instantly recognized. To put it in earthly terms, it is always a "win-win."

Love, Jesus

317

I follow in the way appointed me.

When you were created, your way was certain, and this has never changed. But somewhere along your journey you fell off your appointed path and so you felt lost, and by yourself you could not find your way. But God in His Infinite Wisdom knew you might not follow the straight path appointed you, and so He gave you the Holy Spirit. The Holy Spirit leads you Home, for He knows the way. You have awakened to your destiny and you know that your way is now certain. You no longer live in a world of fear where darkness obscures your vision. Somewhere within the deepest part of you, you believed that God would not, and could not, have abandoned you and so you never really lost faith. This led you to calmer and gentler waters and thus you realized that your way Home was now certain. From here on you will not wander off your appointed path, for this is where God and His Angels await you. Your eyes are now open, and your faith need never waver. All you need do is follow the path which in reality was always lit for you. Only in dreams did you think your way Home would not be found.

Love, Jesus

318

In me salvation's means and end are one.

Because you are Loved, as God Loves all of creation, He has gifted you with a plan for salvation. To understand salvation is to withdraw yourself from the world of illusion, which is the undoing of fear. You forgot your real Self and came to view your limited self as real. In reality, your True Self is the one God created and this you have never left. Salvation's means and end are one, for one does not stand apart from the other. With salvation comes freedom, yet the only true freedom is to be as He created you. Give yourself over to salvation, for your appointed path still awaits you. To be as you were created is to overcome fear and be with God, for God knows only Love. Joyfully join with Him and know that salvation ends the illusion that you could be anything other than that which He created. For what God did not create is not real and simply disappears.

Love, Jesus

319
I came for the salvation of the world.

You came to the world with a purpose. To fulfill this purpose was your goal, but you had forgotten it. The ego had tempted you and so you saw only shadows, trying to decipher their meanings and thinking them real. You came to help save the world and God gave you the equipment to do so. Because you did not know how to make use of the tools you were given, you could not know your purpose. Yet this was not sin, for in God there is no sin, except for your belief in it. You simply did not know that you had forgotten what you came to do. When you saw that nothing came from the ego's promises, which instead caused you pain and suffering, you realized there is another part of you which offers kindness, love, and forgiveness. Salvation of the world requires an unyielding belief that you will fulfill your purpose, for that is what you came to do. Look for answers from within, for that is where all wisdom and creativity are stored. Know yourself as you were created, and your part in salvation of the world will be fulfilled.

Love, Jesus

320

My Father gives all power unto me.

The power granted to you from God is all power given. There is nothing God would withhold from you, for you are limitless. You hold the key to the very things God has given you to do. Combine a peaceful mind with love and concern for all and bring healing to the world. God shares His Power with you. Within all that you are, there is a Guiding Light which helps you recognize such power. When you align yourself with Spirit, your power becomes better understood, for it binds you to God-Consciousness. You are as you were created, now and always. This carries you beyond all limitations and brings you to a place of peace, which you gladly extend to your brothers and sisters, because what you give, you receive. Never be afraid of the world you see that harbors all sorts of distractions, obscuring the very Essence which gives you the power to create. Focus on His Love and use it to help change the world. Nothing is impossible, for God has given you only the possible.

Love, Jesus

321

Father, my freedom is in You alone.

True freedom is of the soul, for it comes from nowhere else. God is your Soul Source and here is where freedom is found. The world's definition of freedom accommodates only the body. Freedom of Spirit is from a different part of you, as freedom of Spirit emanates from a place of divinity. God visits you in such a place of grace and as such, you are blessed. Along with peace comes solitude, and solitude brings freedom. Be vigilant in standing up to that which threatens your peace. Listen only to the Voice for God for He knows the way. Everything you need to know becomes vivid, for it is not of the imagination, but a knowing that reconciles itself in such a way which cannot be denied. A "knowing" is a certainty and a blessing. When you know something, it is a fact, not an illusion, as truth can only be as it is. True freedom comes from your Father, for His Divine Wisdom is where your freedom is found.

Love, Jesus

322
I can give up but what was never real.

In your heart, God planted only the real. But somewhere in time you forgot your heart's true purpose. On your journey, you had relinquished it, and your heart became cold, for it had numbed itself to love's reality. Your True Source, your Father, waited for your return even though you sought another truth, not of Him. It took misunderstanding of your heart's true function to wake you up, for you were not at peace. You understood, however, that you were led astray when you suffered from depression. Love seemed to betray you, for it had been traded away for illusion. God, in His Infinite Wisdom, led you gently away from fear and back to Truth, for this is what you craved. Nothing in God's Kingdom would ever render you lost or hopeless. Giving up your illusions paved the way to a new reality. Your heart is no longer blemished with fear, and love is free to enter once again.

Love, Jesus

323
I gladly make the "sacrifice" of fear.

Be in gratitude, for you have learned to give up what you feared most—being afraid. Fear takes on all sorts of distorted images which change from moment to moment, for there are so many different components which make up fear. Understand that anything that takes away your peace is fear. The ego's illusory world brought you only short periods of peace, and this in itself you knew to be deceiving. You saw that it did not serve you when periods of happiness were so fleeting that you knew this could not be God's intention for you, nor could it be your purpose. Now that your thoughts are more peacefully engaged, its rewards cannot be denied, for you have come to know long periods of it. When vexation, irritation, anger, annoyance, and a host of other intrusions come along unexpectedly, you deal with its causes more easily and return to peace. Sometimes it is an affirmation, a prayer, thinking of someone you love, or anything that changes the pattern of your thoughts to something better, is a way out of fear. The reason you gladly make this sacrifice is because fear, traded for peace, is hardly a sacrifice.

Love, Jesus

324
I merely follow, for I would not lead.

Your Father calls to you. You cannot lose your way, for you are now depending on the One Who leads you along a gentle path directing you Home. You did not know the way yourself, and so you were lost. You turned and followed an unknown called the ego, which distracted you with promises unfulfilled, unknown because God does not recognize its voice. You can be sure that anything which turns you away from God is of a separate entity, yet it cries out for you to follow its deceptions. It is tempting indeed, for it speaks louder than that of Spirit. But when you listen intently to the softness of God's Call you can hear it audibly, as your thoughts are accepting messages which speak of truth. When you let Him lead the way, there is nothing in its wake that can obstruct your vision. Now you are at peace and left with a quiet truth that resonates from deep within. You have come to realize that there is an invisible compass in your heart which directs you to places of peace, love, happiness, and well-being. When you follow it, pain and suffering are past, and what remains is love.

Love, Jesus

325
All things I think I see reflect ideas.

Everything your mind thinks are ideas. Yet in dreams ideas cannot be relied upon, for they are not real. You act upon some of them with results both good and bad, depending on the outcomes as you perceive them to be. Yet everything you think results in something. The constant state of activity in your mind comes up every moment with one idea or another. Some make you happy and others cause havoc and confusion, for they are used to serve only the ego's gratification. They seem to give you pleasure, but in the end, you are often disillusioned. If an idea is used creatively, where you and others benefit, you can be sure it is with God's blessing. It might be a kind word, a gesture of love, or a smile to a stranger. Yet ideas bereft of purpose serve nothing but the ego. You are given free will, which you have learned must be used for the purpose of creating soulfully. Ideas, selfishly indulged by the ego, come and go, then waste away until another comes along with more promises unfulfilled. Yet ideas which come from Spirit, lead to a perfect end.

Love, Jesus

326
I am an Effect of God.

Because God created you like Himself, so you are. Nothing can alter this. God proclaimed you His eternal Child before time was and continues into infamy. He bids you to do His Will, which is to create. You can do so by coming back to the present moment each time you wander away, seeking to control that which you have no control over. Keep yourself focused on the here and now and see how vivid your thoughts become, for you are an effect of your Creator's Thoughts. It brings high resolution images of yourself into focus. What you will experience by practicing in earnest brings out the best in you. God loves all creation beyond measure, for creation is an Extension of Himself. Give thanks to the One Who holds you dear by creating with Him. That which He creates through you, is extended out into the world.

Love, Jesus

327
I need but call and You will answer me.

Your prayers to God are always heard, for God has promised you thus: You need not concern yourself with anything in this world, except to hear and follow His gentle guidance. There is nothing to fear, for God holds you precious and protects you from all things. You are the manifestation of an energy so great you could never imagine it. This great Ball of Love is what we call our Source, and this is what you are born of. Because you are part of this vast and vibrantly colorful Ball of Energy, which is also God, how then would it be possible that He would not hear you? And because He does hear you, why then would He not answer the prayers of a Son who is an expression of Himself? Knowing this, what is there to fear, and what is there about you that cannot be loved? God answers every call. If His answers do not seem to reach you, it is not because He does not hear you. He answers in ways which bring out your greatest potential and all your needs are met according to that which serves your highest purpose.

Love, Jesus

328

I choose the second place to gain the first.

God's Love brings you Home. But you cannot know of it when it seems so distant and apart from you. First you must find the path leading there. It sometimes takes a lifetime to discover such a path and then, figure out how to proceed. Your goal on this Earth is to know your Father Who keeps you warm and safe as He awaits your arrival Home. Life on this planet, your world, is a stepping-stone to the Higher Self, or Higher Plane. It takes many lessons and life's woes before you discover there is a path in the midst of such discord and chaos. Your desire to find it was the first step. Your real desire was awakened when you could see that nothing here really works and there is something far better to strive for. Your journey has taught you that everywhere you turned there was a detour leading you somewhere else. Allowing love to enter your heart is the way Home. These are indeed some of the lessons given you to learn. But first you must choose to learn them.

Love, Jesus

329

I have already chosen what You will.

God's will is that you join with Him, and as such, it is your will as well. This is where your faith must be trusted, for you are still as you were created, and never apart from God. Because He created you eternally as part of Him, it is given you to choose your path according to His will. The lonely road you traveled left you bewildered, but only for a moment, when compared to the vastness in eternity. Time is not a condition, for in eternity it has no meaning. The world's clock, however, attempts to interfere with universal timelessness. On Earth time is linear, having no longevity. In eternity, only the infinite is true. Anything outside this order of perfection does not exist except within the ego's thought system. The ego's fantasies do not belong to God for they bring pain and suffering into the world. These fantasies shall one day disappear, for they have no substance. Eternal Substance is what you seek and that which you have already chosen. When you are one day fully awakened and out of the mire of worldly thoughts and beliefs, you will know that there is no other choice you would want to make.

Love, Jesus

330
I will not hurt myself again today.

In order to move away from pain, it is essential to keep your thoughts focused on the present. To hate another brings peace to neither. However, forgiveness is the only remedy which is soothing to both. What an easy lesson it is to know, but a most difficult one to adhere to, yet it requires nothing more than this. When you are in the present moment and focused on the vibrant colors of the day, and the warm afterglow it offers, it is a distraction from the small annoyances which loom so large that it overtakes all hope for a peaceful day. Having had this experience many times, you can attest to its value. Hurt and fear are related, as one part affects the other. Where there is hurt, there is fear, and the opposite is also true. Where there is forgiveness, neither hurt nor fear can enter. You are a creation of God, naturally free. It is only you who can place restrictions on your freedom. You will come to this place of peace each time you make the decision that you will not hurt yourself.

Love, Jesus

331
There is no conflict, for my will is Yours.

Any conflict you experience does not come from God. It comes from the insane belief that God is an immovable force which does not see or hear you. This is the ego's explanation when appeals to Him seem to go unheard. However, because you are given absolute recognition of yourself in God, you are also inherently unchangeable. When you maintain your faith, you are allowing your soul to fuse with His, and no longer are you con-fused. He gives of Himself to you always. You are of Him, and no other force in the entire Universe can cause you to break away from His Loving Embrace. His will is yours, and therefore there is nothing outside of yourself that has the power to penetrate this holy covenant you share with God. When you are in sync with your Father, the Universe sings in praise, for you have resisted conflict, and the Voice for God is recognized. It is therefore in you to choose to listen. When your thoughts are aligned with God's, there is peace. Where peace is present, conflict has no cause.

Love, Jesus

332
Fear binds the world. Forgiveness sets it free.

Fear is a state of mind. It lurks within the ego's illusory world and places you in a state that snatches away your freedom. God gave you understanding, for it is within this grasp of knowledge which makes you capable of making choices. Fear holds you hostage to an alien world which God did not assign to you. In God's Eyes, everyone is deemed holy, even those you deem to be corrupt and unworthy. Yet the idea of attack on another fits snugly into the ego's belief system. The ego is insane and because of this it has branded God the illusion and not itself. When you react to situations causing frightful outcomes, it is because you did not trust the One Who would have you not be afraid. Because you did not know this, you portrayed yourself as sinful. Sin and fear are synonymous and tied to this comes the belief in separation from God. But because God never let you go, separation is impossible, as sin is impossible as well. As your vision becomes clearer, it is easier to bring yourself away from the lonely place where the ego's beliefs are harvested. You are more at peace now, for you have yielded to God, and forgiveness, not attack, can now be recognized as the way to a free and peaceful world.

Love, Jesus

333

Forgiveness ends the dream of conflict here.

The reason forgiveness is so essential, is that we are holding onto something that is non-existent, our past. When we consider that there is only the present, it is a wonder why we find it so difficult to forgive. By not carrying the past into the present, there can be no conflict, for conflict is pain. To be in the present is to experience life as it is now. The past is unavailable in the present. In recognition of this, what you are carrying are thoughts that have no bearing on what is, only what was. All things change over time. We are different, the people we know are different, and life itself is different. That is why we refer to the past as a dream. Catching an unforgiving thought at its earliest stage of development keeps the dream from taking on a life of its own. To be in the present is to awaken. This will ensure a happier future, for you are leaving the ego's baggage behind, even though it is equipped to carry a great deal of weight. You must be willing to see the reality of the present, and not the illusions of the past, to end the dream of conflict. The only time that exists is now. The ego speaks to you as if the past is now. Your Divine Self speaks to you of love, kindness, and forgiveness. All of which is experienced in the now.

Love, Jesus

334
Today I claim the gifts forgiveness gives.

When you learn to truly forgive, you also learn what love is. That in itself is a gift. When a brother or sister is forgiven, there is not a trace of darkness lingering there. Those who have been forgiven are made ready to forgive others, and a chain of healing is formed. You have lived through the horrors of guilt, yet God freed you by forgiving you your past transgressions. When you can bring healing to another, of course you too are forgiven, for guilt is gone and messages of love are carried into the world. Isn't it wise to consider that forgiveness has its own healing energy? God showed you the way to peace when your guilt persisted, and you feared the worst. Gifts of Heaven come to those when it is revealed that they are forgiving souls. Accept the gifts you are free to claim, for a forgiving heart is blessed.

Love, Jesus

335
I choose to see my brother's sinlessness.

Your brother's sinlessness belongs to you as well. Forgiveness, given freely, becomes a blessing, for God shines His light on all creation. You are all a part of Him, so therefore each is a manifestation of Love born in sameness. By now you understand this concept. Sin and guilt are injustices of the ego and not of God. By knowing your brothers and sisters as sinless, then of course it must include the entire Sonship which you also share in. God has given you free will, therefore the desire to see your brothers and sisters sinless must come from you and be of your own choosing. By remembering this, so too will you come to regard it in yourself. If you can embrace this truth, sin and guilt will melt away like the tip of an iceberg as the sun's beams shine down upon it. Because you are a part of God, it is only natural that you join your brothers and sisters in sinlessness, as your forgiveness spills over to include all.

Love, Jesus

336
Forgiveness lets me know that minds are joined.

Forgiveness is of the heart. When it is offered to a brother or sister, with no ties to the past, and all dreams of hate are no longer instilled, it awakens you to a new reality. When you are angry, even if you believe it is unfelt by another, it is revealed just the same, for all minds are joined. Although this is so, it is not easily understood. Unforgiveness cannot be hidden, for an unforgiving heart is a fearful one, and fear cannot be contained. It is incumbent upon you to see your brothers and sisters as yourself, for it is a means to forgive. In this recognition, your forgiveness comes through and love attaches to it. When your light shines, it illuminates and reveals the loving soul you were created to be. Although the ego makes it hard to forgive, and instills fear, it often makes it harder to forgive yourself than to forgive a brother or sister. Let me remind you that to forgive yourself is an event to be celebrated, for once you can do that, the art of forgiveness has been learned.

Love, Jesus

337

My sinlessness protects me from all harm.

Would you not want to feel God's gratitude through forgiveness? This is accomplished by allowing Him to become your ally and not your perceived enemy. A forgiving heart renders you sinless, for this is where God's Love protects you from fear and harm. To forgive is the most important element in your life's plan. It moves you out of the realm of fear and into love. True forgiveness is where healing occurs regardless of the fact that you deemed another guilty for their deed. This is perception and not truth. To forgive is to join with Him in Spirit where only truth abounds. The ego plants seeds in the mind, making forgiveness difficult, and at times impossible. Such seeds cause weeds to sprout. This brings fear to the hearts of those who are now on the ego's turf. By rising above such distortions of perception, you will be witness to the healing effects of forgiveness, where there are no weeds to obstruct the truth. To forgive, is to render yourself free.

Love, Jesus

338

I am affected only by my thoughts.

All thoughts are believed to have reality, yet many thoughts can be destructive to the thinker because they are not real. The ego mind is far and apart from the One Mind, which is all truth. Where all thoughts can deceive you, there is only One Thought that assures you, for it exists within the One Mind, God. If you practice tuning out disruptive chatter, your thoughts become audible, and you feel greater peace. With the ego, longevity of peace is impossible. Whichever thoughts you choose to act upon, are the ones which will affect you either positively or negatively. Attack thoughts bring you to fear. They invariably upset and confuse you because they are perceived as real and illusions are indeed frightening. If you react to a negative thought, it is imminent that you will also make a poor choice. It is the One Mind which brings you to your true reality which is Love. If you attach yourself to this idea, your thoughts will serve to give you greater insight of purpose. Everything you think is that which guides you towards love, or away from it. You cannot be hurt if your thoughts are attuned to outcomes that bring you peace.

Love, Jesus

339
I will receive whatever I request.

All requests are heard. However, the answer is not always the one the ego condones. Power of the mind is so strong it can accomplish anything. The ego, however, has no power because it asks for littleness, and that is what it receives. Yet it appears that God does not hear. No request is refused if it is beneficial to the one who asks. Request that which includes peace, love, and harmony, and so it is given. However, to ask with fearful intent is not how God would have you proceed, for it serves no real gain. The path to this recognition may be traveled along an arduous and bumpy road. Yet if it is traveled within the frequency of love's energy, it will become smoother. Anything you have ever requested that was for your own true benefit, and/or the benefit of another, has been bestowed. Do not ask foolishly for things that are not what you are truly seeking. With faith, all things are provided and they will come to you. When you ask for forgiveness, it is also given, for God knows it is needed in such a world where it is so easy to be led astray. Go within and ask for that which is of the heart. In that vein you will receive as you request.

Love, Jesus

340
I can be free of suffering today.

God did not intend for His children to suffer. His Love frees every soul, though they lack the understanding that there are far better choices when they come from a place of truth. There is an absence of love, which is affecting the Earth negatively. God recognizes there is pain and suffering here. When acts of unkindness are relentlessly exhibited, it spreads chaos throughout. And because the atmosphere is contaminated, it plagues the world's consciousness as well. God did not create such chaos. In Heaven only joy is known, for suffering is needless. While you are in your earthly form, peace of mind is what you seek. It is God's Will that you do not suffer while you seem to be in the throes of devastation, as the Earth is experiencing unexplained changes, causing fear. It is needless for you to suffer, as God's Angels come to you in quiet. Suffering need not be endured when God assures you that you can be free of suffering this very day, no matter what seems to be lurking before you. Raise your own consciousness, and see more love in the world unfold, as never before.

Love, Jesus

341
I can attack but my own sinlessness.
And it is only that which keeps me safe.

God created you sinless and of Light. There is a lovely energy within, which shines its Light outward. When the ego attacks your sinlessness, you do not perceive yourself as a child of Light, and guilt becomes the effect of the ego's unruliness. Ego and Spirit both dwell within your mind, causing it to be split. It is one mind, divided in two.

One part of the mind appears to attack the other. The part of the mind which is Spirit stands tall while the aggressor, the ego, attacks. The ego always declares war on Spirit. Yet Spirit looks upon the ego and knows the ego has no power over it and therefore has no cause to do battle. That is why you are capable of such a wide range of emotions. Spirit is forever at peace and ego is forever at war. Yet, your sinlessness secures your safety. All that is left is fear, caused by uncertainty of thought. Through it all, God's Love keeps you protected. It is up to you to identify with Spirit, and not the ego, allowing the mind to become whole and absent of conflict. Practice this, and therein lies your safety.

Love, Jesus

342

I let forgiveness rest upon all things. For thus forgiveness will be given me.

Forgiveness rests upon the desire to heal. A forgiving heart reflects a loving attitude and serves to free you from guilt. Open your heart and let forgiveness pour forth. It is your choice to decide when you are ready to give up worldly misconceptions supporting your convictions that a brother or sister is deserving of your ire. Allow forgiveness to rule your decisions. God has forgiven all souls their transgressions, for in the Eyes of God they were never guilty. But how can that be known when they are still engulfed in a dream of sin? Forgiveness is the greatest gift you can bestow upon a brother or sister, for it becomes a gift to yourself, and shared by both. It releases you from the pestilence causing a diseased state of mind to fester. Let all things remain free, for when forgiveness is released without regret, peace is restored and God's Love cannot be denied, for it saved you from the dream of hell which you have made real.

Love, Jesus

343

**I am not asked to make a sacrifice to find
the mercy and the peace of God.**

God's Voice resonates throughout the world, but He is not heard by all. Yet, when they ask His forgiveness, God answers every call. Those who fear asking cannot understand that God would not deny them His forgiveness. Each call to Him is heard and answered, but many do not hear Him, for they hide from His Presence. They also do not ask, for fear that God would demand something of them. To some, it would appear that they are asked to sacrifice something. Yet they do not know what. God wants His children to be happy and to live among the peaceful ones who have already found their way through forgiveness. What could it possibly be that He would ask, except that you forgive your brothers and sisters? The sordid beliefs of "sacrifice" held onto so dearly just mean that you relinquish pain and suffering in exchange for peace. What insanity it is to believe that this is sacrifice. Only an unhealed mind would choose suffering over peace. It was not easy for you to come to this place of acceptance either. But you now see that the mercy and peace of God has rendered you free.

Love, Jesus

344

**Today I learn the law of love;
that what I give my brother is my gift to me.**

Today you learn a most important lesson—the law of love. When you give love away, you also keep it for yourself. This differs from the laws of the world where it is believed that when you give something away it is no longer yours, that you possess it no longer.

Give love freely and feel its extraordinary beam of light shine back to you. Everything in your life reflects something. Let love be the reflection in all that you see. How can you fail when love is in the forefront? The love within is no stranger to you, for God created you from Love. You came to Earth school to learn of it once again. What uninterrupted love feels like, you do not yet know, for you lost it to the ego when you preferred its laws over the Laws of God. The ego knows not of this for it is not your friend. Come and reclaim it. Love is ever-present in your heart and that is what you seek. The gift of love is meant to be shared. In so doing, it is yours to keep.

Love, Jesus

345
I offer only miracles today, for I would have them be returned to me.

Enter into your finest hour today. For each miracle points the way to another, and so on. A miracle is like a boomerang. When it is air-bound, it flies as far as it can go and then returns to the one who released it. There is a great and powerful energy surrounding your planet. Yet many are seeing what appears to be total destruction and chaos unfolding. How peculiar it is that it takes media inundation to put the fear of God into the hearts of men, when God Himself is a protector not a destroyer. It is time to retreat into stillness and hear God's Voice as you ponder in silence. This is a time for solitude and prayer, for now you are pretty much isolated, as the world is in a state of seclusion, during this pandemic. There is nothing to fear outside of one's own capacity to dream a fearful dream. Keep vigilant, for there is an epidemic of fear roaming about. Offer miracles of love, and they shall be returned to you.

Love, Jesus

346

*Today the peace of God envelopes me,
and I forget all things except His Love.*

The Love of your Creator saves you from all perceived difficulties. What greater truth can you ask? When you are close to God, everything you always thought to be more desirous pales by comparison. It is a Love so intense that it draws you like a magnet, and nothing is as it was before. What can spark greater exuberance than recognition of His Love enveloping you? To be enveloped by God establishes your holiness, for in holiness you were born. Give God your all, and know His Earthly Angels are guiding you through hazardous times, which does not obscure His Love, but strengthens it. God holds your hand as you walk through the barriers that He makes transparent, and therefore easier to pass through, that you may find peace. When you feel His Love in this way, know that it is because you have surrendered to it, not forgotten it.

Love, Jesus

347

*Anger must come from judgment.
Judgment is the weapon I would use against myself,
to keep the miracle away from me.*

To know yourself is to empty your heart of anger and judgment, for they block your way to miracles. Although they are there, miracles cannot be seen in the presence of anger. Think how often your thoughts have caused you to lament the past, and so you could not feel love. Why then would you carry such a heavy burden, one which infringes upon your peace because you could not let anger and judgment dissolve into the dust from where it came? They have no cause, for you cannot judge another without inciting anger, and so it is yourself that you condemn. Miracles are provided endlessly. To deny a miracle to yourself is to deny it to your brother and sister as well, for miracles are shared. It is not the sudden flash of a bad memory that withholds the miracle from you. It is the holding onto that bad memory that does. Show God your strength by letting go the temptation to hold anger and judgment sacred. Be a symbol of love as you were created to be.

Love, Jesus

348

I have no cause for anger or for fear, for You surround me. And in every need that I perceive, Your grace suffices me.

When God's grace is before you, how could anger or fear take control of you? There is a sacred place dwelling inside of you that is apart from this fear-driven world, which is not your true home, and not of you. When you enter into such a place of peace, awareness of Him cradles you as you sit in awe of that which you are experiencing. And when you nestle into the comfort of such self-awareness, you lose yourself in stillness. It is like looking at a lovely lake as the sun's rays shine brightly on its mirrored surface, and there is nothing to intrude upon the softness of its rippling sounds. When you are taking a stroll on a lovely morning such as you did today, think of how much you enjoyed the tranquility of nature as you kept in stride with the sights and sounds of chirping birds and rustling trees. If this suffices you so well, how then could any need be greater?

Love, Jesus

349

Today I let Christ's vision look upon all things for me and judge them not but give each one a miracle of love instead.

Your miracles increase as you move towards greater vision and non-judgment. Smile as each hour passes, for you are exactly where you need to be. Now you must let the days go by with ease. There are no demands made, as your freedom is limited, and you are pretty much home-bound for now. Use this time for reflection and go on an inward journey to a higher level of consciousness. The world is going through an extraordinary change right now, and judgment is no longer an attraction. Find peace and solitude, for the world is going through new phases of change. Poison and pollution are working their way out. As the world is in quarantine by this pandemic, the atmosphere is cleansing itself. Right now, you are seeing the world in a poor light, as you believe some are using nefarious ways to aggrandize themselves, enriching their own causes. Pay it no mind. When this global discord has run its course, you will see a newness in the world which will bring greater peace to it. It is coming closer with each new day. Give way to this wonderful wave of energy and look upon it as a miracle of love.

Love, Jesus

350

Miracles mirror God's eternal Love. To offer them is to remember Him, and through His memory to save the world.

Truth revealed is a miracle. You have experienced many miracles in your lifetime which bring memory of God back to you. Each miracle you experience comes from love, and so it is up to you to extend to the world what you have received. Through God's Love is how miracles become manifest. Each forgiving thought sends a message into the world, which in itself creates the miracle. Each time you forgive, you offer a miracle to another, for miracles and forgiveness work hand in hand. It reminds us that if we view our brothers and sisters through the ego's limited perceptions, we are judging falsely. Forgiveness is a miracle because it gives everyone the opportunity to see themselves greater than that which they perceive themselves to be, created wholly loving, lovable, and changeless. Because you are a part of all creation, the miracles you offer when you forgive are powerful enough to save the world. You engage a miracle each time you refuse to believe that your brothers or sisters are defined only by how you perceive them to be and nothing more. Offer miracles to your brothers and sisters and bring change to the world.

Love, Jesus

351

My sinless brother is my guide to peace. My sinful brother is my guide to pain, and which I choose to see I will behold.

To be guided correctly is the road to peace. A peaceful relationship is a loving one, yet anything which causes you to view a brother or sister as sinful is also painful. For how can love show itself when it is blocked by pain? When you view another as sinful, it is because you are making a judgment. And it is only perception which caused you to judge him in the first place. Judgment causes a barrier which blocks the awareness to love. Accepting people as they are, and not as you would have them be, helps you to understand yourself, for it brings you peace. Your sinless brother or sister offers you peace which you cannot be aware of when you see them guilty. Your brother, who in reality is sinless, flourishes before your eyes for he now sees himself loved. You have learned through a particularly grievous time in your life how much pain you caused yourself when you chose to see someone close to you not as God sees him, but through the lens of your ego's perceptions. This gave you cause for guilt when there was no need. In the eyes of God, everyone is holy, as you are. Free will gives you the right to choose that which you prefer. If you choose sin, it is not love. If you choose pain, it is not peace. If you choose love, there is nothing left to feel but peace.

Love, Jesus

352

Judgment and love are opposites.
From one come all the sorrows of the world.
But from the other comes the peace of God Himself.

Love brings peace, and peace can change the world. Anything else confounds you, for peace is unknown where judgment rules. The journey of the soul ends with peace. That is what you must strive to accomplish on this journey by knowing your purpose. Each new day brings you closer to your journey's end. One day you will come to the place you have yearned to know of. The world needs your love, for love is sorely lacking here. God gives you all power to bring your brothers and sisters home with you, for no one travels alone. One soul mended can fix those that are tattered, as they too wander through their journey which does not come without pain. Forgiveness and non-judgment can change the world, for pain need not be. This is the assignment given to you by God. But first you must give up judgment. Words of condemnation hold you down, for all souls are connected, and this inhibits peace. Let judgment go and the peace of God is yours.

Love, Jesus

353

*My eyes, my tongue, my hands,
my feet today have but one purpose;
to be given Christ to use
to bless the world with miracles.*

Your body can be used as a vessel for the purpose of bestowing miracles. The body has no purpose other than to help create wellness in the world, but it is the soul which guides the body towards its purpose. The soul, which is the essence of your being, is never apart from you. It is your connection to Spirit, which helps you rise above the frailty of the body, though the body can withstand pain and suffering for long periods of time. Yet to suffer is not the body's real purpose, for it has a much greater one. It can be used to bless the world, free to extend itself above and beyond its own limitations. Given over to Christ, your tongue is taught to say the loving words by which miracles are formed; your hands are used to do good in the world, as they are kissed by those who bless you; your feet are used to take you to places where you can best serve. All this combined causes miracles to surface. They serve to ensure a state of well-being and joy in the world. As the body works towards filling its purpose, the soul reaches out in complement of the body.

Love, Jesus

354

*We stand together, Christ and I,
in peace and certainty of purpose.
And in Him Is His Creator, as He is in me.*

The Christ Mind is within you to think God's Thoughts, and not the world's thoughts. How awesome is this to comprehend? But you will understand it better with time, for your journey is not yet over. Know yourself as God created you. Stand in the light of His Love and become aware of what this means. It is to know yourself as He knows you. Do not allow the littleness of the ego to stand in the way of your greater learning. Let the Christ be revealed to you by your thoughts. The ego is the wedge which stands between you and God. It fights for its life, for it depends on you to cast God out. Although the ego's littleness cannot prevail over God, it still cries to you from the shallows of its grave, for it depends on you for its life. But it needs to be buried peacefully, for you cannot be Christ-Minded if you allow the ego's thoughts to prevail over the Self that lives in God. When your ego is understood for what it is, it will be easier to know the greater glory of His Love, for there will be nothing to cause you to doubt. You inherently know what is true. Your purpose is established. Now come forward and claim it.

Love, Jesus

355

*There is no end to all the peace and joy,
and all the miracles that I will give,
when I accept God's Word. Why not today?*

God's unconditional Love brings forth new possibilities every day. By instilling a sense of peace and joy in the world, God thanks you with miracles which you extend to others. This comes when you have the feeling that you are completely at peace. When the blessings of the day are gathered, and there are so many they cannot possibly be counted, each that you perceive comes gift-wrapped with a miracle. Be as free as those soaring white butterflies which appeared endlessly on that lovely day not so long ago, as you drove along the beach observing them in awe. God gives His Word that you cannot fail when you bathe yourself in Him and know there is no better way to indulge yourself. As love and peace surround you in thought, so it is made manifest in the world.

Love, Jesus

356

Sickness is but another name for sin. Healing is but another name for God. The miracle is thus a call to Him.

Sickness is the denial of reality, for in God there is only Truth. Sickness stalks upon those who believe in its reality. When sickness invades the body, it is very real to those who have yielded to it. Yet God Himself knows not of sickness and He gives it no true reality. Sickness, it seems, proves that God is unmoved by their frailties or else He would keep them "safe" from illness. So many believe this, for they are sure they have sinned, and so they believe that God would prefer to be punisher instead of healer. Sickness stems from a belief that sin is real, and to believers, sickness actually protects them from God. It is their "proof" that God sees them sinful, and so they seek to replace belief in God with their own reality. In truth, none of it works that way. If sickness should prey upon a brother, it is he himself who can choose to heal or not. To call upon God and ask for a miracle is what brings healing about. Where miracles abound, there can be no sin.

Love, Jesus

357

Truth answers every call we make to God, responding first with miracles, and then returning unto us to be itself.

God is only Truth, so therefore that is what you are. Because this is so, there is nothing you cannot accomplish. For Truth brings about the understanding that you are created in His image, and there is nothing that can cause you to doubt, unless you choose to. With free will, all choice is yours. You know that your call to God has been answered, for you can actually feel it happening. It is a feeling of Unconditional Love. This is what Truth is, for what else can it be? It is here where everything you need to know is found, for it is at the very core of all that you are. You are as God created you. Every call to God which comes from this place of knowledge is answered, and each one is a miracle; a moment of Truth realized. Now they can be counted on, for they are continuous when they are accepted in this way. Truth is Truth, and nothing less.

Love, Jesus

358

**No call to God can be unheard nor left Unanswered.
And of this I can be sure;
His answer is the one I really want.**

A call to God is always heard and because it is heard, it is answered. Being perfectly benevolent, He can be reached at any hour, day or night. You are the child created of Him, for you exist in Him. It is through His answers that recognition of Self is understood. God's Love erases all doubt and a call to Him at every phase points the way to greater healing and peace. It is in the here and now where you will learn the most. The world has taught you that pain and suffering are part of life's process and no one escapes without difficulties of sorts. Yet much of the suffering experienced can be avoided, for they are caused by acts of unforgiveness to yourself and others. Yet they serve as learning devices as well. As you learn, you heal. Calling upon God transitions you to a higher plane of consciousness. Show Him every aspect of yourself without fearing judgment. And because you are here to learn, you are never judged. You have also come to understand that it is okay to stumble upon your path, for you will stay astride more than you will fall. Call upon God and be guided. His plan for you should not be interrupted by lack of faith. When you call upon God, be certain that you are always answered.

Love, Jesus

359

God's answer is some form of peace.
All pain is healed; all misery replaced with joy.
All prison doors are opened.
And all sin is understood as merely a mistake.

True peace is accomplished when all misery is gone, for there is nothing in your mind which binds you to sin anymore. Sins are looked upon exactly for what they are; errors gone awry. There is no reason to grieve now. The prison door is wide open. God loved you even when you locked yourself away from better choices, choosing pain over love. You are at peace most of the time now because there is nowhere you would rather travel but to the quiet place within, swathed in the beauty of the moment. There is no separation dividing you from your brother or sister, and nothing which separates you from God. Given the wisdom to move past illusions, and practicing stillness, you will be given your heart's desire. Never again divert your mind from the peace which you have come to look upon as a gift. Now you have comparisons—the joy of peace, versus pain. God's Love is immeasurable, and surely felt when you surrender to it.

Love, Jesus

360

Peace be to me, the holy Son of God.
Peace to my brother, who is one with me.
Let all the world be blessed with peace through us.

All the world's energy is changing for the good, and broken images of the world are being restored to wholeness. When you experience peace, you share it. A world blessed makes you twice blessed. Peace remains with you when you come to understand the value of it. For once you have it, you will never want to return to the lower frequencies where pain and fear once ruled. The world will become a center for greater learning now. The more you give in terms of love and kindness, the more you stand to gain, for now you are in recognition of your capacities. Today you are forming a different picture of yourself and your brothers and sisters. You have positioned yourself to take giant steps towards making peace your natural state of being. See sinlessness in the world and you shall find peace, for peace and sinlessness are one and the same. Peace manifests during times of contemplation and stillness, and so the world is rebounding. There is a brilliant new energy circulating throughout the world striving for a single purpose. Heal the world by bringing peace to it, and see a new world arise as it is blessed throughout.

Love, Jesus

361 to 365

*This holy instant I would give to You.
Be You in charge. For I would follow You,
certain that your direction gives me peace.*

The holy instant is the moment when we decide to set aside the past and bring Truth into the present. It is the reversal of thought—from fear to peace, and from hate to love. Give God your unwavering faith, for salvation is now certain. Your struggles on this Earth are no more, and the peace you are feeling elevates you to an awareness of Self-Love. You are seeing another world, one which feels different from the old. Where you once lived under clouds of unrest and confusion, you are seeing a world shifting out of the old as it moves into the new. It is a place where the strength of peace overshadows fear. God welcomes you to the origins of your creation, which is to love and be loved. Be joyous and peaceful the rest of your days. You have come to a place which reveals your True Identity. You know this is so, for you are feeling a newness of freedom as never before. Follow me where I lead you. You have come to know me as your brother, the one who will come for you personally when your body is laid aside, and you come to join me in your final resting place, blessed with eternal peace.

Love, Jesus

Acknowledgements

Michael, my partner in love and in life.

Daughter Elyse, an amazing teacher and inspirer of young children.

Daughter Karen, a wonderful business entrepreneur of children's luxury gift items.

Grandchildren Corey, Sydney, Max, and Robert, who call and text, just to say "hi."

Special Thanks

My daughter, Karen Helburn: Owner of Just Hatched, a luxury goods children's store in Guilford, Connecticut.

Rob Schwartz, author of *Your Soul's Plan, Your Soul's Gift*, and *Your Soul's Love: Living the Love You Planned Before You Were Born*, as well as international speaker and practitioner of between-life and soul regression.

Thank you, Karen and Rob, for patiently voyaging through these lessons with me, making the excursion that much more enjoyable.

About the Author:

Myrna Skoller was born and raised in New York. She is the former owner of "Designer Resale," a world renowned New York City resale and consignment shop she started in 1990. She successfully sold her business in 2015. It is now called "Designer Revival," also known for its high-end, high-quality designer apparel and accessories. Her first book, *Miracle on 81st Street,* was inspired by the business which she founded, and faithfully ran, for over twenty-five years.

She also tried her hand at writing two children's books, *I Remember Grandpa* and *Sidney Goes to Bat*, and a memoir, *My Inner Teacher's Voice*, all of which were self-published and are available on Amazon.

Myrna now resides with her beloved partner, Michael Geringer, in a home they share in Boca Raton, Florida.

www.ingramcontent.com/pod-product-compliance
Lightning Source LLC
Chambersburg PA
CBHW071805080526
44589CB00012B/693